**Play
the Game.
Change
the Game.
Leave
the Game.**

Also by Robert Livingston

The Conversation: How Seeking and Speaking the Truth About Racism Can Radically Transform Individuals and Organizations

Play
the Game.
Change
the Game.
Leave
the Game.

Pathways to Black Empowerment, Prosperity, and Joy

Robert Livingston

CROWN CURRENCY
New York, NY

CROWN CURRENCY
An imprint of the Crown Publishing Group
A division of Penguin Random House LLC
1745 Broadway
New York, NY 10019
currencybooks.com
penguinrandomhouse.com

The image on page 146 originally appeared in *The Conversation* by Robert Livingston (New York: Crown Currency, 2021).

Library of Congress Cataloging-in-Publication Data is on file with the publisher.

Hardcover ISBN 979-8-217-08597-2
Ebook ISBN 979-8-217-08598-9

Editor: Paul Whitlatch
Editorial assistant: Katie Berry
Production editor: Craig Adams
Text designer: Aubrey Khan
Production: Heather Williamson
Copy editor: Sibylle Kazeroid
Proofreaders: Muriel Jorgensen, Pam Rehm, and Kevin Clift
Indexer: J S Editorial, LLC
Publicist: Gwyneth Stansfield
Marketer: Tara Gilbride

Manufactured in the United States of America

9 8 7 6 5 4 3 2 1

First Edition

The authorized representative in the EU for product safety and compliance is Penguin Random House Ireland, Morrison Chambers, 32 Nassau Street, Dublin D02 YH68, Ireland, https://eu-contact.penguin.ie.

For our ancestors—

whose survival and sacrifice enabled not only our existence, but our agency and ability to decide how we engage with the game

Contents

Play
the Game.
Change
the Game.
Leave
the Game.

Introduction

From Antiracism to Black Empowerment

The throng of upbeat, smartly dressed men and women had descended on the stately ballroom of the Omni Hotel in Boston for the 2023 Men of Color Leadership Conference. I had been invited to deliver a keynote address to the crowd of over a thousand ambitious individuals, composed of business executives, attorneys, engineers, educators, consultants, and other professionals. I knew they were hungry for inspiration and advice on how they could bolster their chances of success as they climbed the American career ladder. I had originally planned to reiterate what had become my standard DEI presentation on strategies for promoting antiracism in the workplace. But that day I wasn't feeling up to it. Something had changed.

For most of the previous three years, I had possessed boundless energy and optimism for the DEI mission of increasing social justice through education and conversation—which constituted the foundation of my first book, *The Conversation: How Seeking and Speaking the Truth About Racism Can Radically Transform Individuals and Organizations.* In it, I presented a framework outlining what leaders and ordinary individuals could do to promote racial equity in the workplace and society. In the wake of George Floyd's murder, there had been a surge of interest in antiracism. I had spent most of the three years that followed Floyd's death engaging in conversations with thousands of corporate executives and employees, police chiefs and officers, mayors and city managers, administrators of federal agencies and state judiciaries, and nonprofit directors from across the United States.

But by 2023, I had grown frustrated. Leaders in almost every sector had given plenty of lip service to racial equity, but very little seemed to change with respect to outcomes, or even mindsets. It was mostly hand-wringing and performative pledges, I had concluded, rather than real learning and commitment to change. I had become deeply disillusioned by the time the Men of Color Leadership Conference rolled around, and was beginning to believe that all the collective effort to advance antiracism in organizations had been a grand waste of time.

This put me in a difficult spot as a speaker. The conference organizers knew what was in my book, and that's what they had signed up for—a hopeful conversation about the promise of antiracism education. I had been invited to the conference to inspire people, not to demoralize them. However, I had become so disenchanted by broken DEI promises that I did not feel I could continue to make the case that an investment in antiracism that depended on the actions of White people would bear fruit.

I agonized for days over what to say in my presentation. Should I just stick to the "Yes, we can" mantra and tell the conference attendees to keep their heads down and keep on keeping on? It seemed disingenuous and inauthentic, given that DEI efforts had not only stalled but were quickly moving in reverse. The speed and scope of the backlash were astounding—and the reprisals continued long after the conference:

- At least sixty-five anti-DEI bills have been introduced by state legislators since 2023, as reported by *The Washington Post*.[1]

- Multiple large companies such as Meta, Tesla, Lyft, and Wayfair have slashed the size of their DEI teams by 50 percent, with Tesla's billionaire founder and CEO infamously taking to social media in December 2023 to proclaim that "DEI must DIE."

- The iconic tractor company John Deere went from calling DEI one of its "highest priorities" in 2022 to stating in 2024 that it would audit materials "to ensure the absence of socially motivated messages."[2]

- Ditto for Brown-Forman—the maker of Jack Daniel's, Woodford Reserve, and other well-known spirits, wines, and liqueurs—which rolled back its DEI commitments in August 2024 in response to mounting external pressure.

- In June 2023, the U.S. Supreme Court ruled race-conscious college admissions at Harvard and UNC–Chapel Hill unconstitutional, overturning forty-five years of legal precedent. *The Chronicle of Higher Education* later published a tracker of all legislative efforts to thwart DEI at colleges and universities. The list is long.[3]

- The Shenandoah County, Virginia, school board voted to *re*name schools after Confederate leaders Stonewall Jackson and Robert E. Lee after these names were changed in 2020 to Mountain View High School and Honey Run Elementary School. This change reportedly cost hundreds of thousands of dollars in a district that desperately needed funds for computers, books, and other education essentials.

- The school board in the liberal bastion of Concord, Massachusetts, rejected a proposal to name a new middle school after Black abolitionist Ellen Garrison, despite many buildings in the town being named after White historical figures. Currently, none are named after Black historical figures.

- The states of Florida and Texas passed legislation to remove core components of Black history from their public education curriculum. Much of what remained was rewritten or misrepresented.

- Data from the Southern Poverty Law Center (SPLC) indicates that hate crimes have skyrocketed in recent years.

- In January 2024, the first Black president of Harvard University was forced to resign from her position—after only six months and two days on the job—by individuals who appeared to be more focused on a political agenda than her tremendous leadership potential.

Progress had become regress, despite our efforts to the contrary. I contemplated the notion that almost everyone, including me, had assumed that racism could be remedied with factual information, moral appeals, or self-interest incentives. In other words, if we taught White people about Black history or unconscious bias, that would raise awareness and reduce racism. Or if we called out all the harm that racism inflicts, and appealed to White people's morality and humanity, that would increase empathy and decrease discrimination. Or if we helped White people realize that racism actually hurts White people too, then we could appeal to their self-interest. And surely, I had believed, White people would renounce racism if they understood the personal benefits of doing so.

While there is good logic underlying all these assumptions—and empirical evidence showing that appealing to any one of them may move the needle to some degree—they do not address what I have come to believe is the true source of the problem. The real issue is *not* a lack of information, morality, or self-interest. I believe that White people already know in some deep part of themselves that both anti-Black racism and White privilege exist. Most White people also value compassion and kindness and, in their hearts, want to do the right thing. They may even realize, on some level, that ending racism would benefit everyone, including White people themselves.

The problem is that racism does not just reside in the mind; it is in the body as well. I began to realize that racism operates, in many respects, like an addiction—an addiction to White supremacy.

I define White supremacy simply as an endorsement of, or acquiescence to, the notion that Whiteness is superior to Blackness. It doesn't require hatred, cruelty, fear, or avoidance of people of color. In fact, one could engage in antiracist actions and still fit the definition of a White supremacist. Abraham Lincoln is a vivid example of someone who was very sympathetic toward the Black community—and even led a monumental antiracist campaign (i.e., Emancipation)—all while believing Black people to be inferior to White people.

In a speech during his Fourth Debate with Stephen Douglas in 1858, Lincoln stated, "While they [Black and White people] do remain together, there must be the position of superior and inferior, and I as much as any other man am in favor of having the superior position assigned to the white race. I say upon this occasion I do not perceive that because the white man is to have the superior position the negro should be denied everything. I do not understand that because I do not want a negro woman for a slave I must necessarily want her for a wife [crowd laughs and cheers]. . . . So it seems to me quite possible for us to get along without making either slaves or wives of negroes. I will add to this that I have never seen, to my knowledge, a man, woman or child who was in favor of producing a perfect equality, social and political, between negroes and white men."

What this speech clearly delineates is a distinction between cruelty and parity. The progressives of Lincoln's era did not want abject cruelty for Black people, but they did not want social parity either. They all agreed on the inferior position of Black people, even if they disagreed on whether the inferiority was due to nature, nurture, culture, or circumstance.

The last sentence of the Lincoln quote is the kicker. It indicates that the notion of full equality between Black and White people was so foreign and unfathomable to White people that he had never heard anyone even suggest it. His speech plainly illustrates that it is possible to be anti-cruelty, and to some extent pro–human rights, while also believing in the superiority of White people vis-à-vis Black people. White supremacy has more to do with opposition to racial parity than support for racial charity. The ironic result, in Lincoln's case, is sympathy for Black people but empathy with racist White Southerners despite disagreement with their methods.

I argue that the White progressives of the twenty-first century are not all that different from those of the nineteenth century—their real problem is not with White supremacy itself, but rather how it's expressed and delivered. Perhaps a subtler word to describe this quality of White supremacy is "Eurocentrism." For White people, regression to White supremacy, or

Eurocentrism, is a reflexive response. White supremacy is not just a belief but a *need* for White people.

In a 1963 interview televised on the program *The Negro and the American Promise*—later featured in the 2016 documentary *I Am Not Your Negro*—the highly celebrated and influential African American writer James Baldwin stated, "What white people have to do is try to find out in their own hearts why it was necessary for them to have a nigger in the first place because I'm not a nigger, I'm a man. If I'm not the nigger here, and you invented him, you the white people invented him, then you have to find out why."

The "n-word" that I find most emphatic and revealing in Baldwin's statement is "necessary." Baldwin's assertion that White people *need* to believe in the Black bogeyman—and are more than willing to invent one where none exists—is insightful and compelling. The hallmark of addiction is a need (more specifically, a *felt* need: something people believe they need, even if they don't actually need it). When viewed through the metaphorical lens of addiction, both the voracious consumption of White supremacy and the "relapses" following periods of "sobriety" begin to make more sense.

I realize that "addiction" is a strong word with many connotations. Some people might feel more comfortable with a word such as "habit" or "tendency" to describe the allure and persistence of White supremacy (which itself is a term that many people do not like). However, I believe the metaphor fits, considering the perennial appeal of White supremacy, its re-emergence after brief periods of pause, and the perpetuation of harm to others and oneself, followed by feelings of guilt and shame, which, ultimately and ironically, lead to greater consumption rather than cessation.

Having said this, I want to make clear that I use the words "addiction" and "addict" in strictly descriptive rather than evaluative terms. There is no judgment or condemnation intended. Although I further unpack this addiction analogy in the first chapter of the book, the question of *why* racism has proven so remarkably persistent is really of secondary importance. The unfortunate reality is that it *has* persisted. The primary focus of this book is on a different question: Where does racism's stubborn, addiction-like persistence leave Black people?

If White people are addicted to White supremacy, then this changes how we, as Black people, must move forward in our journey toward racial equity. The first thing to understand is that you cannot persuade or compel a person who is struggling with addiction to change. They must decide for themselves that they are committed to ending the cycle of abuse. And recovery requires a process of *rehabilitation*, not simply education. That is Addiction 101. In his book *Understanding and Helping an Addict (and Keeping Your Sanity)*, physician and addiction expert Andrew Proulx writes, "As long as anyone clings to the delusion that they can control [someone else's] substance use, cure the addiction, or 'fix' the addict, then they'll continue to fight a battle they cannot win. They succeed only in expending tremendous energy at the expense of their own needs and sanity."[4]

The second thing to understand is that the impulse to consume White supremacy will persist, as long as the underlying source of the (felt) need remains unaddressed. Although there may be occasional periods of cessation, there will always be a high probability of recurrence. Therefore, we should not have been surprised when, in the years following George Floyd's murder, White supremacy reared its ugly head once again.

Indeed, in American history, we have observed this racism rehab-relapse cycle for centuries. The country witnessed similar backlash after Reconstruction in the 1860s and '70s and the Civil Rights Era in the 1950s and '60s, in the wake of the brutal beating of Rodney King in 1991, and during and following the two terms of the first Black president of the United States, Barack Obama, from 2008 to 2016.

Each historical push toward racial equality was countered by an intractable effort to reestablish White supremacy. It is a process that historian Carol Anderson has described as "white rage" and historian Ibram X. Kendi has referred to as "dueling dualism." What made it so jarring after George Floyd's murder was the sheer velocity of the relapse. In the past, the period of progress was more protracted, with the pro-justice momentum lasting a decade or two before the inevitable about-face. This time, the racial equity honeymoon was over in the blink of an eye.

To be clear, I am not an Afropessimist who believes that it is futile to try to combat racism.[5] Nor do I subscribe to the "racial realism" idea that racism will always be a permanent fixture in American society.[6] Maybe it will be; maybe it won't be. My Black ancestors living in the South in 1850 probably assumed that they would never see the end of the institution of slavery, given that it had been in existence their whole lives, and for the entire history of the country.

However, the reality is that it is incredibly difficult to predict the future, even with full knowledge of the past. If the past always predicted the future, then centuries-old monarchies would never die, world records would never be set or broken, and breakthrough technological advances would never occur. For hundreds of thousands of years, no human had ever gone to the moon—and then it happened. Although White supremacy, and the racism that supports it, are stubborn and formidable, it does not logically follow that they are inevitable or invincible. While I remain hopeful about the possibility of moving the needle in a profound way, I am also aware that the probability of radical change is tenuous. Therefore, we should not put *all* our eggs in the antiracism education basket.

We do not have to be confined to the Sisyphean struggle against racism that we have been engaged in so far—where we exert so much effort to change the mindset and behaviors of the dominant group, only to have the boulder roll back down the hill again. We can simultaneously adopt an alternative approach. In addition to focusing on antiracism, aimed at changing the racially biased attitudes and behaviors of White people— a few of whom *do* show signs of real recovery—let us also focus on Black empowerment, concentrating our efforts on increasing our own capacity for self-determination and prosperity. Upon this realization, my initial discouragement gave way to a Zen-like feeling of serenity and liberation— and hope.

With these insights, which emerged over many months of contemplation in 2023, I finally began to feel energized once again. Soon, I was ready to bring this optimism and inspiration to the Omni Hotel ballroom.

From Antiracism to Black Empowerment

In the wake of my revelation, I decided to switch things up. Instead of focusing on White-centered antiracism, I would focus on Black-centered empowerment. This decision was not without risk. There were dozens of White executives from corporate sponsors in the audience, many of them from white-shoe investment banking and insurance firms such as Morgan Stanley, Fidelity, Liberty Mutual, and John Hancock. Would they withhold funding for future conferences if my talk was too "radical"? I had pondered the dilemma. The last thing I wanted to do was jeopardize the relationship between the conference organizers and their sponsors. But I also figured that the organizers had chosen me for a reason, knowing that my approach is "truth to power."

The central theme of my presentation was that we can't wait for White people to change. That day may never come. We have to empower ourselves. A slide in my presentation deck laid out the three paths to that empowerment:

- Play the Game

- Change the Game

- Leave the Game

What I was telling this sea of a thousand faces in the Omni ballroom was something few people in the DEI world had been saying—racism has always been, and will likely continue to be, a formidable force in the workplace. Therefore, it is imperative that we acknowledge this inconvenient truth and respond accordingly. I then began to elaborate on the numerous ways in which individuals could *play* the game, or work within these systems of White supremacy; *change* the game, or challenge the status quo in an effort to upend White supremacy; and *leave* the game, or carve out alternative spaces for flourishing outside of the central orbit of White supremacy. I emphasized that these paths are not mutually exclusive. Most

Black people will do all three things in the course of their career, to one extent or another, depending on their personal goals and circumstances.

As I delivered my talk—the first time I had publicly made some of these arguments—the crowd was dead silent. I had no idea what they were thinking, or whether the message was resonating. At the conclusion of the presentation, I thanked the audience, then held my breath.

After an instant, I was stunned by the whooping and thunderous applause I received. Judging from the energy in the room, I had struck a chord deep inside folks. As I tried to leave the ballroom, people surrounded me, clamoring to ask questions and discuss the ideas further. I had places to be, but the attendees made it clear that they didn't want me to go anywhere. I stuck around speaking with people for nearly an hour.

Later, after finally making my way home, I spent the evening mulling over what had happened. It was evident that many in the Black community were as weary as I was from the constant lobbying for concern and antiracist action from White people. It was also clear that despite the fatigue, hope endured. Everyone in that room seemed to believe that things can change. We just weren't sure we could depend on White people to change them.

Indeed, Black people have always led the charge for our own freedom and dignity. Although many people tend to think of abolitionists as noble White men and women, the movement was created and led by Black people (Frederick Douglass, Harriet Tubman, Sojourner Truth, etc.). Ditto with the Civil Rights Movement. Ditto with Black Lives Matter. In all these movements, there was critical support from staunch White allies once the movement gained momentum. However, these true White allies have always represented a minuscule proportion of the overall White population. Why should now be any different?

I wrote this book for the multitudes of Black people who feel the same way as those who filled that Omni ballroom—people motivated to put themselves, their families, and their communities on a path to prosperity. The two intertwined themes of this book revolve around accepting the unfortunate reality of the persistence of White racism while also embracing the optimistic reality that there is much that Black people can do to effectively navigate, mitigate, or extricate themselves from the quagmire. This book is about Black self-determination, as individuals and as a collective. One thing I want to make crystal clear from the outset is that although I am focusing on actions that Black people can take, both individually and collectively, Black people are in no way responsible for the racism they endure. Ideally, it is the system that should change.

Racism was created by White people and should be dismantled by them. If you're curious about ways to promote antiracism among White people, then read *The Conversation* for concrete, scientifically validated tips on how to move the needle. However, I also believe that there are other ways to create greater racial equity—ways that do not depend on the goodwill of White people at all. If "the game" is a workplace and society infused with White supremacy, then this book is about how to play the game, change the game, and/or leave the game. It's about how we, as Black people, can own our power and choose our own pathways.

Playing the Game

Playing the game is not necessarily about obsequious ingratiation with White people for the purpose of making them feel comfortable and promoting one's own advancement. Later in the book, I discuss three types of "players"—enablers, climbers, and lifters. Because this book is about Black empowerment, I focus primarily on "lifters." These are Black people who play the game to secure power within an organization and then leverage that insider position to empower other Black people. They essentially play the game to change the game—using a kind of racial jiujitsu to direct the opponent's energy against itself. Playing the game as a lifter can also be about bringing out the best qualities of the organization or society, or identifying and enlisting allies. Being an "outside insider" is not without its challenges, so I will discuss effective tactics for attaining and maintaining these positions. I will also examine the delicate art of leveraging these insider positions to help other Black people without compromising one's racial identity, or physical or mental health. In addition to data, I include wisdom and insights gathered from my interviews with many prominent

African Americans who have played the game and won—people such as Kenneth Chenault, former CEO of American Express, and Deval Patrick, former governor of Massachusetts.

Changing the Game

Changing the game is about the willingness to challenge the game with the *intent* to alter it, even if, in the end, the game isn't actually transformed. This process is more like karate, in which you use your own force against the opponent, whether it's through blocking or counterpunching. These courageous "fighters" take decisive and deliberate action to reform the system in order to establish greater dignity and equity for Black people. Because the system will always resist such efforts, changing the game requires both steadfast determination and savvy strategies for collective organizing. In part III, I will provide an overview of social science research on how to effectively change the game. I also offer sage insights and advice on how to persevere and prevail in the struggle from my interviews with veteran activists, such as the real OG—Dr. Angela Y. Davis, now in her seventh decade of the fight for social equality.

Leaving the Game

Leaving the game is about creating opportunities to exit the ring altogether. However, leaving the game does *not* mean quitting, nor does it imply sitting on the sidelines. It is about discovering, or creating, a new game in a different location and/or with a different set of rules. In the final part of the book, I discuss the three E's of leaving the game: entrepreneurship, enclaves, and exodus. Black entrepreneurship is a form of creating your own game, even within the context of the broader capitalist system. I reveal how Black enclaves, such as Black neighborhoods, Historically Black Colleges and Universities (HBCUs), or employee resource groups (ERGs) can provide sanctuary within mainstream organizations or society. Finally, I examine the prospect of exiting the system altogether whether through ex-patriotism, or the creation of a "Wakanda" within the

United States—such as the Republic of New Afrika proposed in the 1960s—or setting up political enclaves in the South through reverse migration, as discussed in my interview with journalist and author Charles Blow. In all cases, the underlying impetus for leaving the game is not racial separation from White people, but rather distancing oneself from White supremacy.

I will also discuss how leaving the game can sometimes, ironically, better equip one to successfully play or change the game. As you will see in the chapters ahead, these three paths are, in fact, quite synergistic.

Throughout the book, I have sprinkled keen insights and kernels of wisdom gathered from my interviews with other Black luminaries such as Carol Anderson, Kimberlé Crenshaw, William Darity Jr., Anthony Foxx, Eddie Glaude Jr., Ibram X. Kendi, and David A. Thomas. The richness of these perspectives is complemented by social science research—and something else: my own personal history and how it intersects with the book's themes. As you will soon read, I had the unique and transformative experience of growing up in a place called St. Martin's Village—a middle-class, all-Black residential enclave in Lexington, Kentucky.

With regard to my own personal opinions, I have endeavored to remain impartial and objective as to whether, or how, someone should play the game, change the game, or leave the game—opting to allow the research, data, anecdotes, and unique perspectives from Black leaders to speak for themselves. It is also extremely difficult to recommend one "right" path for everyone. Each individual is different. My ultimate goal is not to deliver definitive answers on what Black people *should* do to manage White supremacy but rather to discuss what Black people *can* do—offering an array of options and ideas that will stimulate instructive and productive dialogue within our community. My hope is that this book will inspire and empower the Black audiences that it was written for—primarily African Americans, but also our brothers and sisters in the United Kingdom, Canada, South Africa, Brazil, France, Colombia, Portugal, Bermuda, and other countries where large populations of Black people must exist in workplaces and societies that elevate Whiteness.

For me, it is refreshing to be able to write a popular press book that

White people do not have to understand, or even like. However, this does not mean that the book cannot be useful or informative to White people with a certain level of humility and awareness. This means accepting, among other things, that racism is treated as a structural (rather than individual) phenomenon, and that White people are not centered in this book. Apart from the content of chapter 1, there is very little analysis of White people's problems and challenges, and even less attention given to proposed solutions. Several White colleagues who read the book were deeply intrigued by the notion of White supremacy addiction and immediately asked what my "rehabilitation" plan was for White people. That is for White people to figure out—*if* they are truly committed to change. This book is about Black empowerment.

Finally, in the epilogue, I return to the question of why our society seems perpetually locked in a cycle of racial antagonism, and offer some insights into what a different path might look like. I also go beyond Black empowerment to ponder themes of Black thriving. I examine the profound and provocative topic of what it means to live a good life, and the ways in which the answer varies across geography, ethnicity, and culture. I also identify universal foundations of what it means to lead a joyous and prosperous life—for all human beings.

I have been blessed to have experienced a tremendous amount of joy throughout my life, and I credit the all-Black environment in which I grew up—rife with positive role models and community solidarity—for my ability to even write this book. My hope is that by understanding and embracing pathways for navigating, attenuating, and circumventing burdensome systems of White supremacy, we can ultimately get back to the important business of life: pleasure, purpose, prosperity, and peace of mind.

Part I
Setting
the Stage

One

White Supremacy and Other Drugs

I was delighted a few years ago when "Kaitlyn" and other senior executives at her company invited me to an idyllic lakeside resort a few hours from a major American city to lead a two-day DEI workshop for their employees. Kaitlyn was an ardent supporter of DEI who had moved heaven and earth to get me to speak to her colleagues. No cellphones were allowed. The executives wanted to stay laser focused on their mission to increase racial equity in their organization.

During one of my presentations, I noticed that Kaitlyn seemed especially intrigued by research that examined the effect of "Whitening" résumés. The study showed that a large percentage of Black professionals with ethnically identifiable names—such as Lakeisha Ann Washington—would strategically list their name as L. Ann Washington, for example, rather than Lakeisha A. Washington when it came time to apply for a job. The results revealed that masking their race by using their middle name rather than their first name drastically increased the likelihood of getting a job interview. Prospective employers were more than twice as likely to interview L. Ann Washington as they were Lakeisha A. Washington. This was true regardless of whether the company had expressed a strong commitment to DEI or not.[1]

I attended a dinner that evening with several of the organizers of the event, Kaitlyn among them. She continued to ruminate on the résumé study. I thought her fixation might have been related to the fact that something as simple as a name could have a huge impact on someone's employment opportunities. Or perhaps she was surprised by the finding that companies that purported to highly value DEI were just as likely to discriminate against Black applicants as companies that expressed indifference toward DEI. However, this study resonated with Kaitlyn for personal reasons. She began telling me a story.

"When I was in college, I wanted to join a sorority," she said. "But they turned me down."

I nodded, listening.

"Later, I ran into one of the girls in the sorority, who was shocked to find out who I was." She paused, and then added: "She thought that I was Black!"

Seeing the confusion on my face, she began to clarify. It turned out that "Kaitlyn" was her middle name. Her full name was "Diamond Kaitlyn Wilson" (not her real name), and her family and friends had called her "Diamond" her entire life.

When the all-White sorority saw that a woman named "Diamond Wilson" wanted to join the club, they rejected her on the assumption that she was Black. However, when one of the sorority sisters later met Diamond in person and saw that she was White, she was more than willing to let her in.

"She's now one of my best friends!" Kaitlyn proudly proclaimed, referring to the sorority sister who had initially rejected her when she thought she was Black.

Following that experience, Kaitlyn elected to go by her middle name rather than her first name. Decades later, she still does. I had no idea that her first name was Diamond. Her official e-mail correspondence lists the sender as Kaitlyn Wilson, with not so much as a "D." preceding her first name.

I was floored by several aspects of her story. What stunned me most was how willingly this tireless crusader for racial justice embraced the sorority sister who openly practiced racial discrimination. When I pointed this out to her, she got it. At the same time, she didn't get it at all. She admitted that it was an "imperfect" situation but seemed to understand why the sorority wouldn't have wanted her if she were Black. She insisted that despite their flaws, the sorority members were "good people." In the end,

Kaitlyn reiterated to me her deep commitment to racial equity—and I think she genuinely believed it.

■ ■ ■

My interaction with Kaitlyn was just one of the thousands that I had with White people during my book tour for *The Conversation* from 2021 through 2023—the year that I gave my "Play, Change, Leave" presentation to the Men of Color Leadership Conference at the Omni Hotel in Boston. During those two and a half years, my innumerable encounters and conversations gave me insight into the fact that the problem wasn't really a lack of information. It was something much, much deeper than that.

As a psychologist, I became increasingly aware that the root cause of White supremacy was more motivational than cognitive. In other words, the issue seemed to be grounded in needs, drives, and compulsions rather than beliefs, assumptions, and misinformation. It slowly dawned on me that what I was seeing was much more akin to an "addiction" than a situation of apathy or ignorance. What I noticed across a multitude of interactions was an endorsement of, acquiescence to, or appreciation of the ways in which White supremacy provided comfort, privilege, solidarity, and status—similar to what I witnessed during my interaction with Kaitlyn. I even observed this strong undercurrent of White supremacy amid ostensible efforts to promote antiracism, not unlike the scenario with Kaitlyn.

This paradoxical juxtaposition of DEI allyship and White supremacy was vividly described by Robin DiAngelo—a progressive White woman—in her book *Nice Racism: How Progressive White People Perpetuate Racial Harm.* In one passage, she calls out the "strings" attached to diversity, and how, at the end of the day, what White people are really concerned about is status. She claims that "White progressives who can afford to send their children to private schools do enjoy the small amount of racial diversity these schools typically have . . . but that diversity must be from the right groups and in the right numbers. A little 'diversity' is hip today, but 'too much' and we lose status."[2] Clearly, Kaitlyn's priority was obtaining and maintaining status by becoming a member of an elite club—one that "understandably" would not have wanted her if she were Black (i.e., "low-status"). There is a big difference between racial charity and racial parity, and Kaitlyn was a much bigger champion of the former than the latter.

I will return to Kaitlyn's story later in the chapter. For now, I want to shift gears and elaborate on what I view as the parallels between the psychological processes underlying most forms of addiction and those underlying White Americans' dogged commitment to endorsing and/or defending White supremacy. One of the biggest commonalities is the need to engage in a counterproductive pattern of behavior despite having access to information indicating that it would be better to abstain—and knowing this, perhaps the addict has tried to stop, but failed.

The Nature of White Supremacy Addiction

Imagine you come across a person who is a chain-smoker. You inform them that smoking is highly detrimental to their health. You make it clear that this is not merely your opinion but the conclusion of world-renowned physicians and researchers. You provide the person with studies showing the injurious impact of smoking on their health and longevity. You offer unassailable evidence that the toxic smoke they exhale does harm to other people as well. Finally, you furnish them with a spreadsheet showing the staggering sum of money they squander on tobacco each year. In the end, they are left with a long list of personal, social, and financial reasons to stop smoking. Will they quit?

When it comes to addictions, sometimes information works. More often, it does not. There are at least two problems with the "information as intervention" strategy. The first is that it assumes that the person is unaware of the facts that you are providing to them. Every smoker already knows that smoking is unhealthy. It is impossible not to know, given the hacking cough, shortness of breath, chest tightness, and other adverse symptoms that smokers experience, firsthand, after commencing the habit.

The second problem is that it assumes that the information you're offering will be processed by the smoker in a way that leads to a rational decision. The impulse to smoke is not just in the mind; it's in the body. Like other addictions, the habit is also sustained and justified by a host of defense mechanisms that hinder an objective assessment of the consequences of one's actions. These defense mechanisms include *avoidance* (e.g., "I don't want to talk about it"), *denial* (e.g., "I don't have a problem"), *minimization* (e.g., "It's not that bad"), and *rationalization* (e.g., "It's all your fault").

Similar to smokers' inevitable awareness, I believe that it is nearly impossible to live one's entire life in the United States as a White person and *not* be aware of the existence of anti-Black racism or White privilege. Indeed, research demonstrates that White people are so aware of the societal advantages of Whiteness that they would have to be paid tens of millions of dollars to live their lives as a Black person.[3] What they may not fully appreciate is their own complicity in perpetuating racial inequality, because, like many addicts, they utilize the same defense mechanisms—avoidance, denial, minimization, and rationalization.

As a former smoker, I am all too aware of these tactics. Being a reasonably rational person did not stop me from engaging in all manner of delusion when striving to sustain my habit. I was not a smoker due to any lack of information. For one thing, there was a warning label on every pack of cigarettes—often with a graphic photo—clearly illustrating the grievous effect of cigarette smoke on various vital organs. I was never skeptical of the credibility of the individuals (e.g., the surgeon general) or institutions (e.g., the Centers for Disease Control and Prevention) issuing these warnings. I had the information, and I was motivated to avoid people who might reiterate what I already knew—often engaging in some form of denial, minimization, or rationalization when I did run into them.

Morality was also moot. I didn't start smoking because I turned into a bad person, nor do other people start, or continue, to smoke because they are morally bereft. The same goes for those who are addicted to alcohol and other drugs. Although people suffering from substance use disorders may engage in regrettable behaviors when they are in the throes of active addiction, insufficient morality is rarely, if ever, the underlying cause of addiction. In this way, suggesting addiction as a useful metaphorical lens through which to view racism is neither moral condemnation nor exoneration. It is simply a framework for understanding a persistent and recurring pattern of harmful behaviors that contradict the values and ideals of the person perpetrating them.

Finally, my own self-interest did not compel me to quit smoking. I was fully aware that ending my habit would have benefited me physically, socially, and financially. And yet, I remained a smoker.

There are striking parallels between the psychological processes that characterize both addiction and racism. Like smokers' failure to quit, White people's compulsive engagement with racism is not for lack of information, morality, or collective self-interest. If we think of White supremacy, and the racism that sustains it, as an addiction, then it should come as no surprise that informational, moral, and self-interest-related appeals—all the tactics that antiracist educators have employed to date—have failed to produce dramatic shifts in racial equity. Understanding that White people's addiction to White supremacy—to maintaining the myth of the legitimacy of White exceptionalism—is not simply an idea, ideal, or ideology but a profound *need* will go a long way toward developing shrewd and healthy coping strategies.

This need-based component of White supremacy is central to its characterization as an addiction. *The Merriam-Webster Dictionary*'s primary definition of addiction is "a compulsive, chronic, physiological or psychological *need* for a habit-forming substance, behavior, or activity having *harmful* physical, psychological, or social effects" (italics added). In short, an addiction is characterized by the need to engage in behavior that produces harm for oneself and/or others.

Ironically, not only is engagement with the behavior harmful, but disengagement can also produce negative consequences, at least in the short term. Consistent with this idea, the *Webster*'s definition continues by asserting that failure to indulge in the habit can result in a person experiencing "well-defined symptoms such as anxiety, irritability, tremors, or nausea." This "damned if you do, damned if you don't" aspect of addiction often leads to a vicious cycle of repetition.

Indeed, repetition is explicitly stated in the secondary definition of addiction in *Webster's*: "a strong inclination to do, use, or indulge in something repeatedly." This "something" could be anything, as the National Health Service (NHS) in the United Kingdom indicates: "Addiction is most commonly associated with gambling, drugs, alcohol and smoking, but it's possible to be addicted to just about anything, including: work . . . internet . . . shopping." Addiction is further connoted by the idea that one tried to stop but simply couldn't.

In summary, there appear to be at least three core characteristics of addiction:

- Need

- Harm

- Repetition

The need component of addiction distinguishes it from ordinary attitudes and preferences.[4] There is a big difference between liking whiskey and needing whiskey. Similarly, there is a difference between believing that Black people are inferior to White people and *needing* to believe that Black people are inferior to White people. History suggests that White people's need to believe in the inferiority of Black people is even stronger than White people's actual belief in the inferiority of Black people.

For example, White people needed to tell themselves that Black people were dirty and disease-ridden in order to justify the desire for separate public facilities. Yet White people had no problem with their children being cared for by Black people, despite the close physical contact. While this scenario shows a stark contradiction with respect to the alleged fear of contamination, it reveals crystal-clear consistency with regard to hierarchy and group status. In short, equal-status contact is shunned, whereas subservient contact is embraced.

Similarly, White people insisted throughout the era of enslavement that Black people were unintelligent, yet they were willing to go to great lengths to prevent Black people from learning to read and write. If someone were truly compromised intellectually, the pertinent question would be whether it is even possible to teach them to read and write. Clearly, that was not the question in White people's minds. Again, the *need* to believe in the inferiority is greater than the actual belief in that inferiority. This harkens back to the rationalization function of addiction. White people needed to believe in the inferiority and deficiency of Black people in order to justify oppressing and exploiting them.

But *why* do White people have such a deep-seated need for White supremacy and/or Black inferiority? Part of the answer lies in the very foundation of personhood and freedom for White people in the United States, a society in which freedom has been defined in contrast to slavery, and personhood by Whiteness vis-à-vis Blackness. This idea was succinctly summarized by the Nobel Prize–winning novelist Toni Morrison, who wrote that "nothing highlighted freedom—if it did not in fact create it—like slavery."

Scholars Sanaz Mobasseri, William Kahn, and Robin Ely have theorized about the ways in which this need for race-based inequality and exploitation impacts the workplace, and American society more broadly. They argue that early White Americans, most of whom fled to America in search of freedom from their European oppressors, had a particularly strong need to believe in the possibility of their own freedom and prosperity—a belief buttressed by the undeniable "unfreedom" of enslaved Black people. In the scholars' paper "Racial Inequality in Organizations: A Systems Psychodynamic Perspective," they write:

> The early European settlers were drawn by the promise of freedoms and economic opportunities that had been unavailable to them in the class-locked, religiously restrictive societies of their home countries.... American ideals provided the cultural foundation for capitalism—a "free" market economy that produced not only things to be sold to others through voluntary agreements but also selves— "self-made" new American men. However, these ostensibly self-made men were made at the expense of [Black] bodies who were denied selfhood.... To conceal these pernicious features of capitalism, racial categories were socially constructed, [and] reified by

slavery. . . . The establishment of a racial hierarchy, which positioned Whiteness at the top and Blackness at the bottom, thus redefined American freedom.[5]

The very definition of freedom and the "American Dream" in race-based terms created not only an economic need but a psychological, even existential, need for White identity—an identity that did not exist in these settlers' countries of origin. Whiteness itself became a path to self-worth—for many, the only one they had. Without Black people beneath them, White people risked losing their very identity. This centrality of Whiteness to one's personhood raised a question: Was it even possible to conceive of being a free White person without invoking the presumed inferiority of Blackness? The answer appears to have been no.

Mobasseri, Kahn, and Ely go on to argue that even poor White people in America "were able to use the privilege of Whiteness to differentiate themselves from actual slaves and to dull the indignities of their circumstances. 'Freedom' was thus predicated on dominance, replicating the very imperial system these new American men claimed to have rejected. . . . In short, the privilege of Whiteness, relative to the 'stain' of being Black, enabled White Americans to ward off any sense of potential un-freedom."

In many ways, this analysis provides a response to James Baldwin's inquiry, included in this book's introduction, about why White people found it so necessary to have a "nigger" in the first place: Their very sense of personhood and freedom depended on it. If the entire value of one's existence is conditioned on the superiority of Whiteness in relation to Blackness, then this racial hierarchy will be reinforced and defended at all costs.

Toni Morrison also contemplated the social utility of this presumed Black inferiority for White immigrants arriving in America:

In becoming an American, from Europe, what one has in common with the other immigrant is contempt for me [as a Black person]. . . . Becoming an American is based on an attitude: an exclusion of me. It wasn't negative to them—it was unifying. When they got off the boat, the second word they learned was "nigger." . . . Every immigrant knew he would not come at the very bottom. He had to come above at least one group—and that was us.[6]

What all this suggests is that although White supremacy exists in every Western nation, the *need* for White supremacy is particularly strong in the United States due to its unique history of race-based slavery, the centrality of a particularly exploitative form of capitalism, and the critical importance of Whiteness in defining personhood and freedom.[7] The brazen hypocrisy of a national creed that preaches freedom, liberty, and meritocracy while practicing slavery, oppression, and "inheritocracy" is galling. However, the preservation of White supremacy required the wholehearted embrace of—even the unapologetic doubling-down on—such hypocrisy and contradiction.

At the same time, I want to make clear, as Isabel Wilkerson did in her masterful book *Caste: The Origins of Our Discontents,* that Black-White racism is not the only game in town. People may also be addicted to other forms of ethnocentrism, or to patriarchy. Nevertheless, without White supremacy, White Americans find themselves in an existential vacuum searching for an identity that aligns with the social, cultural, economic, and political foundations of the society in which they live.

This leads us to a different question, which pertains to the acquisition of White supremacy addiction. Although most addictions are acquired through conscious and deliberate pathways—such as voluntary initiation due to curiosity, experimentation, or peer pressure—sometimes an addiction can be acquired through the environment, without any agency or awareness on the part of the person afflicted with it. One illustration of this environment-to-individual process is an infant born to a parent with a substance use disorder. If the womb represents the diffuse system of society and the infant represents the individual afflicted with the addiction, then White supremacy can pervade both the system and the individual, as they are inextricably interconnected. Thus, the individual doesn't have to decide to stick a needle in their arm, so to speak. The addiction is something that is transmitted environmentally and intergenerationally. The "substance" is so deeply and diffusely embedded in every fiber of American society that the acquisition of the addiction does not require voluntary initiation.[8]

However, once it is in place, it becomes part of a norm and culture that define reality for those afflicted with it. Robin DiAngelo has argued that the socialization of White American children—even (or especially) the poorest ones—includes the tacit or explicit message that they are better than Black people.[9] In *Nice Racism,* she writes:

> The moment the real meaning of poverty crystallized for me came one day when I was seven and my mother took us to visit another family. My sisters and I played with their children while the adults visited, and as we were leaving I was the last one out the door. As I passed through I heard one of the children ask her mother, "What's wrong with them?" . . . The mother held her finger to her lips and whispered, "Shhh, they're poor." . . . I was acutely aware that I was poor, that I was dirty, that I was not "normal," and that there was something "wrong" with me. But I also knew that I was not Black. We were at the lower rungs of society, but there was always someone on the ladder, just below us. . . . I can remember many occasions when I reached for candy or uneaten food lying out in public and was admonished by my grandmother not to touch it because a "colored person" may have touched it. I was told not to sit in certain places lest a "colored" person had sat there. The message was clear: if a Black person touched something, it became dirty.[10]

The message is clear indeed. White people *need* Black inferiority—the "nigger" that Baldwin referred to. As DiAngelo's passage indicates, one inherent challenge of this need resides in the fact that White people realize, deep down, that it is a contrived and manufactured superiority complex— one that is often disconfirmed by the evidence right under their noses. However, the delusion is maintained by nonconscious processes. Like most forms of motivated reasoning, rationalization, and wishful thinking, the process of delusion loses power if people attempt to engage in it consciously. Rather, it is an automatic motivation to suppress—a process that operates outside of conscious awareness, intent, or control.

For over a century, the concept of self-deception has presented a conundrum for psychologists because the same person serves as both the deceiver and the deceived—making it a knotty and puzzling psychological phenomenon. Nevertheless, we know that people are very adept at performing this psychological sleight of hand—making it possible for them to believe whatever they want to, even while "realizing" on some nonconscious level that what they "believe" is not actually true.

■ ■ ■

For behavior to qualify as an addiction, there must exist not only need but also harm and repetition. Historically, we have seen nothing but repetition. We have also witnessed tremendous harm. White people have shown an extraordinary propensity for destroying Black bodies in order to uphold White supremacy. That tendency persists today—reflected in White people's willingness to inflict harm not only on Black bodies, but on their own bodies, in the service of upholding White supremacy.

As an example, Marc Morial, CEO of the National Urban League, recounts an instance when his father, Dutch Morial, a state legislator, witnessed virulent opposition to a proposal to end the practice of separating blood by race in the local blood banks of Louisiana in the 1960s. Despite the fact that the proposal would surely save more lives—including White lives—it was vehemently opposed by Rep. Archie Davis, a White legislator in Louisiana, who famously claimed, "I would see my family die and go to eternity before I would see them have one drop of nigger blood in them."[11]

Decades later, sociologist Arlie Hochschild traveled to Louisiana to interview people who, many would say, vote against their own self-interest. They love to hunt and fish but support politicians who pollute and destroy their wetlands and natural resources. They have small businesses but support policies that strengthen large corporations that put mom-and-pop establishments out of business.

In her 2016 book, *Strangers in Their Own Land: Anger and Mourning on the American Right,* Hochschild investigated this paradox, seeking to understand why so many poor White conservatives were fervently in favor of Donald Trump. The short answer is that many people were voting according to how they *felt* as opposed to what they thought. In other words, it wasn't that they didn't have concerns about his policies, his personality, or even his mental stability. It was that they had a deeper need to be seen, and to be granted respect and superiority, in a world where they felt they were losing status to Black people.[12] This made them willing to harm themselves politically (and medically and financially) in order to reap the emotional and psychological benefits of Whiteness.

This phenomenon is not new. It is an example of what W. E. B. Du Bois called the "psychological wage" of Whiteness. Simply put, White people are willing to forgo certain political, economic, and health benefits in exchange for the ego-based rewards that Whiteness itself confers. Make no mistake—these harmful decisions are made in the service of protecting White privilege even if it means metaphorically cutting off one's nose to spite one's face.

In her 2021 book, *The Sum of Us: What Racism Costs Everyone and How We Can Prosper Together,* author Heather McGhee investigates what she calls the "solidarity dividend," or what White people also stand to gain from supporting antiracist policies perceived as benefiting Black people, as well as what they stand to lose by allowing racial resentment to fuel opposition to policies aimed at establishing racial equality. The iconic example, depicted on the cover of the book, is the integrated swimming pool, a contrast to many White communities' decision to drain their public swimming pools during desegregation rather than keep the pools open and allow Black children to swim in them. The result was that White kids ended up with no neighborhood pool either.

However, eminent Duke economist William A. Darity Jr. has a different interpretation of the notion of the solidarity dividend. He argues that "McGhee's book perpetuates the mythology of mutual deprivation of blacks in general and non-elite whites" when in actuality it is primarily Black people who face systemic deprivation.[13] In addition to the "psychological" wage of Whiteness, he makes the case that there is a "material" wage of Whiteness as well. He argues that it is often the case that poor White people endure only temporary inconvenience, while society makes other arrangements for them (e.g., the New Deal). The deprivation of Black people, on the other hand, tends to be more permanent, as Black deprivation is the way that American society was designed to operate. Even today, Whites with only a high school education have more wealth than Blacks with a college degree.[14] He concludes by stating:

> I wish McGhee's analysis was correct. If it were, there would be no essential reason for anti-black racism to persist. If we could just enlighten non-elite whites about their "true interests," we could move forward toward the good society. Lamentably, her analysis is incorrect. Whites gain financially both in relative and absolute terms from the American system of racial hierarchy. . . . [A racially just society] will require intense and sustained struggle—and finally, a majority of white Americans trade white privilege in exchange for a just society. We cannot produce a racially just society without diminishing the relative position of white Americans . . . but we may be able to avoid diminishing their absolute position.[15]

Darity's last point is particularly important. If "winning" is defined in relative terms (i.e., to be successful, I must have more than you) rather than absolute terms (i.e., to be successful, I must have sufficient resources for me), then there is really no way to get White people engaged with solving the problem of racial inequality. Returning to our previous arguments, if White people need Whiteness, *and* White people need Blackness to be in an inferior position for Whiteness to even mean anything, then this presents an eternal zero-sum game in which any gain for Black people will be seen as a loss for White people.[16]

There is recent scientific data showing that White people tend to construe not only "winning" but fairness in relative terms. This means that White people will oppose policies that close the gap between Black and White people even if those policies simultaneously benefit White people.

In a 2022 paper titled "If You Rise, I Fall: Equality Is Prevented by the Misperception That It Harms Advantaged Groups," social psychologists Derek Brown, Drew Jacoby-Senghor, and Isaac Raymundo showed that dominant group members are less threatened by increased equality within their own group—equality among White people, for example—than increased equality between groups (e.g., increased equality between Black and White people).[17] This can prompt White people to vote for policies that enhance inequality between Black and White people even if it hurts White people in the process.

Conversely, they may also vote against policies that financially benefit White people if those policies also increase equality between Black and White people. In another paper, titled "Majority Members Misperceive Even 'Win-Win' Diversity Policies as Unbeneficial to Them," Brown and Jacoby-Senghor showed that majority group members perceived diversity as a zero-sum game—believing that policies that help underrepresented minorities actually hurt majority group members, even if, in reality, these policies helped majority group members too.[18]

In essence, it may be difficult for White people to conceptualize a "win-win" situation when other racial groups are involved. What is both interesting and important is that the findings of these studies were not explained by ideological differences among dominant group members. In other words, liberals and conservatives tended to see the situation in the same way.

The willingness to perpetrate self-harm can go to even greater extremes. In his book *Dying of Whiteness: How the Politics of Racial Resentment Is Killing America's Heartland,* Vanderbilt University medical professor Jonathan Metzl recounts the physical harm that White people are willing to impose on themselves in order to preserve White supremacy. As a physician, Metzl witnessed firsthand how racially motivated resistance to "Obamacare" by members of poor White communities directly contributed to their mortality. As one patient told him—echoing the sentiments of Louisiana legislator Archie Davis when faced with the desegregation of blood banks—"Ain't no way I would ever support Obamacare or sign up for it. . . . I would rather die."[19]

Like Hochschild, Metzl describes these seemingly irrational reactions as being the result of perceived self-victimization, and a desperate desire to recapture some honor or status that they *feel* they have lost. However, as suggested by the Brown and Jacoby-Senghor studies, all that is required for White people to *feel* victimized or dishonored is greater racial equality. Not doing better than Black people is inherently offensive to White people because it violates the sacred covenant of White superiority that has always been integral to White Americans' identity. Black progress, even in relative terms, is a direct assault on the White ego. Metzl explains that these extreme political positions are often "playing to anxieties about white victimhood" and that "dying for a cause" amounts to a "modern-day form of kamikaze."[20]

In short, the "cause" for which White people are willing to crash the plane or throw themselves on the sword is the preservation of White supremacy. And they are willing to incur tremendous harm to themselves—including death—in the service of this pursuit. This is clearly consistent with one of the defining features of addiction. But not everyone is so extreme or dramatic in their consumption of White supremacy. The addiction can show up in different ways for different people—just as alcohol can produce different kinds of drunks: happy, mean, morose, comatose, or high-functioning. In the next section, I will discuss three distinct ways in which White supremacy addiction can show up.

The Dolphin, the Ostrich, and the Shark

As Kaitlyn's story illustrates, it is possible to hold egalitarian values while being complicit in the preservation of White supremacy. The Abraham Lincoln example cited in the introduction illustrates this paradox quite convincingly. Both Kaitlyn and Honest Abe are examples of what I refer to as "dolphins." Dolphins have strong humanitarian and prosocial values that lead them to want to help others and seek social justice. However, multiple lines of social psychological research, such as *aversive racism theory,* support the notion that White people can be committed to antiracist values while engaging in racist behaviors.[21] The charity of egalitarianism is not always accompanied by a desire for parity in racial outcomes.

As discussed in the introduction, White supremacy does not have to be characterized by hatred, violence, or cruelty. It is about the active or passive maintenance of racial hierarchy and disparity. This can show up in counterintuitive ways, including philanthropy. Many scholars, such as Ibram X. Kendi, have analyzed the historical and contemporary role of the "White savior"—who provides assistance to people of color in order to feel powerful or exert control.[22] Other Black writers have observed that philanthropy itself can be a way to elevate one's personal power and social status.[23] As Charles Blow opined:

> Among the wealthy who are thus inclined, they give a little and expect to be praised a lot. Philanthropy serves as a badge of benevolence, a kind of shield to justify excess, to enjoy privilege and the spoils of a system of white supremacy. Even more manipulative and self-serving, it offers a way of gaining cultural currency among the elite, to move up the social ladder from nouveau riche and nearer to old money.[24]

The point is that White supremacy can arrive in any number of beautifully wrapped packages. Harvard sociologist Marshall Ganz, who was a White organizer and participant during Freedom Summer in Mississippi in 1964, discusses the process of learning and adjusting his own perspective of what it really means to be helpful in the struggle for racial equality. In his book *People, Power, Change: Organizing for Democratic Renewal,* he states, "I began to learn the difference between justice and charity. Charity asks, 'What's wrong? Let me help!' Justice asks, 'Why is it happening? Let me change it!' When you ask [this latter question], you get pushback."[25]

He hit the nail on the head. Most White people are asking how they can help, rather than why help is needed in the first place. An honest answer to the latter question would require not only a deep social examination but also a level of self-examination that most White dolphins are not comfortable with. So they don't attempt to change the system—the same system that serves them—in any profound way. That is what Kaitlyn taught me.

You may be wondering how dolphins can genuinely value egalitarianism if they are addicted to White supremacy. The short answer is cognitive dissonance—a disconnect between how one wishes to view oneself and how one actually behaves.[26] Dissonance is also relevant to addiction. According to Dr. Andrew Proulx, cognitive dissonance is a strong component of addiction and tends to set in motion a whole series of defense mechanisms, such as those mentioned earlier in the chapter (i.e., avoidance, denial, minimization, and rationalization).

In fact, dolphins are so dependent on these defense mechanisms that they often respond in the most reactive and explosive ways when the discrepancy between their ideal values and their actual behaviors is pointed out.[27]

Another manifestation of White supremacy addiction is the "ostrich." Unlike the dolphin, who struggles with dissonance, the ostrich does not have strong intrinsic values around equity and inclusion, and is relatively unconcerned about social justice. Like an ostrich that buries its head in the sand, these people tend to look the other way when they witness racism, or when the topic of racial inequality surfaces. What most concerns them is pursuing their own self-interest. If that means supporting DEI, great. If it means opposing DEI, no problem.

Perhaps the most straightforward manifestation of White supremacy addiction is the "shark." Unlike dolphins or ostriches, sharks are neither invested in egalitarianism nor indifferent to it. They are invested in *anti*-egalitarianism, or social *in*equality. What they value is power—power to dominate others, rather than power to uplift others. They prefer having a hierarchical food chain, as long as they are the apex predator. Therefore, sharks commit considerable energy and resources to preserving, or even enhancing, the racial hierarchy. In empirical terms, these are people who score high on the social dominance orientation scale, a personality variable that measures preference for social hierarchy.[28]

Interestingly, philanthropy is not the sole domain of dolphins. Sharks can also give. In fact, research has shown that charitable support can be a way to preserve the racial hierarchy through appeasement.[29] Strategically

showing generosity, particularly in the face of civil unrest, can be an in-
sidious way to preserve "peace on the plantation," so that harmony and
oppression can exist simultaneously.

No matter what the particular manifestation of White supremacy is—
dolphin, ostrich, or shark—at the end of the day, the ultimate result is the
perpetuation of racial inequality.

■ ■ ■

Kaitlyn upheld the legitimacy of White exceptionalism, even while showing an ostensible commitment to promoting racial equality. Most White
people make excuses for racism, regardless of their social values. And it's
not simply the case of "nobody's perfect." Racism is justified by White
people in a way that other socially undesirable behaviors (e.g., pedophilia)
are not. Part of the reason is that most White people can personally relate
to overt White racists, on some level, even if they find their actions dis-
tasteful.[30] Egalitarianism is an ideology that has more to do with people
being treated with equal dignity, kindness, and respect, rather than social
groups having equal positions in society. Egalitarianism is about process—
more specifically, process *in theory*. Parity, on the other hand, is about actual outcomes. It is about the worthiness of equal status, not simply equal
compassion.

Charles Blow highlighted this distinction in a vivid and compelling
way during my interview with him, arguing that (progressive) White people often "object to [racial] cruelty, but it's in the same way they object to
animal cruelty—not because they believe the dog is equal; they just don't
want to see anything suffer." The chief takeaway is that it is possible to be
pro-egalitarianism without being pro-parity.

In a similar vein, it is possible to be sympathetic without being empa-
thetic. Returning to the passage from Abraham Lincoln's speech, what
we see is profound sympathy for the suffering of enslaved Black people,
without an ounce of real empathy.[31] In fact, when the newly freed Blacks
began to follow General Sherman, Lincoln asked, "What do these Negros

want?"[32] This question reveals a profound lack of not only empathy but also imagination. What would anyone want in such a situation? They want protection. They want opportunity. They want dignity.

On the flip side, Lincoln's speech shows a disconcerting ability to empathize with the perspective of White confederates. He fully understands their views regarding the inferiority of Blacks—he just does not approve of their brutality. He is bothered by the cruelty, *not* the White supremacy per se. To build on Blow's analogy, just because a pet is not equal to its owner, it doesn't give the owner the right to mistreat it. Lots of people get very angry and upset when they see a dog being brutalized, even if those same people acquiesce to disparate treatment, such as a restaurant's decision to allow humans but not allow dogs. The chief question with regard to White supremacy is one of parity, not kindness.

During my book tour for *The Conversation,* I realized that my PRESS (Problem Awareness, Root Cause Analysis, Empathy, Strategy, Sacrifice) model—which served as the organizing foundation of the book, had a weak cornerstone. The centerpiece of the model—empathy—was frequently unsatisfied, despite awareness of the problem and the availability of viable strategies to fix it. Strategies are only activated and executed when racial empathy is present—which, historically, only seems to have occurred in instances of cruelty.

If we think about every major social movement focused on racial equality in which White people were active participants, they have all occurred in the context of abject human cruelty, not racial disparity per se. The most recent example is the gut-wrenching murder of George Floyd. Police brutality was never rare—such extreme cruelty vividly captured on camera was. Without the cruelty, racism becomes mundane and palatable, if not preferable, to White people. Indeed, research has demonstrated that White people, as a whole, are relatively indifferent to racism—even clear-cut racism—when it doesn't involve cruelty.[33] In the Kaitlyn scenario, there was racial exclusion, but not cruelty, making the situation "imperfect," but still acceptable.

In the absence of visible cruelty, there may even exist greater empathy between White dolphins and White sharks (e.g., Abraham Lincoln and

Robert E. Lee) than between either group and Black people. White dolphins and White sharks have many of the same needs—as described in depth in this chapter—and oftentimes congruent perspectives. They both understand, on some level, how a White officer might have felt afraid when encountering a Black person on the street—due to their own shared fear of Black people. They also understand how an employer might see a Black person as a "diversity" hire, political correctness aside—due to their own (latent) assumptions about White superiority. As previously argued, there can be multiple manifestations of the same intoxication.

■ ■ ■

For me, arriving at the conclusion that racism operates like an addiction was liberating, even empowering. Although progress is entirely possible, it is important to understand the limitations of our ability to control the behavior of other people.[34] At the same time, I understand, and appreciate, the fact that not everyone will agree with my metaphorical diagnosis. The portrayal of White supremacy as an addiction will either resonate with the reader or it won't. The relevant point is that White supremacy is a recurring feature in American society despite multiple efforts to eradicate it. That is irrefutable. So, the key question centers around the resources and strategies that Black people can employ to deal with this reality.

That is where I will turn my attention for the remainder of the book. Before plunging into the substance of playing, changing, and leaving the game, I will set the stage by describing my own introduction to Black self-determination—the all-Black neighborhood in which I grew up. In the next chapter, I return to my childhood years to give the reader a better sense of who I am and the factors that led me to become a champion of both DEI and Black empowerment.

Two

St. Martin's Village: Creating "Ease of Spirit"

St. Martin's Village was a cocoon that allowed me to develop my wings while ensconced in the warm embrace of a protective and loving Black community. Known to locals simply as "the Village," the Lexington, Kentucky, neighborhood where I spent the bulk of my formative childhood years was a middle-class Black enclave with modest 1960s ranch homes, wide streets, mature trees, and manicured lawns. Before turning to the rest of the book—and exploring the three pathways of playing the game, changing the game, and leaving the game—I feel compelled to reflect on the ways in which my childhood shaped my own perception of the standing and significance of Black people in America.

Both my neighborhood and the broader Black community were filled with role models. My pediatrician was Black. My dentist was Black. Our insurance agent was Black. There were Black teachers, principals, engineers, nurses, small business owners, and police officers who lived in St. Martin's Village, as well as cooks, postal clerks, and factory workers.

One of the police officers was married to my Aunt Lynn—one of my mother's eight siblings—who lived around the block from us. My friends and I would ride to their house on our bikes, uninvited and unannounced, during our cycling adventures. We would rummage through their pantry for snacks, then head to the fridge for ice and apple juice to fill our water bottles. On the way out, we'd greet their droopy-eyed, floppy-eared dog, Hannibal—a bloodhound named after the legendary African general who led an army toward Rome mounted on elephants. On other days, we would make similar stopovers at the homes of other extended family members and friends in the neighborhood.

My third-grade teacher, Mrs. Hunt, also lived in St. Martin's Village. One thing I remember about Mrs. Hunt was her impeccable sense of style. She was always dressed to kill, often in a two-piece polyester leisure suit with a silk blouse and pearls. She drove a Jaguar XJ6 that never had a speck of dust on it, thanks to her devoted husband, who could be seen with a bucket of soapy water, a pile of towels, and a green garden hose nearly every time we rode our bicycles past their house. "Hi, Mr. Hunt!" we'd yell. He'd smile and wave back. It was a carefree existence.

Growing up in St. Martin's Village, I never feared White people. I never harbored hatred toward White people. And most important, I never felt an ounce of envy toward White people. There was no reason to; I had everything I needed. In fact, I do not remember thinking about White people at all, except as either an abstract concept or specific White individuals. I certainly never thought of Whiteness as a basis for social hierarchy, with Black people being less powerful than White people. If anything, I assumed the opposite.

I later discovered that my experiences in St. Martin's Village were a far cry from those of many Black children raised in predominantly White communities. I cringe when I hear some of my friends—who are Black parents living in White neighborhoods—telling their kids not to run down the street yelling while they are playing, or forbidding their teenage children from ringing the doorbells of neighbors when they are selling raffle tickets for school fundraisers. Their wariness is understandable. Black people have been shot in White neighborhoods for ringing doorbells, or simply jogging down the street. It is a sad and stark contrast to the unfettered freedom I enjoyed.

In St. Martin's Village, not only would my friends and I ring the doorbells of random neighbors to sell cookies, chocolate bars, and raffle tickets, but sometimes we'd do it just to have a little fun. On occasion, we would play "ding-dong ditch," where we'd ring someone's doorbell, then scatter and hide before they got to the porch. The game was especially gratifying if the constant goading would provoke an otherwise mild-mannered neighbor to scream into the summer darkness, "Y'all badass kids better not ring my doorbell again or I'm gonna call your mommas on you!" They would linger outside for several seconds, seething amid the chorus of chirping crickets while they scanned the horizon for any sign of the culprits. Satisfied, we'd move on to the next victim.

There was always mischief. In Whitney Young Park—named after a fellow Kentuckian who was a leader in the Civil Rights Movement—we'd highjack the smoothly paved tennis courts and use them as our own outdoor roller rink, given the popularity of roller boogie in the late '70s and early '80s. Black adults trying to do what the courts were built for—play tennis—would give us the side-eye, the hand on the hip, or even the death stare, depending on how boisterous we became. To smooth things over, we would collect stray tennis balls during our disco laps around the court, receiving subtle nods of gratitude as we returned the balls to their owners.

I was never worried for a second that our antics might lead to real danger. The thought that I might get shot for ringing a doorbell, or have the police called on me for turning the tennis court into a roller rink, never entered my mind. That kind of fear is unhealthy, even traumatic, for a child. In the worst-case scenario, a displeased parent would be waiting for us when we got home. Being a hellion should be a rite of passage for every kid, not a death sentence.

The Black environment of my childhood in St. Martin's Village was filled with not only love, inspiration, joy, and protection but also *patience*. Looking back, I am blown away by the abundance of patience possessed by the village that raised me. It is a level of patience that White people rarely show toward Black children. This patience and tolerance also gave me the space to embrace my rambunctious personality and explore my unique talents—without hesitation or apology. In a nutshell, it gave me an unwavering sense of confidence.

In his book *The Devil You Know: A Black Power Manifesto,* Charles Blow explains how growing up in a nurturing Black environment provided him with a deep sense of security and self-assurance:

During my schooling, all of my spaces were safe. Almost every class-room I ever walked into, a Black person was the smartest person in that room, so as an adult I continued to believe that into every room I walked I could be the smartest person there. The security and com-fort of being inculcated and enveloped by Black culture, not just becoming "woke" to it as intellectual pursuit, a form of activism, or need for demonstrative rebellion, produced in me an overwhelming confidence and also an ease of spirit.[1]

His reference to an "ease of spirit" deeply resonates with me. It bril-liantly captures the freedom that Black environments provide—the ability for a Black child to simply be.

The History of the Village

Despite its critical impact on my development, I realized while writing this chapter how little I knew about the origins of my childhood neighborhood. So, I called my father—a brilliant man with a reverence for history—and asked if he could fill me in. He was more than happy to oblige. In addition to giving me an extensive oral account of the early days of St. Martin's Village, he sent me a series of newspaper articles published over the course of several decades. One of them was a fascinating piece from the *Lexington Herald-Leader* with the headline "Lexington Subdivi-sion Opened American Dream to Black Families in the 1950s." This article chronicled prior efforts to construct prosperous Black neighborhoods in Lexington, and how St. Martin's Village came to be. As the article details:

When rumors circulated in 1925 that black-owned land off North Limestone [Street] would be developed into a subdivision for blacks, more than 200 white citizens gathered in a nearby church and organized a successful effort to block it. But after World War II, Lexington's business leaders realized their little college and farming town needed to attract industry if it was to have a strong economy and viable middle class.[2]

And attract industry it did. In 1956, IBM built one of its largest plants in Lexington, creating thousands of jobs. Because IBM was an early adopter of what was then referred to as "Affirmative Action" (a precursor to DEI), this also resulted in the creation of good-paying jobs for members of the Black community. A *Washington Post* article documented IBM's impact on Lexington's economy, noting that "the company forced up local wages; brought more attention on education; and provided jobs not only for many people, but also for minority workers, who had had few career options before." According to Carl B. Cone, a former chair of the University of Kentucky's history department who was quoted in the article, "It really was the beginning of Lexington's industrial revolution."[3]

On the heels of IBM, industry poured into the area. Toyota constructed a large plant tasked with building the Camry, which also brought thousands of jobs and professional opportunities for the Black community. Other large manufacturers that relocated to the area were Trane, Xerox, Square D, WABCO, and Tempur-Pedic. The advent of manufacturing, combined with the existing agricultural, equine, and educational sectors, created a vibrant economy that supported a burgeoning Black middle class in Lexington.

This intensified the demand for new residential development, which led to the creation of St. Martin's Village, as well as other thriving Black subdivisions on the west side and north side of Lexington. As the *Lexington Herald-Leader* article reports:

> The big break came in 1955, when Joe Fister teamed with Chuck Seeberger and Joe Tuttle to build a 200-lot subdivision for blacks on 40 acres of farmland Fister owned on Price Road off Georgetown Road. St. Martin's Village was named for St. Martin de Porres (1579–1639), a mixed-race monk in Peru who is the patron saint for those seeking interracial harmony. The main street was called De Porres Avenue. "This will be as good as any subdivision in Lexington," Seeberger said in a 1955 *Lexington Herald* article that carried the headline, "First Negro Subdivision Planned on Fister Tract."[4]

One resident interviewed for the article commented: "It's a family-oriented neighborhood; almost like a big extended family. . . . We all grew up together. We were always in each other's houses. . . . We even got to know each other's relatives from out of town when they would visit. It's home."

This description is highly consistent with my experience of St. Martin's Village as a tight-knit community. In addition to the close interpersonal relationships, there was a strong sense of Black solidarity. My parents—who are both native Lexingtonians—were especially committed to championing Black businesses and education, being entrepreneurs and college graduates themselves. This stalwart support was due not only to their empathy with Black business owners but to their deep commitment to racial justice. As a result, they demanded that White businesses that received their dollars also support the Black community.

Lessons in Black Advocacy and Solidarity

On one memorable occasion when I was about ten years old, my mother, her best friend, and her best friend's daughter—my godmother and godsister—and I were at the mall one afternoon in late summer doing some back-to-school shopping. On the way home, my mother decided to swing by a nearby car dealership to check out a new model that she had been eyeing. When we entered the showroom, a stout, friendly White salesman bounded up to us with a big smile and hearty greeting.

"Good afternoon, folks! How're y'all doing today? Are there any questions I can answer for you?"

"Good afternoon. I'm doing well, thanks," my mother replied warmly. "I can't complain at all. Just a little bit worn out from all the shopping for these kids." Then she added, "Actually, I do have a question," before dropping what I thought was a bombshell at the time: "Do you have any Black salespeople?"

After a brief moment of silence from being caught off-guard, the salesman uttered, "Uh . . . yeah . . . sure. No problem, ma'am. Hold on just a moment. Let me find you someone, okay? I'll be right back."

My godsister, who was a year younger than me, and I were suddenly overwhelmed by the giddy, awkward discomfort that so often afflicts tweens. We exchanged wide-eyed gazes with our mouths agape in embarrassment, before burying our faces in our palms and bursting into nervous laughter.

My mother turned to us with her own wide-eyed gaze and half whispered: "What's the problem?" as our preadolescent giggling continued. Once we had settled down, she turned to us again and stated in a very matter-of-fact tone, no longer whispering: "I'm not going to buy a car from any dealership that doesn't have Black salespeople."

That moment has always stuck with me. The notion that we not only can, but should, demand representation in places where we spend our money has had a lingering impact on me. With the benefit of hindsight, I can begin to piece together how aspects of my childhood shaped me as a scholar, a writer, and a human being. My "truth to power" outlook didn't just happen by accident.

There was also proactive advocacy for Black representation when it came to the school system. My string of Black teachers was not a random outcome. My parents went to the school to request that I be put in their classrooms. They wanted me to be taught by as many Black teachers as possible, just as they had been during segregation in the 1950s and '60s. My Black elementary school principal, Mrs. Weathers, had been my mother's classroom teacher decades prior, in a segregated school, before becoming the head administrator in my integrated school. And she lived in St. Martin's Village as well, down the street from Mrs. Hunt.

Throughout my K–12 public school experience, there was Black representation at every level in every school—from the students, to the teachers, to the guidance counselors, and up to the principals. My junior high school homeroom and social studies teacher, Mrs. Akins, was a well-known and respected member of the community, given that her husband was the pastor of one of the local Black churches. She was close friends with my guidance counselor, Mr. Ferris—also Black. They both had a great relationship with the head principal, Mr. Cordoves, a swarthy Cuban man with a heavy accent. When I got into trouble—which was often—he would never suspend me or send me to detention. He would just stare me down with pursed lips and thick, furrowed eyebrows for what seemed like an eternity before releasing a deep sigh and beginning his tirade. "Mister Rrrobert," he would say, rolling his *r*'s. "Why you always here in my office because you acting like a clown in class? You are very smart. Why can't you learn and be a good student?" He would then throw another weighted stare my way, awaiting a response. I would shrug my shoulders.

Then, almost immediately, his demeanor would soften and he would begin to tell me a story—a variation of the same story he would recount every time I was in his office—about how he'd come to the United States from Cuba. It was a tall tale involving an epic journey over land and sea that had him swimming in the ocean and battling sharks. It contained not only nostalgic snapshots of the joy and vibrancy of the life he left behind in Cuba, but also an appreciation of the educational opportunities that existed in the United States. Opportunities that he insisted I not take for granted. I am not sure how or why he ended up in Kentucky. However, I have no doubt that he endured many encounters with discrimination, due to his towering height, dark complexion, and heavy accent. This might have been one of the reasons he had such a good relationship with the Black teachers and students at the school.

He was fearless as well. I remember that ahead of one of the school's dances, he warned the students against any "dirty dancing" they might be planning. He was plugged into the Black community, so he knew that George Clinton's funk classic "Atomic Dog" had just been released and there were two new sexually suggestive dances that were all the rage—one aptly named "the dog," and its counterpart "the alligator" (a horizontal interpretation of "the dog"). The dances were more about posturing than anything else, and we assumed that Mr. Cordoves might be sympathetic to a bit of feisty, but innocuous, sensuality due to his provenance from the land of salsa and merengue. He was not.

That evening came, and the DJ avoided playing "Atomic Dog" for hours. But the raucous crowd of a couple hundred students and their guests from other schools became restless. Caving in to the pressure, the DJ finally dropped the tune. When the synthesizer bass hit the two large subwoofers perched on the gym stage, the crowd exploded with excitement. Throngs of students grabbed a partner, hit the dance floor, and assumed the position. The bump and grind was on.

I distinctly remember the stupefied facial expression of one of the White teachers as she gasped in dismay, wholly unsure of what to do next. Mr. Cordoves, his face scrunched into a scowl, began frantically signaling to the various teachers to separate the students. The teachers were met with no cooperation or compliance from the gyrating adolescents. Finally, Mr. Cordoves had seen enough. In a fit of frustration, he stormed the stage, unplugged the music, grabbed the microphone, and let the jeering and booing crowd know, in no uncertain terms, that there would be no more "doggy dog," and that the party was over. He turned on the lights and herded everybody out of the gymnasium.

Despite the occasional flashes of fury, I remember him as a compassionate man. Looking back, I believe that hearing his fascinating stories about Cuba, sprinkled with Spanish words that I couldn't understand, is one of the reasons I became interested in Spanish and Latin American Studies, with a focus on Afro-Latinos. Another reason is that my high school Spanish teacher was a Black man.

During that time, in the 1980s, Lexington had four public high schools: Bryan Station, Henry Clay, Tates Creek, and Lafayette. My high school, Bryan Station, was the one that raised eyebrows among White people because it was the only predominantly Black high school in town. Even to this day, when I meet White Lexingtonians and they ask where I went to high school (a surreptitious way to discern social class), there is the inevitable pause followed by "Oh" and the figurative clutching of the pearls when I proudly proclaim it was Bryan Station.

My high school classmates and I had always assumed that Bryan Station was about 75 percent Black. But my yearbook suggests it was closer to 50 percent Black. No matter. It was the high school that people in Lexington saw as the "ghetto" one. In fact, even some Black people did not want their kids going to Bryan Station because of its reputation for "drama." This is consistent with research showing that White people, and Black people, associate Blackness with being low status.[5]

One of the distinctive and fascinating qualities of my high school, which had an impact on my educational experience, was how race intersected with class. In addition to St. Martin's Village, there were five other predominantly Black or all-Black "middle-class" neighborhoods in Lexington: Oakwood, Oakwood Estates, Radcliffe, Winburn, and Green Acres, all located on the west or north side of town. Combined, there were a few thousand people living in these communities. What is interesting is that *all* high school students in these Black neighborhoods were sent to Bryan Station, which created a not only large, but also relatively well-resourced, population of Black kids.

Almost everyone in town, regardless of their race or social class, went to public schools. All the high school students in most of the wealthy White neighborhoods were sent to Henry Clay or Tates Creek. In fact, Kentucky governor and prospective Democratic vice-presidential candidate Andy Beshear attended Henry Clay. Every single high schooler in a middle-class Black neighborhood was sent to Bryan Station. However, only a tiny handful of wealthy White high schoolers went to Bryan Station. This created a level of economic and social equality at Bryan Station that is rarely seen in integrated public schools.

Academic achievement was not seen as an exclusively "White" thing in my high school. I always had Black students in my advanced classes. Although I graduated in the top 10 percent of my high school class, there were a dozen or more Black folks who graduated ahead of me. I was a Black National Merit Scholarship Finalist, but I wasn't the only one. There was nothing exceptional about me. At my thirty-year high school reunion in 2019, there was a slew of successful Black professionals—physicians, lawyers, engineers, veterinarians, corporate executives, entrepreneurs, politicians, and a musician who plays with T. D. Jakes. You name the occupation, it was represented.

At the same time, social class did not create rigid fault lines within the Lexington Black community because most of us were only one or two generations removed from poverty. This means that we all had close family and/or friends who lived in under-resourced neighborhoods. I had lived in one myself—Aspendale, a large housing project on the east side of town where I spent the first five years of my life living with my maternal grandmother while my mother finished college. My grandmother was a pillar of the community—a very strong, and equally kind, woman whom everybody adored and nobody dared to mess with. She loved to garden, and even in the projects managed to grow seven-foot-high sunflowers in the ten square feet of earth in front of her home. I still remember that sunflower garden—a towering and majestic solar constellation hovering above me each day as I entered her house of love.

This relative absence of socioeconomic fault lines within the Lexingtonian Black community is very different from a city like New Orleans, for example, where the Black population has been divided along color and/or class lines for centuries. In Lexington, on the other hand, the advent of industry in the 1950s and '60s—combined with pro-justice legislation during that era—led to an economic boom and a substantial Black middle class, almost overnight. These fortuitous circumstances predated my birth in the early 1970s and did not run its course (largely due to Reagan-era policies) until I had become a young adult in the late 1980s.

In short, I just happened to be born in the right place at the right time. Historically, it was a time in America when both the overall wealth gap and the racial wealth gap were the lowest they had ever been. My developmental years occurred during a "sweet spot" for Black people. In many ways, my life is a fluke. In other ways, it was no fluke at all. Our story is not only about enslavement and struggle. Black people have always flourished when given the opportunity, just as the Greenwood neighborhood of Tulsa did half a century prior to my birth (until White people violently destroyed it). Many other Black enclaves across the country continue to thrive today.[6] These pockets of Black solidarity and achievement represent one reality of our community, and mine has indelibly shaped my worldview on Black empowerment, as well as my vision of what is possible.

A number of Black writers, including Toni Morrison, James Baldwin, Charles Blow, and Austin Channing Brown, have identified one of the most damning consequences of racism to be the stifling of Black creativity, imagination, and vision of what is possible. Therefore, one of the most powerful forms of Black resistance is not succumbing to the cynicism of grim expectations for what we, or our communities, can achieve.

The Gift of Armor in the Broader World

It wasn't until I emerged from my cocoon and went off to a college in the Deep South that was only 8 percent Black that I started to get a real idea of what "the game" was all about—White people feeling comfortable, superior, and in control. What an eye-opening experience that was! It was fascinating to hear what White people truly thought of Black people. For example, it was my first time learning that many White people assumed they were doing Black people a favor by allowing us in their social space.

I applied to several universities but ended up at Tulane in New Orleans, which had two points in its favor: a warm climate and a lively jazz scene. Tulane had awarded me a full-tuition scholarship, as well as a National Merit Scholarship that covered most of my room and board. The summer before our freshman year, Tulane invited me and other Black and Latine honor students who had declared an interest in science, engineering, or medicine (I was pre-med at the time) to participate in a program called ASIST (A Summer in the Sciences at Tulane). A group photo from 1989 that was sent to me in 2024 by August Martin, an old friend and ASIST participant, shows that there were about sixteen Black students and seven Latine students in the program. During that summer, we took field trips and were matched with mentors at Shell, Martin Marietta, and other large employers in southern Louisiana. We also took summer classes in calculus and computer science with Tulane professors.

During the same summer, there was a concurrent program called FSB (Freshman Summer Bridge). It was designed to provide support to students who needed extra help making the academic transition from high school to college. They took classes on time management and study skills, as well as an introductory college math course. The ASIST program and the FSB program were administered by the same office on campus, and the participants were housed in the same dormitory and attended the same social events (tours of the French Quarter, crawfish boils, trips to Biloxi Beach, etc.). What is intriguing and amusing is that the FSB cohort was predominantly White—with about two dozen White students and just a couple of Black and Puerto Rican students.

In effect, what Tulane's Educational Resource Center had done—intentionally or inadvertently—was put a group of academically gifted Black and Latine students in the same space as a large group of White students who needed academic assistance. Once again, I found myself in an integrated environment where Blackness was not subservient to Whiteness—at least in my mind.

Many of the FSB students were humorous and laid-back, albeit in a smug, self-assured way. A few of the White guys started referring to the FSB as the "Fucking Stupid Bastards" program, often with a goofy grin on their face. They seemed fascinated by the presence of so many able and ambitious people of color. Some of the more curious FSB participants expressed interest in hanging out with our group, and even asked if we would be willing to help them with their math homework. Other White folks in the program seemed resentful of the whole situation and wanted nothing to do with us.

I was also intrigued by the diversity within race. In Lexington, everyone was "plain old" Black or White with relatively little ethnic diversity within either race. In other words, most of the Black people were African American descendants of enslaved people who had been in the region for centuries, and the vast majority of the White people were the descendants of Irish, English, French, and Scottish immigrants who had been in the region for centuries.

In New Orleans, I was exposed to a diversity of White people that I had never seen before: French-speaking Cajuns, olive-skinned Italians, East Coast Jewish students, and many other groups—all with different food traditions, cultures, accents, and even physical features than those of the White people that I had grown up with. I have always been naturally curious about the world, and had traveled quite a bit prior to arriving at Tulane. Therefore, I wanted to explore friendships with many different types of people, which I thought would be a noble gesture on my part. In high school, all my close friends were Black. And we, the Black folks, were the "cool" kids. So, in a way, I felt I was doing the White kids a favor by opening myself up to cross-racial friendships.

However, they saw things differently. To them, hanging out with a

Black person *lowered* their status. So they were doing *me* a favor. *Wow.* I smile even as I type these words remembering my shock and amusement upon learning this. The news was much more intriguing than threatening. At that point in my life, I had developed a strong sense of self—my coat of armor was quite thick. Their questions or comments about Black people struck me as incredibly uninformed and a bit droll—not unlike a three-year-old child's claims that there are monsters hiding under the bed. *Poor kids,* I would think. This attitude is how I was able to approach the dense, highly charged material in my previous book, *The Conversation,* in such a dispassionate way. Because I did not grow up experiencing racial trauma, I am able to interact with racial ignorance and hostility with the self-assurance of knowing that I am not the one with the kooky ideas.

What was particularly disconcerting for me was noticing, over time, that I was beginning to hear more and more nutty ideas and justifications for racism. The White people on campus and in the city would boldly claim that their racism was due to all the crime in New Orleans. I did not grow up in a city with a lot of crime, so this "reasoned racism" deviated from the knee-jerk "backwoods" racism that I would occasionally see growing up. It was almost an attempt to convince me, through pseudo-logical, persuasive appeals. They would argue that it was Black people, not White people, doing almost all of the mugging and the murdering in the city. Or they would argue that Black people did not value education, and point out the cafeteria workers as examples of happy-go-lucky servants from a bygone era, or the Black bus driver who spoke non-standard English. They were seen as the "real" Black people. They thought that the ASIST Black folks were exceptions. They attempted to make a case for how reasonable and rational it was for White people to fear or despise "those" Black people, and even wondered why I didn't feel a bit embarrassed by the existence of "those" people.

This contrived perversion of reality is what ultimately compelled me to change the course of my advanced education. "Those" Black people were exactly like me—perhaps even better. The cafeteria workers at Tulane walked through the door with their heads held high in a defiant spirit of joy, despite the racialized indignities that they suffered on a daily basis.

That's real power. They showed a special kindness and affection toward the Black students, beaming with pride when they saw us coming through the lunch line. I remember one person in particular, Ms. Iona—whom many of us would affectionately refer to as Mama Iona. She was one of the lead cafeteria ladies and would always ask us, "How you doin' today, baby? You hungry?" before giving us a little extra food or something she'd made. It was an extension of the "Village" where I grew up. Mama Iona once told one of the cafeteria workers from Central America that I was studying Spanish, and that person started videotaping (on VHS) episodes of *Simplemente María* and other Spanish-language soap operas to help me with my listening comprehension.

These people who were being disparaged by outsiders were showing me genuine love in so many ways. So why would I have ever felt embarrassed by their existence? If anything, the shame should have been flowing in the direction of those who posed the question in the first place. What the White people lacked was the awareness of how they were culpable or complicit in the creation or perpetuation of the very situations that they were condemning. And what I was lacking at the time was the awareness that White people already knew, on some level, their role in creating the Black caricatures in their minds that they so willfully denigrated. Baldwin was right—they *needed* the "nigger" and were happy to assign any Black person to that role. Their comments were not the product of an objective observation of reality, but rather symptoms of a deeper yearning and motivation to paint the world in a particular way. This process of distortion was asymmetrically applied to themselves as well—producing an overblown sense of their own aptitude and ability.

One day, while I was writing this chapter, it occurred to me that I should look up some of the "FSB bros" from the summer of 1989 to see where they are today. Two that I remembered in particular were tall, athletic, good-humored, and brimming with confidence. I looked them up and found that *both* of them were top executives (each having held the title "president") at fairly large companies, one in textile manufacturing and the other in . . . aerospace! To this day, it is always astounding to me to see talented Black folks experiencing imposter syndrome when underqualified White folks do not. The FSB bros—particularly those from affluent backgrounds—felt very secure about their future, which authorized their self-deprecating humor about being stupid. In a way, they were telling us that their intelligence didn't matter. In her book *Mediocre: The Dangerous Legacy of White Male America,* author Ijeoma Oluo writes that "by making whiteness and maleness their own reward, we disincentivize white men from working to earn their privileged status."

Hence, it makes sense that the ASIST students were no threat to the FSB students, regardless of how much we knew. They were telling us that it was quaint for them to see these bright Black students who were working so hard. They were intrigued by us and wanted to get a closer look. Their status was not threatened by hanging out with, or even getting tutored by, smarter Black kids—even if it appeared to put them in the numerical minority, or in a position of intellectual inferiority. They understood, consciously or unconsciously, that the larger structures in which we lived and operated still conferred power to them. It was their "birthright."

Even in this context of Black intellectual superiority, we were still paying attention to the White people. They had successfully penetrated our social circle and sated their racial curiosity. It became clear that what White people need is for Black people to acknowledge them. They demand relevance. A Black person simply doing their own thing without giving White people any attention or validation is highly unsettling to White folks. This placed me in the unfamiliar and uncomfortable position of having to manage the White gaze.

During that time, I thought there were three different types of White people in the FSB program—the "cool" ones who were down with Black people, the "standoffish" ones who were polite but indifferent, and the "racist" ones who couldn't stand us. Today, I realize that they were three facets of the same stone. All three camps of White people had internalized White supremacy, albeit in different ways—and all of them would have been threatened by Black power at scale.

The threat of Black power and excellence creates the need for strategy— a need I was blissfully unaware of during my early years in St. Martin's Village. Black people, just as I did upon arriving at Tulane, must learn the strategies of effective engagement with White people. They must learn how to play the game. In part II, I will discuss the various ways in which we, as Black folks, deal with the demands of navigating predominantly White environments in a manner that allows us to be who we are while also getting what we want.

Part II
Playing the Game

Three

Doing the Dance

In his famous essay "Just Walk on By: Black Men and Public Space," journalist Brent Staples writes about whistling classical music in public spaces to make nearby White people feel more comfortable:

> I employ what has proved to be an excellent tension-reducing measure: I whistle melodies from Beethoven and Vivaldi and the more popular classical composers. Even steely New Yorkers hunching toward nighttime destinations seem to relax, and occasionally they even join in the tune. Virtually everybody seems to sense that a mugger wouldn't be warbling bright, sunny selections from Vivaldi's *Four Seasons*. It is my equivalent of the cowbell that hikers wear when they know they are in bear country.[1]

This practice of making White people comfortable as a means of increasing Black safety was portrayed in the 2024 satirical film *The American Society of Magical Negroes,* which depicts a society of Black guardians who use their magical powers to "fight white discomfort every day. The happier they are, the safer we are." Although the film, starring David Alan Grier, is a comedy, it echoes the all-too-real threat evoked by Brent Staples' metaphor of the bell and the bear.

Of course, this cowbell dance occurs in various facets of real life as well. Black students and professors in Boston report donning university sweatshirts when walking through White neighborhoods in the hopes that their college affiliation will attenuate any fear that White passersby might experience. A more serious example of the cowbell dance occurs anytime Black people have encounters with the police. The cowbell is so essential during these interactions that Black parents have "the talk" with their teenagers about how to speak and behave if they are ever pulled over.

Sometimes playing the game requires more than a melody, a sweatshirt, a soft voice, or hands on the steering wheel. At one of my jobs, I had a wonderful colleague named "Mabel" who was a very prominent Black scholar in her field. She was also an "auntie" for me and many other young Black professors working at the university. Because I had developed a deep fondness for her, I was devastated when she informed the department that she had been diagnosed with late-stage cancer and would be entering a hospice care facility. Although Mabel was unmarried with no children, she had a sister with whom she enjoyed a close relationship. Her sister had flown to town to be with her full-time, and I would always run into her when I visited Mabel at the hospice center.

During one of the visits, a nurse entered the area where her sister and I were chatting and announced, "Your mother would like to speak with you." I looked around, feeling a bit confused. Was the nurse talking to me? Had she erroneously assumed that I was Mabel's son? Seeing the perplexed look on my face, Mabel's sister whispered to me that she would explain later and proceeded to follow the nurse to Mabel's room. Upon her return, Mabel's sister informed me that Mabel was not her sister but was, in fact, her mother. They had spent several decades passing as sisters because Mabel did not want the fact that she was a young, single Black mother to diminish people's perceptions of her talent or negatively impact her professional opportunities.

As a Black woman educated in the 1960s and '70s, Mabel "played the game" the way she felt she had to in order to realize her professional goals and take care of the people she loved. Other members of the department found out that Mabel had a daughter—and a son, too—weeks later when *The New York Times* published an article after her death. Indeed, White supremacy can impact not only who we portray ourselves to be—in a fundamental way—but also how we connect to other people in our lives.

■ ■ ■

Everybody plays the game to some extent, albeit in different ways and for different reasons. Playing the game is, by far, the widest of the three pathways. It is the one that we are all thrust onto, given our existence—and need to survive—in a world in which the rules were not written for us. As you will discover throughout the book, even changing the game and leaving the game often require some level of playing the game. Although the Wall Street game is not identical to the academic game, which is not the same as the professional sports game or the DC political game or the nonprofit game, these pursuits have much in common when it comes to the obstacles and challenges that Black people must navigate. The biggest commonality is a set of rules and standards that embody patriarchy and White supremacy. Therefore, the paramount question for Black professionals is *What do I have to do to survive and prosper in a game that was not created for me?*

Sadly, our realization that certain games, in particular, were not created for us can steer us away from our dreams. We may feel unwilling to pursue a specific career or interest because we don't think we would fit in. I can remember vividly the ostracism that Venus and Serena Williams faced early in their careers because of their hair beads, their close relationship, and other racialized factors. Their father, Richard Williams, knew how they would be perceived in the tennis world and did a masterful job of inoculating them against that toxicity and building their resistance. However, many Black parents would have advised their kids against country club sports altogether—and understandably so—knowing the increased hassle and hostility their children would endure in such an environment, compared to that of a relatively more hospitable sport, such as basketball.

Similar choices are made in the professional domain, as Black people sometimes choose career paths based not on their talents or passions but on their perceptions of the chances of surviving and thriving in a particular domain. I have encountered many Black people who decided against careers in art, interior design, oenology, gastronomy, or other fields perceived as being especially unwelcoming to Black people.

To be sure, there is no escaping the game—regardless of which field we choose. Therefore, it is essential to understand what our options are. In the four chapters comprising this part of the book, I will discuss various components of playing the game: (1) "doing the dance," or strategically monitoring and regulating one's behaviors—particularly those that code as Black, (2) "being twice as good," or maximizing one's knowledge and skill, (3) understanding the importance of "who you know" and the art of creating diverse social networks, and (4) becoming a "tempered radical." The latter term refers to Black folks who obtain power in mainstream organizations and institutions with the intention of changing them from the inside.[2]

Let's begin by focusing on the strategic choreography of one's appearance, speech, and behaviors in predominantly White spaces. New York University law professor Kenji Yoshino has coined the term "covering" to refer to the tendency for people from marginalized social groups to conform to mainstream standards. In his book *Covering: The Hidden Assault on Our Civil Rights,* he writes: "Everyone covers. To cover is to tone down a disfavored identity to fit into the mainstream."[3]

To be clear, covering does not involve *hiding* one's race, as was the case when very light-skinned Black people would try to "pass" as White people, a practice that was common for centuries. Covering is more about *dialing down* certain aspects of one's racial identity in order to fit White standards. An example of covering might be Michelle Obama's decision to straighten her hair while serving as First Lady, in contrast to wearing the locks, braids, and other Afrocentric hairstyles that she does today. She never hid the fact that she was Black; rather, she "toned down" her Blackness.

Code-switching—or speaking in a less ethnic or regional dialect—is another common form of covering. During my interview with Charles Blow, he told me about a television diction class that he happened to stumble into in college. He recalled the instructor saying that a good anchor sounds like they can be from anywhere and nowhere. "So I then would watch TV and repeat whatever the anchor said, after they said it, to get rid of my Southern accent," Blow said. But he added, "I have four brothers, and they still sound like they're from the South. No less smart than me, and I think some of them even smarter than me . . . but until those people who don't change everything get the same respect as people who do, I don't believe you that you're egalitarian."

Yoshino argues that the demand to cover is a form of White supremacy because it requires that all racialized groups "act White" in order to fit in. He writes:

> Americans have come to a consensus that people should not be penalized for being different along [social category] dimensions. That consensus, however, does not protect individuals against demands that they mute those differences. . . . Covering has enjoyed such a robust and stubborn life because it is a form of assimilation.[4]

Yoshino describes four axes of covering, along with examples: appearance (clothing, hairstyle), affiliation (listening to NPR, speaking unaccented English), activism (being more politically mainstream or whitewashed and/or being wary of more progressive groups), and association (not having friends from your own racial group). A 2013 Deloitte study found that a whopping 79 percent of Black employees across a range of industries reported covering along at least one of these axes.[5] The majority of these respondents believed that their leaders expected them to cover, despite the fact that covering had a detrimental impact on many respondents' sense of self.

Interestingly, 93 percent of respondents overall stated that their organization articulated inclusion as one of its values, and fully 78 percent of these respondents felt that the organization lived up to those values. This suggests that people do not necessarily view pressure to cover as an effort to exclude them, but it nevertheless created an extra burden of assimilation. As the report put it, "The question was not whether they were included, but on what terms they felt their inclusion rested. Often that perceived social contract involved managing aspects of their identity in a way that the dominant group would not have to do. These individuals felt they had to work their identities alongside their jobs."[6]

Many Black respondents of the survey report that even being seen with other Black people could risk giving the appearance of a "clique" or "posse," thereby making White people feel uncomfortable. To be clear, none of these organizations had formal rules against the assembly of more than two Black people at a time, nor were there informal admonishments against posse gathering. Rather, Black people intuitively knew that such behavior would make White people nervous and uncomfortable, and so they "covered" by avoiding the behavior whenever possible. Notably, none of the White respondents expressed any concerns about associating with other White people at work, or about how assemblies of White people socializing might make others feel.

Covering has also been institutionalized in formal ways. Yoshino argues that covering is an assault on basic civil rights because the practice of not allowing people to fully express who they are is baked into our legal system, through policies that target behavior rather than identity. He summarized it as the difference between "being" and "doing." In other words, the law recognizes that Black people cannot choose to *be* a different skin color; however, they can control whether they *engage* in certain cultural practices, such as wearing an Afrocentric hairstyle or speaking in a nonstandard dialect.[7] Being Black is permissible; "doing" Black is not. Indeed, covering in the workplace is required for people from any stigmatized social group.

For example, Yoshino recounts the story of a lesbian woman who was out of the closet at work but was not allowed to bring her wife to any work functions because it was deemed "inappropriate," despite the fact that heterosexual couples were allowed to bring their spouses. Being gay was permitted, but "doing" gay was not. This employee decided to litigate but ultimately lost in court because "once the court determined she could assimilate, it assumed she should do so, without regard to the legitimacy of the demand for assimilation."[8]

Yoshino found that the same distinction between "being" and "doing" applied to race as well as sexual orientation, with "doing" being much more susceptible to punishment. He describes the legal stance in the following way:

Because the federal Constitution and Title VII of the Civil Rights Act of 1964 both protect race much more robustly than [sexual] orientation, I expected individuals to fare better against race-based covering demands. This proved overly optimistic. The courts have made the same distinction between being and doing in race cases that they have made in the [sexual] orientation cases, protecting the immutable but not the mutable aspects of racial identity. A racial minority fired for her ancestry or skin color will win her suit in a hot second. But a racial minority fired for refusing to cover a cultural aspect of her racial identity will generally lose.[9]

Regrettably, people from stigmatized social groups are forced to assimilate to White, heteronormative standards at work, or risk not only "insider" status but loss of employment altogether. This is true even for, or perhaps *especially* for, Black people in positions of power.

Several writers and scholars, such as Ellis Cose and Jim Sidanius, have asserted that it is often affluent Blacks who are the most susceptible to experiencing racism simply because they are operating above their prescribed station. In his book *The Rage of a Privileged Class,* Cose recounts stories of hazing and disrespect that many high-ranking Black leaders face, particularly from White subordinates. And Sidanius' social dominance theory, developed with social psychologist Felicia Pratto, discusses the *out-of-place principle.*[10] The ironic finding across all these perspectives is that the more power Black people obtain, the more (not less) racism they experience.

Consistent with this idea, Yoshino and his colleagues found in a 2024 Deloitte study that C-suite executives and senior managers report a rate of covering that is 6 to 14 percent higher than that of the ranks that fall below them (i.e., managers, salaried staff, and hourly staff).[11] Of all the respondents who had been promoted within their organization, almost all of them (96 percent) reported that their need to cover either increased or stayed the same after the promotion. Therefore, the need to cover did not go away once people obtained a higher position. This finding suggests that achieving elevated status or power within an organization is no shield against the demand to dial down your ethnicity. The Obamas covered more when they were in the White House than they do as private citizens. The same cannot be said of Donald Trump.

For Black leaders, playing the game includes an array of tactics aimed at defusing White people's negative perceptions of Black power. My colleagues at Duke and Northwestern and I have investigated the extent to which "disarming mechanisms"—physical, psychological, or behavioral traits that attenuate perceptions of White people's perceptions of Black people as threatening—facilitate organizational success for Black executives in corporate America.[12] The term "disarming mechanisms" references a broad category that can involve anything from "whistling Vivaldi," to code-switching, to voting Republican, to having a baby-faced appearance.

In one study, we obtained evidence of a "Teddy-bear effect" in which Black male Fortune 500 CEOs tended to be more "baby-faced" in appearance than White male Fortune 500 CEOs, as well as being more baby-faced than Black people who were not top-level executives. Like attractiveness, baby-facedness can be accurately judged by people's subjective perceptions—even though there are also objective ways to assess these traits, such as facial symmetry for attractiveness and face-width-to-height ratio for baby-facedness.[13] Among Black male CEOs, those who were the most baby-faced led the largest Fortune 500 companies and had the highest salaries. Interestingly, we observed the opposite trend for White male CEOs—those who were the least baby-faced led the largest companies and earned the most money.[14]

Baby-facedness is a liability, not an asset, for White males. This is because White males do not need to be disarmed. As discussed in earlier chapters, they are "entitled" to wealth and power and should therefore look the part. While a baby face might make White men appear warmer and friendlier, it also makes them appear weaker and less competent—like a baby. For White male leaders, it's all about looking strong and powerful. For the Black male leader, it's about appearing docile and nonthreatening.

While our study did not include Black women (at the time, there had been only one Black woman Fortune 500 CEO), other studies have examined how Black women disarm themselves in the workplace by virtue of how they wear their hair. One study by Christy Zhou Koval and Ashleigh Rosette showed that Black women who straightened their hair were perceived as more refined, respectable, polished, and professional than Black women with natural hairstyles.[15] This led to the Black women with straight hair being recommended for interviews more often than the Black women with natural hair. This bias against natural hair was especially prevalent in more conservative industries, such as consulting, compared with more creative industries, such as advertising.[16]

Eminent legal scholar Kimberlé Crenshaw coined the term "intersectionality" to describe the ways in which multiple social categories intersect to impact perceptions of members of different socially disadvantaged groups.[17] In other words, the experiences and challenges faced by Black women are often different from those encountered by White women, or Black men, and an intersectional lens helps us to better recognize and understand those differences.

In our own organizational research, Ashleigh Rosette and I have found that covering demands tend to differ in predictable ways for Black men, Black women, and White women. We found that there are three qualitatively different types of social disadvantage:

- Stigmatization

- Marginalization

- Subordination

We found that Black men are stigmatized—meaning that they generate high levels of both attention and vigilance from White patriarchy, as well as highly negative emotions, such as fear, anger, contempt, or disgust. On the other hand, Black women are marginalized—meaning that they are largely invisible. They do not attract the same level of vigilance as Black men, due to a lower perceived threat, nor do they elicit strong negative emotions, such as fear.[18] However, invisibility is a double-edged sword, offering both advantages and disadvantages, as the research of Valerie Purdie-Vaughns and Richard Eibach has shown.[19]

In contrast, White women are subordinated, rather than stigmatized or marginalized. They elicit neither the same level of threat as Black men, nor the same level of indifference as Black women. Unlike Black women, they are highly visible to, and monitored by, White men, given the relevance and centrality of White women to their lives. However, White women are not permitted to possess high levels of power within White patriarchy. Research on benevolent sexism shows that White women are very much liked by White men—in fact, White men tend to like White women more than they like other White men. The real question, however, is whether they *respect* White women as much as they respect White men. They don't. Research strongly confirms that all the affection and protection exhibited by White men toward White women is conditional on White women's willingness to assume a submissive role vis-à-vis White men.[20]

In short, these three distinct types of social disadvantage—stigmatization, marginalization, and subordination—create qualitatively distinct challenges in the workplace for different groups. These challenges can also shift over time for a particular group. Research conducted by organizational psychologist Kecia Thomas and her colleagues has found evidence of a "pet-to-threat" effect for Black women. When they first arrive on the job, Black women are celebrated, and treated with warmth and benevolence—the "pet" phase. Although they are often praised for the diversity that they bring to the organization, they are also exploited as tokens, and their skills and talents are underutilized. As time progresses and Black women ascend the ladder, White men's perception of them shifts from a "pet" to a "threat" to the status quo. Black women are deprived of the authority and legitimacy that their positions deserve, and are often underpaid and overworked.[21]

Because perceptions are dynamic, doing the dance requires flexibility and agility—even for individuals from the same stigmatized group, across different stages of their career. Because of this hassle and complexity, some may choose to choreograph their own moves.

From "the Dance" to "the Stance": Strategic Authenticity

Playing the game does not always require dancing to someone else's beat. You can also decide to do your own thing. The word "authenticity" is commonly invoked to describe something that represents a genuine, unvarnished reflection of what is beneath the surface. Despite the ostensible clarity of the definition, there is astonishing variability in how people perceive the authenticity of others. For example, ponder the question of whether Donald Trump is "authentic." Some people will immediately evaluate him as someone who is extremely authentic and "tells it like it is," whereas others will insist that he is a phony and a con man whose entire career is grounded in chicanery. This stark disparity in the perception of the authenticity of a single individual, for whom people have access to the same objective information, speaks volumes about the nebulous nature of the construct.

It is important to recognize that authenticity and audacity are not the same, even though people sometimes misperceive the latter as an indicator of the former. An individual who feels free to criticize or insult others while concealing their own flaws and misdeeds is not really "keeping it real." Nevertheless, brazenness often codes as authenticity, just as research has shown that dominance is often mistaken for competence.[22] Therefore, one challenge for perceivers of authenticity is to have clarity around what they mean by "authentic" and to ensure that they are using valid criteria in their assessment of it.

The challenge for people seeking to act in an authentic way is to determine how to be authentic in the workplace without threatening regulations, norms, or a general sense of propriety.

NYU Stern School of Business professor Julianna Pillemer has written about what she calls the "paradox of self-presentation" regarding people within organizations who "desire to be seen as simultaneously true to self and professionally appropriate in workplace interactions."[23] She and other scholars draw a clear distinction between *feeling* authentic and *behaving* in an authentic way,[24] and research has shown that feeling authentic does not necessarily mean that a given individual will be seen by others as *being* authentic.[25] Therefore, one must be mindful of the fact that our own perceptions of who we are may not correspond with others' perceptions of who we are. When this disconnect happens, it raises the valid question of what authenticity really means.

A second consideration that one must carefully weigh is the balance between what is authentic and what is potentially detrimental to one's own, or others', well-being in the workplace or society. There are times when authenticity—however one defines or measures it—is not advantageous to oneself or anyone else. There are also situational factors to consider, such as the culture of the organization or level of danger in the environment.

My interview with the icon and activist Dr. Angela Y. Davis—which we'll return to later in the book—nicely illustrates the complexity of the various motives for the dance. During our conversation, I brought up a humorous, but serious, scene in Ava Duvernay's documentary *13th* where lawyer and political analyst Van Jones talked about the authenticity that Dr. Davis displayed in a California courtroom during her 1972 trial. Guns that were registered to her had been used in the armed takeover of a courthouse by two activists, Jonathan Jackson and George Jackson, during which four people were killed. Jones commented that Davis was facing serious time, and the possibly of the death penalty, yet she walked into the courtroom with a big Afro and her fist in the air, when most people would have gone to the beauty shop for "a nice press and curl" and put on some "little white church gloves" in the courtroom and started praying to Jesus.

I asked Dr. Davis about this iconic display of authenticity in the courtroom, as well as her take on other forms of covering, such as codeswitching. Here are excerpts from her longer response:

> I wore my hair natural not so much because it represented Blackness but because it was what women in the movement were doing. Wearing a natural [hairstyle] at that time was a very conscious decision, but it wasn't simply about an essential identity. It was about politics. It was a political statement, and I certainly did not want to disguise

my politics and my political statements in the courtroom, so it never even occurred to me that I should present myself differently. . . . I think that ways of representing how one imagines oneself to the world are really important, but I think they change with changing times. . . . I wore a straight-haired wig during the time I was underground, but that was literally a disguise. . . . I guess I would say we're always somewhat strategic. For example, if I'm speaking to elementary school students, I speak differently from how I would speak if I was speaking to high school students, and then different from [how I would speak at] the university. A talk at a rally is totally different from teaching a graduate seminar, even though one might be addressing the same subject. So, I think I'm conscious of my environment, not so much because I think I need to disguise myself, but because I want to communicate. And I think those kinds of translations are often necessary in order to guarantee that one can truly have a relationship with the other person . . . not because one is trying to hide something.

Dr. Davis also discussed how these adaptations are sometimes necessary due to changes in the social and cultural environment. She recounted a story about having to remove a "Black is beautiful" bumper sticker from her car because she was almost run off the freeway several times during an era in which Blackness was becoming increasingly threatening. She was aware of that perception and felt that Blackness should be threatening to the extent that it caused people to imagine and create a new world—one with which they were not familiar but which nevertheless contained greater social justice. While her political existence was about agitation and activism, she had the presence of mind to pick and choose her battles. She ultimately decided that it wasn't worth being run off the highway for a bumper sticker.

Let's zoom out. The point here is that it is important to know *why* you're dancing, and whether it is a sort of strategic jiujitsu, a genuine desire to connect with other people, an act of self-expression to show others who you are, or some combination of all these. The idea underlying the notion of strategic authenticity is that strategic choices and authentic behavior are not mutually exclusive. The idea that "real" authenticity means saying or doing whatever you want, whenever you want, is too rigid and simplistic. We do not live in a social vacuum. We live in a very complex and dynamic world with many different people and situations that require a certain level of flexibility in how we behave. Putting on clothing before taking a public bus or subway is not being inauthentic, even if you enjoy lounging around your house in your birthday suit.

It is also important to mention that not everything that appears to be dialing down one's ethnicity is necessarily inauthentic. Sometimes people are just quiet, or agreeable, or proper in their speech or mannerisms. As Yoshino himself concedes: "The covering concept might assume too quickly that individuals behaving in 'mainstream' ways are hiding some true identity, when in fact they might just be 'being themselves.' "[26]

After speaking with various Black leaders in corporate America, I discovered that for many, their success is a product of their willingness to simply be themselves. Ken Chenault, the former CEO of American Express and current chairman of General Catalyst, is a prime example. He told me during our interview that "a mistake that so many Black leaders make is that they are uncomfortable letting people know who they are and what they believe in. They just want to fit in." He further argues that "if you subjugate yourself, it makes you inauthentic and also signals [to others] that you're not comfortable in your own skin." Kenji Yoshino agrees with this assessment, arguing that "oftentimes when we bring our full selves to work, that's when we find our power."

But Chenault also talked candidly about his own ability and propensity to code-switch. He saw it as a way of living in two worlds, much as bilingual people are able to communicate in different languages when they travel or speak to different family members. He also saw living in two worlds as providing the advantage of helping him understand people from a different culture, much in the same way that Nelson Mandela was able to understand the psychology of White Afrikaners after spending decades in prison. For Chenault, the authenticity comes from having solid core values and a clear sense of who you are. He told me:

One of the things that was very helpful to me, and I think you're certainly very aware of it, is having grown up in a two-parent household with parents who not only emphasized education but really talked about the importance of Blacks getting into positions of leadership. That certainly had a very strong impact. But I also went to a predominantly White school in a different town, so the code-switching was something that I was doing since I was four years old. I think what was important was an understanding of who I was and the pride that was instilled, because if you code-switch, you can lose yourself. So having those core values and beliefs was important.

Something that I also learned from that experience is how to be myself, but at the same time, how to understand the [White] mindset. You know, one of my favorite autobiographies is Nelson Mandela's.... As you know, he understood the apartheid mindset and was able to convert his jail guards, who [ultimately] became [his] followers. I want to be careful [in how I convey this] because I wasn't trying to be manipulative. I wasn't plotting. But I had to be comfortable both in the Black world and the White world at an early age, and I became very adept at that.

Another Black CEO, whom I happen to know personally, is Patrick Tannock, who was the head of AXA XL Insurance in Bermuda and the first Black chairman of the Association of Bermuda International Companies. He is known for being a champion of Black talent, hiring numerous Black executives for his organization. At a reception that he once hosted for me in the AXA boardroom overlooking the azure waters of Hamilton Bay, all the invitees were Black. During a dinner later that week, one Black professional who was not in attendance at the AXA dinner commented on how "inappropriate" he thought Patrick's decision had been. He felt there should have been White people there as well, for the sake of optics.

The comment struck me as classic association-based covering—where individuals dial down their ethnicity by not associating with too many people from their own group. But Patrick is confident and authentic in both his demeanor and his unapologetic commitment to promoting Black employees. Sometimes such boldness can appeal to White people. As Ken Chenault mentioned, it signals that you are comfortable in your own skin. In addition, White people may feel that their willingness to associate with such "authentic" Black people provides them with bona fides that certify that they are not like other White people, who might be uncomfortable in the midst of such swagger and realness. They walk away satisfied that they are truly open-minded and unprejudiced. Like Ken Chenault, Patrick also attended a predominantly White private school but received strong messages of Black empowerment both at home and through the "Liberation School" run by the Black Berets—which he describes as the Bermudian version of the Black Panthers.

People's response to authenticity also depends on whose brand of authenticity they are reacting to. It is important to realize that who some Black people really are just happens to be more palatable to the mainstream than who other Black people really are. Both Ken and Patrick are charismatic, affable, confident, good-looking, and extremely comfortable in their own skin. They are also incredibly intelligent. Thus, the person they authentically happen to be is also a person who happens to "fit" into mainstream environments. Another Black person's "authentic self" might not fit as well. Therefore, it's not just a question of whether someone is authentic or not—but also of whether their unique flavor of authenticity matches the environment they are in.

Regardless of whether a Black person does the dance or the stance, their manner of self-presentation is not the only factor in determining whether they are successful in playing the game. Unlike the FSB bros I encountered at Tulane, Black people cannot successfully play the game by relying on their charm, swagger, and social network alone. There has to be some real horsepower under the hood. In the next chapter, I will discuss the various types of competence that every Black professional must possess in order to effectively play the game.

Four

Twice as Good Yet Half as Far: Mastery Versus Performance

From a very early age, Black people are taught that we have to be twice as good to get half as far. Actor and comedian Chris Rock said that his mother once told him, "You can't beat a White man, but you can knock him out." In other words, our performance needs to be far above and beyond that of our White colleagues. Even so, that's often not enough. Even when we score a knockout or hit a home run at work, we are often asked to do it again—to prove that the first time wasn't a fluke. Therefore, managing how we acquire and display our knowledge and skills is another aspect of playing the game.

For Black people, competence is absolutely necessary, but it is not sufficient. For White people, it is sufficient but not necessary. In other words, if you are a White male and you're really good, then you're golden. On the other hand, if you're a White male and you're *not* that good, often you are still allowed a seat at the table—particularly if you have the right look or network. As it turns out, it is not just the FSB bros from my Tulane days who are able to rise to top executive positions within their organizations despite their mediocrity. Brilliant thinkers such as Ijeoma Oluo and Koritha Mitchell have written about the ubiquity of White mediocrity as evidence that White supremacy is frequently prioritized over meritocracy.

Of course, none of this is to suggest that there are not highly competent White people—or incompetent Black people. The point is simply that the consequences of competence, or incompetence, are vastly different for Black and White people. Underqualified White people are hired or elected all the time, and it is hardly ever accompanied by outrage. On the other hand, even overqualified Black people are often labeled as "DEI hires."

Research corroborates this conventional wisdom. Ashleigh Rosette and I assessed the degree to which making a mistake on the job negatively impacted Black and White professionals in leadership roles. The results revealed that White male leaders could commit errors with relative impunity, as mistakes were seen as reflecting human error, not lesser competence. In contrast, Black leaders were heavily penalized for making mistakes.[1]

We found this was especially true of Black female leaders, who suffered a "double jeopardy" effect due to the stereotypic image of a "leader" being someone who is White and male (look no further than the long line of White male Fortune 500 CEOs or American presidents before and after Barack Obama). Because Black women possess neither Whiteness nor maleness, their mistakes were interpreted as proof that they were wholly unsuited to the leadership role in the first place. Mistakes also lowered perceptions of leadership suitability for Black men and White women, though to a lesser degree than for Black women.

Even when Black people overachieve, some still internalize the stigma of "imposter syndrome." Boston University professor Koritha Mitchell has extended this idea by arguing that Black folks are made to feel unworthy of their professional position or achievements due to a phenomenon that she calls "know-your-place aggression" (similar to Sidanius' out-of-place principle mentioned in the previous chapter). As Mitchell describes it, Black folks can feel that they will never be good enough, while White people who were never adept to begin with are given a green light. Being aware of this dynamic, Mitchell argues, is not only a vindication of self-worth but an important form of self-care:

> Know-your-place aggression is a continuing American tradition, so I always strive to equip marginalized communities to withstand the hostility that never fails to accompany their victories. . . . I also believe that noticing white mediocrity is a form of self-care. . . . To put it plainly, when I look around my campus and the profession more

generally and ask myself, "Would that person even be here if they weren't white?," I most often find myself answering, "Nope!" As a result, I am less likely to run myself ragged by holding myself to higher and higher standards because I remember that I have already done more to earn my position than most members of the profession. As important, I am less likely to let others' assessments of my performance overwhelm me when I remain cognizant of how seldom they use actual criteria with each other. Surely, I am not alone in having noticed that requirements are most passionately discussed when someone who isn't white, male, and/or straight is being evaluated.[2]

Taken together, this research presents an unfortunate predicament for Black people. On the one hand, playing the game involves acquiring and displaying signals of competence, which are far more critical to the success of Black people than White people. On the other hand, our competence is not fully recognized or rewarded—due to the need to keep Black people in their place, as discussed in chapter 1. In many ways, these contradictory findings summarize the two components of the dictum: (1) You have to be twice as good, and (2) you only get half as far—because the system is constantly putting you "in your place."

In the next section, I will unpack what it means to be "good"—drawing a distinction between performance and mastery. Subsequently, I will address the question of why, despite a surplus of intellectual capital, Black people manage to get only half as far.

What You Know Versus What You Show

Researchers have shown that there are two conceptually distinct, but interrelated, forms of competence: mastery and performance.[3] Mastery goals involve *learning* as much as you can about a given topic. Performance goals are about *demonstrating* competence through concrete tasks and outcomes. If you are taking a Spanish class, a high level of mastery would entail becoming fluent in the language. A high level of performance might be earning an A+ in the class. Thus, mastery and performance are related but not identical. There are people who get an A+ in Spanish but cannot communicate with native speakers in a real-world context. On the other hand, a student who is fluent in the language might end up getting a B in the class, for any number of reasons. Mastery is driven by an intrinsic desire for knowledge and growth, whereas performance is motivated by status, reward, or the desire to outperform other people in the environment. Both mastery and performance have been shown to predict positive achievement-related outcomes. In a nutshell, what's important is not just how you perform but what you actually learn.

However, individual and situational factors can determine the extent to which one is prioritized over the other. Just as some teachers find it frustrating that students are often more concerned about grades than about learning, managers can be put off by employees who are more focused on their next promotion than on developing the necessary technical and professional expertise to excel at their jobs. On the flip side, managers can become frustrated with employees who are constantly developing skills but never producing results, or with those who are obsessed with getting it right versus getting it done. While quality is important, these managers believe that too heavy a focus on mastery can allow the perfect to become the enemy of the good.

I think it is important for Black professionals to develop *both* mastery and competence, while understanding that neither is equivalent to "natural" talent. Growing up in the Black community, I was sometimes told that "truly" smart people didn't have to study—because they already had the knowledge, as if by magic. However, it is possible to be intelligent and ignorant at the same time. And that is what can happen if an intelligent person does not take the time to learn new information or practice a skill.

It is also problematic to assume that people who spend a lot of time in the library studying are obliged to do so because they are not "naturally" smart. In his book *Outliers: The Story of Success,* Malcolm Gladwell suggests that exceptionally high achievement in any particular domain requires an investment of approximately ten thousand hours of practice and honing.[4] Simply having natural talent is not enough. Any Olympic gold medalist or superstar professional athlete will proudly confirm that they had to practice innumerable hours to reach the pinnacle of their sport. Contrary to popular belief, they were not simply born with superstardom.

L. Duane Jackson, a friend and colleague of mine who is one of a handful of Black architects and real estate developers in the United States, told me about the critical importance he assigns to mastery. He was so dedicated to learning all that he could about his complex profession that he spent an extra year and a half in architecture school at MIT. He describes his investment in learning with a memorable phrase: "I had to immerse myself in the education of myself." He insists that this investment in the mastery of his craft has paid immense, compound dividends over the decades-long course of his career.

Similarly, the former mayor of Charlotte and U.S. Secretary of Transportation Anthony Foxx explained to me how mastery was critical to his success. Foxx was the youngest person in history to serve as mayor of Charlotte, at age thirty-eight, and the first Black Democrat ever elected to that position. He told me:

> I was a policy nerd, like, for real. I was very focused on thoroughly understanding the substantive levers of policymaking. So, for example, in the first six months on [the] City Council, we faced a budget cliff. I took it upon myself to learn the budget—like, not just learn the line items, but learning how one thing affects the other. You know, if you adjust the property tax this much, what does that get you in terms of borrowing capacity? What does it get you in terms of operating capacity? So, for the first six months, I just dove into understanding the budget as thoroughly as I could, which gave me the ability to actually craft a budget for the city during my first term, which I did. And this budget actually garnered the support of the City Council. We were even successful in overriding the mayor's veto of that budget, and it did things like get our street resurfacing improved, allowed us to continue our efforts on affordable housing, put more police officers on the street, and several other things along those lines. And I think that people got the sense that I was a serious

policymaker. I was probably less of a backslapper as a politician. I wasn't, you know, out to give a bunch of rousing speeches and that sort of thing. I think I was more the kind of somebody you would go to to try to solve a problem, but not the person you would go have a beer with.

Anthony Foxx's strategy for playing the game—in a city that was predominantly White—was mastery. He needed to be "twice as good" when it came to understanding the complexities of fiscal policy—so much so that he became the go-to person. His superior knowledge also enabled him to assume a leadership role with respect to crafting and proposing a sound budget that actually worked. This mastery of the mechanics of municipal governance gave him the credibility and legitimacy necessary to garner support for his run as mayor.

What is interesting about Foxx's case is that, by politician standards, he is relatively shy and soft-spoken. He tends to listen more than he speaks. As he himself acknowledges, his ascent did not require the backslapping, schmoozing, or grandiose displays of charisma that we so often associate with politicians. However, it would be erroneous to assume that his success was attributable to mastery alone. As I will explain later in the chapter, his social network played a role too. He is also someone who comes off as very authentic, and is willing to stick to his values.

In one memorable experience as mayor, Foxx faced a dilemma around a controversial transit project that would have served a working-class Black neighborhood. Here's how he described his thought process:

I think that one has to decide what winning is. You know, when I was running for mayor of Charlotte, there was a project that was heavily maligned. It was a transit project that was going to run through the spine of the Black community, and there was a lot of resistance to it because these areas were underinvested in, highly poor, and so many people thought the line was going to be a train to nowhere. And my pollsters came to me and said, You know, this is a loser. A lot of people agree with you, but slightly more of them *dis-agree* with you. And at that moment, it would have been smart for me to just say: This is a problem. I care about this project, but I don't care about it more than I care about winning. And I could have just punted it. But to me, "winning" would have been hollow if I would have felt like I could get into this position and not be free to do the things that I thought were right for the community or the city.

For Foxx, his decision to go through with the transit project paid many downstream dividends. First, it bolstered the perception of his integrity and authenticity. He believes that when politicians always follow the polls, and never their hearts, "it starts to settle with people as a lack of core belief." Second, in many ways, his successful execution of the transit project, along with his reputation as someone who is a masterful policy expert, led to his subsequent appointment as the U.S. Secretary of Transportation under the Obama administration from 2013 to 2017. He was confirmed unanimously by the Senate in a 100–0 vote.

His story suggests that in addition to building mastery, part of the game requires clarifying for yourself, and others, what the specific performance goal is. What would success look like in a particular situation?

In her illuminating book *Strategize to Win: The New Way to Start Out, Step Up, or Start Over in Your Career,* Carla Harris—one of the highest-ranking Black executives at Morgan Stanley—has referred to this process as "defining the win." She recounts a situation in which she was able to achieve something that nobody in the company had ever done before. However, she and her boss were not on the same page with respect to what high performance, or the "win," entailed. The situation involved securing a meeting with a highly desirable firm to discuss a product. Because she had to move heaven and earth to try to land this meeting—and ultimately succeeded in doing so—she was satisfied that she had scored a win. However, to her boss, a "win" was actually getting the firm to *buy* the product, not simply opening the door of opportunity by landing a meeting with the client. She recalls:

I knew that there was real value to my firm in getting the exposure, since this was a client that the firm did not have a relationship with and it was a good candidate for other products that we sold. Where I failed, however, was in getting my manager to define the "win" up front. Since I did not find out what was important to her in the end or try to redefine what should have been important, I left myself exposed to her definition of what success looked like and left my effort and my performance vulnerable to being undervalued or not valued at all.

What I should have done was gone to my manager and got her to agree that the "win" would be in obtaining the meeting, and getting the client to agree to a follow-up meeting would be yet another "win." I should have stressed the fact that no one at the firm had *ever* gotten an audience with this client to discuss this product and that that in itself would be a huge win. . . . If I could [have] convince[d] my boss to redefine what would be valued, then I could have given myself a chance to earn performance currency. Since I could not control whether the client would ultimately buy the product *and* no one else at the company had ever visited the client before, I should have separated the decision to buy the product from the decision to take the meeting.[5]

In addition to agreeing on what the "win" or performance goal is, it is equally important to identity the competencies that are needed to achieve the win. Carla Harris identifies four general skills that all Black corporate professionals must hone early on in their careers to consistently attain high performance:

- **Presentation** skills—the ability to speak to groups of people in a confident and compelling manner.

- **Management** skills—the ability to effectively motivate and direct others to complete projects.

- **Analytical** skills—the ability to understand and interpret data and quantitative reports.

- **Selling** skills—the ability to influence others and convince them to buy your ideas and agenda.

According to Harris, you can acquire these skills through (1) education and seminars, (2) on-the-job experience and special assignments, or (3) mentors, sponsors, and other social relationships. These general skills, combined with your technical skills, intellect, experience, and strong delivery will, over time, give you what she calls "performance currency."

Simply put, performance currency is the reputational and professional capital that you earn by doing your job well and delivering stellar results on discrete assignments. Harris argues that, like all currency, it can be exchanged for desirable goods such as pay raises, promotions, a seat at the table, a captive audience of people who are willing to listen to you, or an introduction to important people. Or it can be cashed in for grace, forgiveness, and another chance if, and when, you mess up.

When you do make a mistake, Harris advises against denying it or doubling down. As previously mentioned, White men can often get away with brazen denial or passing the buck when they make a mistake. Not true for women and people of color. Here's how Harris advises people to recover from mistakes: "1) own up to making it; 2) articulate what you learned from it, either to your boss or in a public way; 3) correct the error; and 4) endeavor not to make the same mistake again."[6]

Another aspect of what it means to be twice as good is adopting what Harris calls an "under-promise and over-deliver" mentality, which means that you should always plan to deliver more than what is asked or expected of you. She suggests, "If your boss asks for an assignment by 2:00 p.m., you should strive to have it completed by 11:00 a.m. If you are asked to create a summary of the research on a company, you may also want to hand in a summary on that company's biggest competitor and a quick comparative analysis of the two."[7]

Getting Half as Far

The second part of the "Twice as good yet half as far" maxim stipulates that our competence often gets us only so far. Although competence is rigidly demanded of Black folks, we do not get rewarded for it in a manner that is commensurate with our performance—or equivalent to the rewards that White people receive for the same level of performance. There is copious research on a phenomenon called performance-reward bias, which documents the ways in which women and people of color are under-rewarded, relative to White males, for equal performance.[8]

One study found that the same performance evaluation scores led to higher rewards for people from dominant groups compared with those from marginalized groups. Another study showed that teams comprised of female founders were able to raise only half the money of similar teams comprised of male founders, despite the fact that they generated 10 percent more revenue.[9] The irony is that men who hire these overqualified women often feel as if they have done the women a favor. And women themselves often feel gratitude toward the men who make these promotion decisions. Nevertheless, we know that many organizations are willing to promote women and people of color only when the organization is on the precipice of disaster—something known as the *glass cliff phenomenon*.[10] As absurd as it sounds, people from marginalized communities are expected to be grateful for the opportunity to be underpaid and set up for failure.

Not only is high performance by people from marginalized groups under-rewarded and underappreciated, it can also be perceived as threatening. In a fascinating study, White asset-allocation managers evaluated venture capital funds led by a highly competent Black or White fund manager. The asset-allocation managers evaluated the competent Black fund manager—who had a solid track record of high performance—more negatively than the White fund manager with a similarly competent track record. Further analysis shed light on what may have been driving the more negative evaluation of the highly competent Black fund managers—envy. Results revealed that after reviewing the highly competent Black fund manager, the White asset managers rated their own social status as being lower. However, they did not think less of themselves after evaluating the competent White fund manager.[11]

Black people are well aware of the backlash that their high performance can produce. Research indicates that Black employees and students often downplay their achievements out of fear of negative consequences. In one study, researchers provided feedback to Black participants indicating that they had excelled on a standardized test (a portion of the LSAT) and were given the choice to publicize their stellar result. Results showed that the Black students who scored highest on the test were the most reluctant to make their scores public, out of fear of negative backlash.[12]

This tendency is even expressed in literature. In the National Book Award–winning novel *James,* author Percival Everett describes a scene in which the protagonist, Jim, an enslaved man in the South, is giving a class to young people about how to "play the game" around White people, encouraging them to show less knowledge than they actually have:

> "You're walking down the street and you see that Mrs. Holiday's kitchen is on fire. She's standing in her yard, her back to her house, unaware. How do you tell her?"
>
> "Fire, fire," January said.
>
> "Direct. And that's almost correct," I said.
>
> The youngest of them, lean and tall five-year-old Rachel, said, "Lawdy, missum! Looky dere."
>
> "Perfect," I said. "Why is that correct?"
>
> Lizzie raised her hand. "Because we must let the whites be the ones who name the trouble."
>
> "And why is that?" I asked.
>
> February said, "Because they need to know everything before us. Because they need to name everything."

Apparently, a house burnt to the ground is preferred to a Black person who knows more than a White person.

Due to the perils facing the "uppity Negro," Black people are cognizant of the punishment they may receive for showing off—even when they have the competence to back it up. This holds true even in domains that are stereotypically associated with Black people. In a study of people's responses to NFL players, organizational scholar Erika Hall and I found that Black NFL players were punished for celebrating after touchdowns whereas White players were not. Although both Black and White players who celebrated were seen as being more "arrogant" than Black and White players who did not celebrate, only the Black players were punished for their arrogance. In fact, the data suggested that, if anything, White players were rewarded for being arrogant.[13] So, perhaps the old saying should be modified to advise Black people to be "twice as good, but three times as humble."

■　■　■

Competence, performance, and humility are only a part of playing the game of upward mobility. In addition to the adage that "you have to be twice as good to get half as far," we have all heard that "it's not what you know, but who you know." Moreover, the further you advance in your career, the more decisions will be determined based on social relationships rather than mere competence. Notwithstanding, so many of us continue to believe that all you have to do to obtain success is keep your head down, work hard, and maintain a high level of performance. In a true meritocracy, that might be true. However, we don't live in that world.

For better or worse, politics play a huge role in determining where people end up. Part of that political landscape is your social network and how these relationships provide access to information, resources, and social support. Even in the case of Anthony Foxx, whose mastery of policy played a central role in his political success, his social network was also extremely important:

My grandparents had been teachers in the segregated school system in Charlotte. So, when I went to the grocery store or to church or just around the community, there were always people who would associate me with my grandparents. The fact that they had standing in the community gave me a bit of a launching pad for my political career. . . . I ran into a gentleman who was probably in his late sixties when I was running for mayor, and he said, "Your grandfather was my principal when I was in high school." It wasn't really that unusual to hear a story like that. And then he proceeded to tell me that because he hadn't had a person in his family go to college before, he relied on my grandfather to help him fill out his applications. I said, "Wow, that's amazing, great story." He said, "No, there's more to the story. I had to also apply for financial aid, and I had to go to Raleigh state capitol to get my papers finalized. I didn't have a way to get to Raleigh. But your grandfather gave me the keys to his car." And I thought that sounded like my grandfather, but it also sounded like public service. And, you know, when your roots are that deep in a community, it gives you a starting place to run for office.

Foxx is not the only one who has benefited from a personal network, or a proxy network through a friend or family member.

In the next chapter, I will take a deep dive into the power of social networks, which are critical to not only playing the game but changing and leaving the game as well.

Five

The Necessity of Social Networks

Mary served on the board of the United Way in the early 1980s. One of her fellow board members was John Opel, the CEO of IBM. At the time, the company had envisioned the possibility that everyone in America could have their own personal computer, or PC, which they could use for household budgeting, video games, and other activities. This was an audacious notion considering that a computer in those days could be as large as an entire room. Because IBM was facing challenges, including several antitrust lawsuits, the company decided it might be wise to outsource the software division for the PC project. Mary listened intently before recommending that John talk to her college-aged son, Bill, who was quite familiar with software. The rest is history.

It is very possible that Microsoft might have never come into existence without the powerful network of Mary Gates, who became the first woman to chair the United Way's board of directors. Despite his brilliance, Bill Gates had no college degree, and limited real-world experience, in a field rife with competitors. What he knew—with respect to his software knowledge—was important to his success. However, *who* he knew (or rather, who his mother knew) was even more critical. What the Microsoft example illustrates is that you don't have to possess a deep, intimate relationship with someone to obtain access to resources and opportunities. Research has shown that even relatively casual relationships, or "friend of a friend" connections, can provide immense professional benefits.

Stanford sociologist Mark Granovetter pioneered the study of social networks, demonstrating the power of "weak ties," or acquaintances. In a landmark paper, he and his colleagues showed that weak ties were more instrumental to landing a job than strong ties (e.g., close friends)—an idea that was controversial and revolutionary when he introduced it in the early 1970s.[1] One of the reasons that weak ties are so instrumental is that they link people to vast and diverse networks that are outside their immediate circle—thereby expanding reach and access. These ideas were further expanded by Brian Uzzi, a sociologist at Northwestern University, and many other scholars, as well as being popularized in the book *The Tipping Point: How Little Things Can Make a Big Difference* by Malcolm Gladwell.

Building social networks is yet another crucial component to successfully playing the game. The first thing to understand is that not all networks are created equal. Two distinct individuals who happen to know the same number of people can still have vastly different access and opportunities due to the *types* of networks they are embedded within. A "clique" is an insular network, characterized by strong ties, and has the advantage of high levels of trust. A perfect illustration can be found in the popular 1990s sitcom *Friends,* starring the late Matthew Perry as Chandler Bing. In the series, Chandler had exactly five friends, and those friends were all friends with each other, without having many friendships outside of this inner circle of six.

In contrast, a "broker" or "connector" network is formed when someone

CLIQUE NETWORKS

BROKER NETWORK

is connected to different types of people and networks. Unlike Chandler Bing's network, the people in a broker network are from distinct, relatively nonoverlapping networks. The person at the epicenter of this network is referred to as a broker, connector, or boundary spanner. The diagrams above illustrate the difference between "clique" and "broker" networks. In the clique network illustrated on the previous page, you know three people and are connected with only those three people. The broker in the second diagram also knows only three people. However, because those three people are from diverse social networks, the broker is actually connected to *eleven* people rather than just three people. Spanning boundaries increases social connectivity.

What Granovetter and other social network researchers have shown is that the downstream impact of these different types of networks is astounding. To vividly illustrate this networking phenomenon, I will analyze a historical event that took place not far from where I currently reside. Both Paul Revere and William Dawes rode off into the Massachusetts countryside in the spring of 1775, during the dawn of the American Revolution, to warn the colonists of the impending British invasion. Today, most people have heard of Paul Revere, but few have heard of William Dawes. Nevertheless, they rode similar distances and spoke to approximately the same number of people to warn them that the British were coming. What differed between the two riders, however, was the type of network that the people they spoke with were embedded in. Dawes conveyed the sensational news to people who were in clique networks—the equivalent of Chandler Bing's. Chandler then told Rachel, who told Phoebe, who told Ross and Joey, before Joey told Rachel again, who later conveyed the news to Monica, who repeated it to Ross. The news got stuck in what is called an "echo chamber" and did not travel beyond this bubble.

Paul Revere, on the other hand, seemed to intuitively understand that delivering the news to the brokers in each town would produce a more impactful outcome. Such brokers in colonial Massachusetts might have been a tavern owner, the head clergyman, or the town's doctor, for example. These are people who would have been connected to a large *diversity* of people and networks within the community—the old and the young; the rich and the poor; the butcher, the baker, and the candlestick maker. From the mouth of a broker, the news is destined to reach exponentially more people, leading to the creation of a larger militia and solidifying the historical impact of Paul Revere's legendary ride.

One of the earliest empirical demonstrations of this Paul Revere effect was a creative and fascinating study by social psychologist Stanley Milgram in the 1960s (you may recall Milgram's famous "obedience to authority" shock experiment from Psych 101).[2] Milgram's social networks study was inspired by his travels. Wherever he roamed—whether in Europe or South America—he often encountered other travelers who were acquainted with someone in his network. It seemed like an unusual coincidence given the billions of people in the world. He reasoned that the connectivity between people may be much higher than previously assumed. Perhaps it's a small world after all.

To test this "small world" hypothesis, he randomly chose a person in Boston and asked several dozen people in Omaha, Nebraska, to get a letter to the Bostonian. If they knew the Bostonian, they could send it to him directly. If they didn't know him, their task was to send the letter to someone who they believed might know him—or someone who might know someone else who would know him. The researchers were interested in whether the letter would ever arrive, and if so, how many links it would take to get it there.

Milgram discovered that it took an average of six links to get the letter to the Bostonian—which is one source of the popular cultural reference to "six degrees of separation." Even more important, the researchers found that about half the letters traveled through the same four people. These were the brokers, or connectors. Similar studies on the small-world phenomenon were conducted decades later and have obtained similar results.[3]

■ ■ ■

As Black people, we need to be fully aware of the importance of social networks, and the dynamics of how they operate, when playing the game. Whether the game is sales, politics, or online influencing, being able to leverage the power of social networks is critical to achieving your objectives. The adage "It's not what you know, but who you know" is too simple. It not only matters who you know, but who *they* know too. How many different *types* of networks are you plugged into? These diverse networks may be especially important given the circuitous path to success for people from stigmatized social groups.

Research has shown that the metaphor of a corporate "ladder" may be more applicable to White men than to women and people of color. For women and non-Whites, it appears to be a series of corporate "lily pads." In other words, people from stigmatized social groups tend to advance by moving from corporation to corporation, with advancements occurring after each move, rather than by being repeatedly promoted vertically within the same organization. For instance, one study revealed that top-performing female CEOs were almost twice as likely as male CEOs to have been hired from outside of the company.[4] Because the path to promotion may be fundamentally different for women and people of color compared with White men, it is even more critical to develop a diverse social network.

For people of color, this means building relationships both within our ethnic enclaves (the safe space) and within the broader, mainstream community (the brave space). This is what political scientist Robert Putnam refers to as "bonding capital" (within our groups) and "bridging capital" (across groups).[5] One function of the enclave is to safeguard your emotional well-being, whereas professional opportunities are typically more plentiful in the mainstream. Due to the asymmetrical power structure of the society in which we live, White people in America can have highly successful and prosperous lives without ever having to interact with Black people. In contrast, few Black people have the luxury of playing the game well without knowing how to deal with White people.

Although meeting different types of people may mean expending tremendous energy and sacrificing comfort, it is a crucial element of playing the game. As Professor Marshall Ganz writes in his book *People, Power, Change:* "Relationships with people like us can be very supportive but can also close in on themselves, isolating us in echo chambers and limiting our creativity. Relationships with people not like us may require more work but can open us to diverse sources of information, a rich variety of perspectives, and greater creativity."[6]

One of the obstacles to building networks is the view among many people of color that networking is "dirty" or disingenuous. Organizational scholar Tiziana Casciaro and her colleagues conducted research on the ways in which networking can make people—especially less powerful people—feel dirty.[7]

They identify two broad network categories: personal and professional. They also identify two broad approaches to building a network: spontaneous and instrumental. Spontaneous networking occurs with no premeditated purpose. Instrumental networking is done with a specific goal in mind. From these variables the authors created four types of networking:

- **Spontaneous Personal Networking**—developing supportive or close relationships with people whom you met by chance or without looking for them.

- **Instrumental Personal Networking**—developing supportive or close relationships with people whom you sought out deliberately with the goal of fulfilling a need for emotional support, companionship, friendship, or matrimony.

- **Spontaneous Professional Networking**—developing relationships with people within your organization or industry whom you met "organically" without searching them out, perhaps by bumping into them at the coffee machine or in the cafeteria, for example.

- **Instrumental Professional Networking**—developing relationships with people within your organization or industry whom you deliberately and strategically sought out to help with a problem, serve as your mentor or sponsor, or assist you with some other professional goal.

Of these four types of networking, the only one that produces moral ambivalence for some people is the fourth one—instrumental networking for the sake of professional ambition. Because actions that are motivated by self-interest rather than altruism or concern for another person's welfare are seen by many as being less morally pure, instrumental networking in a professional setting makes some people feel "dirty." As Casciaro and her colleagues argue, "Instrumental networking clearly has a selfish intent, because the person initiating the relationship is doing so to obtain certain benefits. [Moreover,] because this intent is clear to the initiator, but perhaps not to the other person, the initiator may feel guilty."[8]

People who feel that instrumental professional networking is dirty are much less likely to engage in it. In turn, not engaging in instrumental networking results in a lower likelihood of advancement at work. The authors argue that "those who engage in more frequent instrumental networking will increase their chances of accessing valuable information, resources, and opportunities, and thus improve their job performance."[9] People who are powerful are more likely to engage in instrumental professional networking than people who are less powerful, further increasing the power of people who already have it and reducing the likelihood that people without power will ever get it.

These researchers gained access to a large corporate law firm with hundreds of attorneys distributed among twelve different practices within five offices across North America. The attorneys completed a survey that assessed the frequency of their networking, their feelings of dirtiness, and their job performance—measured by billable hours. The researchers also examined the rank of the attorney within the organization. Their results revealed a strong and significant negative correlation between how dirty the attorneys perceived instrumental professional networking to be and how frequently they engaged in instrumental professional networking. Not surprisingly, those who saw it as being dirty were much less likely to do it than those who did not see it as being dirty. What is interesting is that there was also a significant positive relationship between networking frequency and professional performance. Those who networked more often had more billable hours in the firm. Finally, there were a number of social variables that predicted who was more likely to see networking as being dirty. Women, introverts, and people with less power in the organization were all more likely to see instrumental networking as being more dirty.

Dartmouth professor Stacy Blake-Beard challenges the idea that networking is dirty, even when less powerful people seemingly have less to offer. She makes clear that the right networks are always mutually beneficial—even if both parties are not benefited in the same way, or to the same degree. I can offer an example from my own life that speaks to this.

As a hobby and creative outlet, I have been rehabbing and renting or flipping houses for many years now. However, it is an activity that requires considerable financial capital—resources that I did not always have. On one occasion, someone in my network happened to see the before and after of one of my rehab projects, and was impressed by the results. He offered to completely fund my next real estate venture, with the agreement that he would recoup his initial investment in the end, and we would split any profits fifty-fifty. Although he assured me that he wouldn't be terribly upset or disappointed if the project lost money ("It's just money," as he put it), I was not sure I fully believed him.

Either way, the fact that I was using someone else's money—at

0 percent interest—put a tremendous amount of pressure on me to perform well. I was very careful in selecting the right project, in the right geographical location (Florida, in this instance), at the right time (this was after the market crash in 2009). The project ended up being highly profitable, for both of us.

One potential interpretation of the arrangement is that the investor was an altruist who offered to help me out. After all, he completely funded my real estate project and assumed all the risk, while I did not invest a penny and only stood to profit. However, another way to look at it is that he believed that I could do something for him, too, and he was willing to gamble on my talent. In the end, he ended up making far more money than he could have made in any bank account or stock market at the time, and he did not have to lift a finger. Venture capital is not altruism.

There are two takeaways from this story. The first is that my social network allowed me to access interest-free capital that I could not have received from any financial institution, no matter how good my credit was. The second is that no one was exploited. It was a mutually agreeable and mutually beneficial arrangement.

Plenty of relationships that have seemingly asymmetrical power dynamics can be beneficial to both parties. I can attest that I learn as much from my students as they learn from me. Similarly, it is not just mentees or sponsees who benefit from mentors or sponsors. Those who help junior people in their organization benefit as well. During an interview I conducted with Princeton professor Eddie Glaude Jr., I asked him to look back on his long and illustrious career, with all its awards and accolades, and tell me what his proudest achievement has been. He said, "One of the things I'm most proud of, as a scholar, and as an administrator, is that every junior person I hired at Princeton was tenured. That's a small thing, but it's about the lifting that we talked about, right?"

His response speaks volumes about the gratification and reward that mentors and sponsors receive from people who too often assume they have nothing to offer. Giving back to the next generation can produce deep fulfillment because it enhances people's sense of purpose and service to the community. Accepting an opportunity from a mentor is not "dirty" in any way, provided that you do the best job you can—and provided that you also pay it forward one day. In the next section, I will closely examine the concepts of mentorship and sponsorship.

Mentorship Versus Sponsorship

Who you know is not just about large, interconnected social networks but also about one-on-one relationships. Your close interpersonal connections with mentors and sponsors are critical to professional development and advancement. Although the terms "mentor" and "sponsor" are sometimes used interchangeably, there are noteworthy distinctions between the two.

Mentors provide you with knowledge about the job and the organization, emotional encouragement when you need it, and social support when you're feeling lost. On the other hand, sponsors provide you with a professional platform to enhance your visibility within the organization, a shield to protect you from personal attacks and criticism, and a catapult to launch you into your next promotion. Sponsors put their reputation on the line to lobby for your success by supporting you when you happen to be absent from the room—or are not allowed to be in the room. Research has found that women and people of color are over-mentored and under-sponsored.[10] The chart below provides a common summary of the distinct roles of mentors and sponsors.

MENTORS	SPONSORS
Can be at any level	Are typically senior managers
Provide feedback and emotional support	Provide exposure to other top executives
Increase a mentee's sense of competence and self-worth	Protect a mentee from negative publicity or damaging contact with senior execs
Focus on professional development	Fight to get their people promoted

Often the strengths and skills of mentors and sponsors are quite different. As London Business School professor Herminia Ibarra and her colleagues note:

> It's hard to do a good job of both mentoring and sponsoring within the same program. Often the best mentors—those who provide caring and altruistic advice and counseling—are not the highfliers who have the influence to pull people up through the system. . . . Sponsors are typically selected on the basis of position power.[11]

At the same time, one should not view mentorship and sponsorship as being mutually exclusive, despite the title of Sylvia Ann Hewlett's popular book *Forget a Mentor, Find a Sponsor: The New Way to Fast-Track Your Career.* Professor Blake-Beard warns that too much emphasis on sponsorship over mentoring can impair the quality and authenticity of the relationship. As she explained to me: "It's a problem when I feel like I can't be vulnerable because I need you to position me. And it irritates me when people sell sponsorship as a quid pro quo. Sponsorship is one component of mentorship."

So, how do you find a sponsor? The first step is realizing that you need one. As I mentioned in the last chapter, many people assume that hard work and talent alone will lead to promotions and professional success. The second step is realizing that you don't find a sponsor; they find you. Because of the precious political capital that sponsors spend on their protégés, and the reputational risk they assume in doing so, it is unlikely that someone will be an effective sponsor if they do not wholeheartedly believe in you. Nevertheless, there are things you can do to increase the likelihood that they will want to sponsor you. The first is to ask for meetings and face time with potential sponsors. Be authentic and let them discover who you are. If they don't know you, they cannot, in good faith, sponsor you. Also, focus on both mastery and performance. The more you impress them, the more likely they will be to take a chance on you.

Another tactic is to use strong ties to establish weak ties. In other words, ask mentors and others who know you well to promote you throughout *their* network. It also circumvents the "humility" tightrope that people of color must walk between being self-promoting and being self-effacing. Let someone else do the bragging for you. Finally, keep in mind that sponsors do not have to look like you—they only have to believe in you. In fact, in many cases sponsors are from different race *and* gender categories.

I have conducted several studies assessing the paths of Black executives in Fortune 500 corporations. To do this, I pose questions in three stages. First, I ask: "How many sponsors, or people critical to advancing your career to the next level, would you say you've had in this company?" Second, I request that Black executives list each of their sponsors by writing their first and last initial (e.g., J.L.). Third, I read out the initials of each of the sponsors (e.g., J.L.) and ask them to tell me the race and gender of that person (e.g., Black, male).

By collecting the data in three stages—with race and gender being last—I hope to get responses that are untainted by social desirability, or the impulse for those I'm interviewing to tell me what they think I want to hear. Asking about race and gender last also reduces the likelihood of priming respondents to think about people based on their race or gender. The data that I have obtained is remarkably similar across each of the organizations where I have collected data. In one particular Fortune 500 company, Black executives' aggregate responses yielded a total of over a hundred distinct people that the executives saw as being critical to advancing their careers (i.e., sponsors). I use the word "distinct" because many Black executives named the same individual as being critical to their careers.

Of these people whom Black executives saw as being critical to their advancement, almost 60 percent were White. This finding reveals a couple of things. First, it confirms that sponsors do not have to look like you. Interestingly, many Black men had White female sponsors—that is, someone of a different race and gender. The second thing it revealed is that Black sponsors are doing extra duty. Although the Black employee population of this corporation is less than 10 percent—and even lower at the executive level—just under 40 percent of the sponsors of Black executives were other, higher-ranking Black executives. These are the "tempered radicals" empowering other Black employees within their organizations, and that's the subject of our next chapter.

Six

Playing the Game to Change the Game: Tempered Radicals

In the last few chapters, we've explored different ways of playing the game: doing the dance, achieving mastery and performance, and developing strong networks. It all begs an important question: To what end are we playing the game? The answer undoubtedly varies for different individuals. For some, it may involve pursuing excellence while at the same time forging a path that others can follow. For others, it may be purely self-serving. When it comes to playing the game, I have conceptualized three types of Black players: enablers, climbers, and lifters.

Enablers preserve the system of White supremacy. The primary goal of enablers is assimilation, often through ingratiation with White people. This coalition with White people usually requires denying the existence of racism in the modern day, culturally disparaging other Black people, and/or opposing policies designed to produce greater racial justice. Enablers commonly label such policies as "divisive." Although enablers are frequently rewarded for their complicity—which also makes enabling a way to "climb"—I argue that their striving to become part of mainstream White America is not simply a strategic means of gaining greater prosperity for themselves, but also consistent with their ideology and worldview. U.S. Supreme Court Justice Clarence Thomas might be considered an example of an enabler.[1]

Climbers empower themselves in an opportunistic and individualistic fashion. They are driven much more by ambition than by assimilation. They tend to be relatively apathetic and apolitical in their pursuit of status. Although their main priority is themselves, they may sometimes lend a hand to other Black folks—especially if it is convenient and/or if it increases their standing in the eyes of powerful others who could benefit them. By the same token, they typically shy away from confronting White supremacy if it could interfere with the attainment of their personal objectives. Basketball legend Michael Jordan might be considered an example of a climber.[2]

Finally, lifters are those with a strong commitment to using their position as insiders to empower other people of color. In the Black community, these individuals are often referred to as "race men" or "race women"—individuals who make great efforts to uplift not only themselves but the entire race. Like climbers, they may also enjoy status and achievement. However, their values compel them to use their power and position to extend opportunities to others beside them and behind them. Because of their intrinsic values, lifters will help other Black people even when it is inconvenient or unpopular. Basketball legend LeBron James could be considered an example of a lifter.

The boundaries between these categories are not rigidly defined. Enablers can climb, and someone could climb individualistically while also lifting others. It is even possible for lifters to enable White supremacy. Early twentieth-century notions of "uplift" (i.e., respectability) and the phrase "lift as we climb" referenced the perceived duty of elite Blacks to provide "defective" Black people with a viable plan for self-correction. As Columbia political science professor Frederick C. Harris wrote in an article titled "The Rise of Respectability Politics":

> Even though respectability evolved as an elite ideology, it operates as common sense in most quarters of black America. Indeed, it even has its own lexicon. The word "ghetto," for instance, which a generation ago was used to describe poor, segregated neighborhoods, is now used to characterize the "unacceptable" behavior of black people who live anywhere from a housing project to an affluent suburb. Economic power is a needed development, of course, and one that can be used to leverage political power. But the politics of respectability has been portrayed as an emancipatory strategy to the neglect

of discussions about structural forces that hinder the mobility of the black poor and working class.[3]

Traditional notions of uplift enabled systems of White supremacy by putting the onus of improvement solely on individuals, without any attention to the structures that produced those individual outcomes. Lifting connoted fixing indigent people whose existence was considered embarrassing to elites, not helping under-recognized people understand and break through a system of oppression. In contrast, I refer to "lifting" as an intrinsically motivated investment in helping others in the Black community, broadly construed, fulfill *their* dreams. It is about empowerment, together as a community—not "saving" another person to make oneself look better.

Although the three categories are not mutually exclusive, it is still possible to draw a conceptual line between them: Enablers uphold the status quo, climbers empower themselves, and lifters elevate the group. What differentiates enablers, climbers, and lifters is not their level of professional skill or diligence—as evidenced by the Michael Jordan/LeBron James example. It is the strength of their commitment to the Black community. Because this book centers on pathways to Black empowerment, I focus most of the attention in this chapter on lifters.

A broader question is whether playing the game—even as a lifter—can ever lead to Black empowerment, or whether by playing the game we ultimately become complicit in its perpetuation. The Black feminist poet and professor Audre Lorde is often quoted as saying that "the master's tools will never dismantle the master's house." However, when we examine the deeper context of her quote, we discover the expression of a sentiment much richer than the surface-level interpretation that playing the game only perpetuates the game.

The Master's Tools

In her speech titled "The Master's Tools Will Never Dismantle the Master's House," Lorde discusses the ways in which the feminist movement is defined by White patriarchal heteronormative ideals that create a hierarchy among women, leading to the exclusion of women of color, LGBTQ+ women, and those from under-resourced communities—people like Lorde herself. By adopting such "mainstream" standards, the movement undermines its goal of liberation by fracturing its own community—and in doing so, paradoxically strengthens the "master's" capacity for oppression.

One example that she gives is how patriarchy seeks to define, control, and channel women's emotions. In opposition to patriarchal standards that dictate that nurturance be directed toward husbands and children, she urges women to create their own non-patriarchal standards of nurturance and mutual support. She claims, "For women, the need and desire to nurture each other is not pathological but redemptive, and it is within that knowledge that our real power is rediscovered. It is this real connection which is so feared by a patriarchal world. Only within a patriarchal structure is maternity the only social power open to women."

Therefore, she perceives the "master's house" as a *conceptual* prison that imposes stringent limitations on how marginalized groups must think and behave. Leaving the master's house involves both freeing one's mind and embracing the collective power of the entire marginalized community—a community that ironically marginalizes its own members in accordance with hierarchical criteria (e.g., skin color) established by the master. Lorde writes:

> Without community there is no liberation, only the most vulnerable and temporary armistice between an individual and her oppression. But community must not mean a shedding of our differences, nor the pathetic pretense that these differences do not exist. Those of us who stand outside the circle of this society's definition of acceptable women; those of us who have been forged in the crucibles of difference—those of us who are poor, who are lesbians, who are Black, who are older—know that *survival is not an academic skill*. It is learning how to take our differences and make them strengths. *For the master's tools will never dismantle the master's house.* They may

allow us temporarily to beat him at his own game, but they will never enable us to bring about genuine change. And this fact is only threatening to the [marginalized people] who still define the master's house as their only source of support.[4]

Amid the abundant substance of this fuller account of Lorde's famous quote, three themes stand out. The first is the critical role of community. There is no dismantling the master's house without solidarity—solidarity despite the diversity within every marginalized group. The second is the ability to flip the script—to transform what society sees as a weakness or defect into a strength or asset. The third is the importance of not defining the master's house as one's *only* source of support. Audre Lorde's quote is not a condemnation of the master's house as much as it is a petition for greater solidarity, inclusivity, and freedom of being among those who are not of the master's house.

As a product of the Black residential enclave of St. Martin's Village in Lexington, Kentucky, I identify very strongly with all three points. I grew up surrounded by a cohesive and supportive Black community, the belief that Blackness conveyed strength and beauty, and an inherent understanding—from autonomous, entrepreneurial parents—that the master's house was not the sole, or even primary, source of support. Accepting the master's house for what it is (and is not) and *using* the master's tools—without feeling *dependent* on those tools—is empowering when playing the game.

Dr. David A. Thomas, president emeritus of Morehouse College, explored the complexity of operating within the master's house in a 2022 talk at Harvard Business School titled "Morehouse Men: Colluding While Undermining the Master's House 'Brick by Brick'?" It is a thoughtful presentation that ponders the paradox of what it means for Morehouse College to stand in opposition to the master's house while also, in some ways, emulating it. Is Morehouse merely a melanin-rich replication of the master's house, or is it something altogether different? Thomas believes that it is different, and that something powerful emerges when Black students attend Historically Black Colleges and Universities (HBCUs) such as Morehouse:

For these young men, part of what happens during this most important developmental period is that they come to know that the master's house is not their only source of support. . . . Ninety percent [of our graduates] go work in predominantly White organizations just like those who graduate from Harvard and Yale. [It's about] being able to make the choice when you are out in that world about where is the point at which the master's tools are no longer appropriate if you really want to make a difference. It's about not being so tied to the master's house.

And we can ask the question: What is the master's house? I would say that it is both a psychological and a material space. The psychological space of the master's house is designed to undermine one's sense of Blackness as a value. If we get real about it, there are many Black people who have never been in a space of Black excellence as an expectation. And therefore, they think that excellence can only be measured by the master's tools, only be brought about by the master's tools, as opposed to knowing when to use the master's tools but also knowing when to walk away from them.

So you take, for example, Dr. King. He walked away from the master's tools. In his period, the master had two tools—the courts and violence. He chose nonviolence—which was not the master's tool—to transform. And I think that what happens at a place like Morehouse is something foundational that prepares [young Black students] disproportionately, compared to those who go to predominantly White institutions, to go out and be tempered radicals.

Dr. Thomas suggests that being freed from the psychological walls of the master's house enables students to enter the material walls of the master's house with a mindset that better positions them not only to achieve personal success but to be "tempered radicals" who advocate on behalf of their race.

The term "tempered radical" was coined by organizational psychologists Deb Meyerson and Maureen Scully to describe individuals from stigmatized social groups who are able to successfully penetrate and navigate "mainstream" environments and acquire a level of legitimacy as "insiders" within these organizations.[5] They are then able to use this insider position to advocate for "radical" social change that will benefit other members of their stigmatized identity group.[6] Thus, a tempered radical is a type of lifter who has managed to obtain a position of power and influence within mainstream organizations and institutions.

Meyerson and Scully use the word "tempered" for various reasons. One is to signal temperance or moderation, reflecting the fact that tempered radicals adopt a slow and steady approach to social change. This stands in contrast to "untempered" radicals—who operate outside the mainstream and often adopt more disruptive, "burn-it-all-down-now-and-start-from-scratch" approaches (e.g., defunding the police rather than implementing reforms). The authors also use the word "tempered" in the sense of physics, such as how tempered glass becomes more durable after being alternately heated up and cooled down. They believe that existing between two worlds creates greater resilience. Finally, they use "tempered" to refer to temperament—the ability both to maintain one's equanimity and composure under stress, and to show outrage when warranted.

Tempered radicals find themselves toggling between two worlds—a situation that produces both challenges and opportunities. As Meyerson and Scully note: "Tempered radicals speak to multiple constituencies, which poses the problem that they will be seen as too radical for one and as too conservative for another. . . . Some observers may be confused about who the tempered radical is or what she 'really' stands for."[7] However, their existence in two worlds does not necessarily mean that all tempered radicals are constantly "covering." As discussed in chapter 3, Ken Chenault and Patrick Tannock are but two examples of tempered radicals who maintained a high level of strategic authenticity.

A different challenge for Black tempered radicals is how to operate in White society—even authentically—without losing legitimacy within the Black community. Almost every Black hero or prominent civil rights leader we can think of today, including Dr. Martin Luther King Jr., Whitney Young, Jesse Jackson, Barack Obama, and even Malcolm X, was labeled a "sellout" by somebody at some point during their adult life.[8] However, because none of these individuals ever denied their Blackness—or embraced a White supremacist agenda—it would be unfair to classify them as enablers. And because most of them worked for the betterment of the entire race, albeit in vastly different ways, they are not simply climbers. The thorny question is whether they are perceived by the Black community as having done *enough* or having done it in the "right" way.

Dr. King was a tempered radical who tussled with this tension throughout his lifetime, as someone at ease in both the Oval Office and the pulpit of the Black church. Being an insider, he was often criticized by more untempered radicals (e.g., Malcolm X) for not fighting hard enough, in their minds, and for being too conciliatory toward White people. Barack Obama faced similar dilemmas throughout his presidency, which he often managed by framing progressive policies (e.g., the Affordable Care Act) in a race-neutral way. In fact, he tended to shy away from conversations about race altogether. As professor Frederick C. Harris has written:

> Obama's general silence on issues of race and poverty has also contributed to the current malaise in black politics. The president seems to be committed only to social policies "that help everyone," rather than also considering targeted policies that address the conditions of poor black and Latino communities. As president he has spoken less in his first term (particularly during his first two years in office) on issues of race and poverty than any Democratic president in a generation or more.[9]

Although tempered radicals are careful to play the game in a manner that maintains their insider status, Meyerson and Scully argue that they can still be effective at producing change in at least two ways. One is by making *incremental reforms* to policy. It is important to realize that change is not an all-or-nothing proposition. Even in the absence of major changes, small wins can be significant.

Peter Frost and Carolyn Egri argue that "a series of small wins is 'less likely to engage the organizational immune system against deep change.'"[10] In other words, you can strategically assemble a package of small wins that takes the organization by surprise, whereas a huge win would have seemed overwhelming. One example they give is that instead of pushing for an overhaul of work and family policy, tempered radicals lobbied for "flex time," then "on-site child care" followed by other, smaller components, which when combined had a big impact. Similarly, although the Affordable Care Act did not eradicate racial health disparities, it made paying for healthcare more manageable for many Black (and White) people. Thus, we must recognize that small, or medium-sized, wins can reduce the size of big problems.

It is also important to bear in mind that wins that seem small when viewed from a broader societal perspective are actually not so small when we assess the real impact they can have on individuals. In other words, our actions can profoundly affect the lives of everyday people even if they do not transform the system. This is illustrated in the parable "The Star Thrower" by Loren Eiseley. In this story, a man is walking along a beach littered with starfish that are stranded but still alive. He begins collecting them one by one and returning them to the sea. Another person sees him and questions the sensibleness of his actions, pointing out the miles of beach and millions of starfish strewn across the sand. The skeptic tells the man that his efforts are noble but make no difference given the innumerable starfish in need of help. Undeterred, the man states, "It makes a difference to this one," and continues his endeavor to return starfish to the water.

It is easy to fall into the trap of believing that our individual efforts do not matter, even when we receive cards, e-mails, and phone calls from people telling us that we have made a tremendous difference in their lives. We who do this work should never underestimate all the social justice warriors we are inspiring, and the ripple effects that are produced.

This brings us to the second way in which tempered radicals generate social change—by simply being there. The *mere presence* of Black people in positions of power can send torrents of inspiration through the entire Black community. As the saying goes, "You can't be it if you don't see it." Children growing up with a Black man in the White House were transformed in immeasurable ways—the full impact of which may not be seen for decades. Something similar happened in Rwanda, which initially had a quota for the representation of women in their national legislature. The percentage of women grew from 33 percent to 64 percent because seeing is believing. There is similar evidence that mixed-income neighborhoods are beneficial to those from lower socioeconomic backgrounds who wouldn't otherwise see a wide range of professional possibilities represented.

These three distinct forms of change—institutional, individual, and inspirational—help to explain why some Black people disagree about the impact of Obama's presidency. Many argue that Obama's presidency was transformative to society (inspirationally), while others argue that his presidency did little to ameliorate the plight of Black people (institutionally). Both perspectives are valid. It comes down to how you define "impact."

Despite the institutional, individual, and inspirational benefits that tempered radicals can produce, all is not rosy. Being an insider can take its toll on the physical and mental health of tempered radicals. Having only a few insiders can also lead to tokenism, which can fracture and weaken the Black community as a whole. In the next section, I take a closer examination of the personal and social costs of tempered radicalism.

The Perils of Insider Status

What are the cons associated with tempered radicalism, both to the tempered radicals themselves and to the Black community? During my interview with the celebrated Black economist William Darity, he questioned whether we can ever really be on the inside, and spoke of the toll that this perceived "insider" position can take on one's health. Although he is a Distinguished Fellow of the American Economic Association, he confessed that he has never *felt* like an insider in mainstream economist circles. He also questioned whether tempered radicals are actually more durable—like tempered glass—or whether a better metaphor is glass with hidden cracks that run deep beneath the surface. He spoke candidly about not only his heart attacks but about the fact that a long list of other prominent Black economists had suffered heart attacks at a relatively young age.

One question is whether there is a way to be an insider while preserving one's physical and mental health. It might require taking breaks from the dance floor. One Black woman whom I spoke with, who is an "insider," spoke about her personal policy of "not doing White on the weekends." Some may find this social practice jarring or even offensive. But she is clear that it is something she needs to do for her mental health, and that it's more about sheltering herself from the harmful effects of White supremacy than about harboring any antipathy toward White people per se. She has essentially created an ethnic bubble, or enclave, for herself (we will discuss the concept of "enclaves" in greater depth in chapter 11).

Sheltering herself from White supremacy may be an important self-care practice. Multiple researchers have argued that racial health disparities have more to do with how society treats people from marginalized groups than how well those individuals take care of themselves. Health scholar Arline Geronimus uses the term "weathering" to describe the gradual, deleterious effect of societal marginalization on the health and aging process.[11] Linda Villarosa also gives a compelling and comprehensive summary of the detrimental physical impact of racism in her book *Under the Skin: The Hidden Toll of Racism on American Lives and on the Health of Our Nation,* finding that the stress associated with managing racism can lead to a number of harmful conditions such as high blood pressure, stroke, and heart attacks.

In addition to the dangers to mental and physical health, how might tempered radicals, paradoxically, weaken the social power of the entire Black community? There are several scholars who argue that the tokenization that occurs when people become tempered radicals may strengthen and stabilize White supremacy. Legal scholar Derrick Bell has argued that "society's stability is enhanced rather than undermined by the movement up through the class ranks of the precious few who too quickly are deemed to have 'made it.'"[12]

Similarly, economist Albert Hirschman argues that "integration, particularly in the token way in which it has been practiced up to now . . . elevates individual members of a group, but paradoxically, in plucking many of the most promising members from a group while failing to alter the lot of the group as a whole, weakens the collective thrust which the group might otherwise muster."[13]

In short, it is difficult for individual Black people to be successful without being a "success story" for White people. And success stories undermine resistance and political unrest by bolstering the illusion that the system is fair. As Charles Blow told me, "White supremacy always looks for the exception, because then it can maintain the rule. They can say, Oh, that's just the exceptional Negro and they will bend the rule. They will let you be the exception so that they can maintain the rule against everyone else." This allows White people to use Black success stories to pander to the myth of meritocracy.

As if that weren't enough, research by organizational psychologist Rosalind Chow and her colleagues shows that White people often adopt a deliberate practice of appeasement—strategically promoting a small number of Black people to positions of power when there are periods of social unrest in order to create the illusion of progress so that they can maintain the status quo.[14]

For all these reasons, and more, successful Black people on the inside have a social responsibility to disrupt the system, not simply pursue their own self-interest. Many tempered radicals do this by enlisting "untempered" radicals, or people who do not succumb to pressure to work within the system. These are the outsiders—the agitators. These individuals confront the game head-on in an effort to challenge and upend the system. As a friend once told me, "It's not the soap that gets the laundry clean—it's the agitation."

Furthermore, history has shown that these untempered radicals, and others who create what the late Congressman John Lewis called "good trouble," are often critical to the ascension of tempered radicals. Numerous appointments of Black people to mainstream positions have been due to the civil disobedience and demands of activists/untempered radicals who would not take "no" for an answer.

■ ■ ■

Many tempered radicals believe there is a fine line between tempered and untempered radicals, and that the two can work cooperatively. For example, Deval Patrick—the first, and only, Black person elected as governor of Massachusetts—believes that change is facilitated by "insiders" and "outsiders" working together. One story that he shared with me during an interview for this book took place in the 1990s when he was a civil rights attorney working with the Clinton administration. At the time, President Bill Clinton was contemplating his position on Affirmative Action in the wake of waning public support as well as Supreme Court challenges to the policy. Not unlike with their notorious crime bill and the disastrous "Don't Ask, Don't Tell" policy, the Clinton administration was considering taking a more conservative stance against Affirmative Action, reasoning that their liberal base would still stick by them.

As a relatively untempered radical (compared to insiders in the Clinton administration), Patrick was able to be more forceful and sincere in his communications with Clinton and Vice President Al Gore regarding how damaging a full-press opposition to Affirmative Action would be to society, and to their political base. The Clinton administration listened to his candid outsider viewpoint, and they got the message loud and clear. The result was that they did not gut the policy but instead adopted the "mend it, don't end it" approach to Affirmative Action.

Later, in his role as an insider while serving as Massachusetts governor, Patrick believed it was important to have diverse viewpoints at the table, including those of untempered radicals, whenever key decisions were being made. Despite being the first Black governor in the nearly four-hundred-year history of Massachusetts, Patrick felt that it was critical to stay focused on the work itself and not the prestige of the position. During my interview with him, Patrick told me:

What I have tried to do is not be so tickled that I was the first Black "this or that," that in the end I just kept the seat warm. And sometimes that means you [have to] get in people's faces. I will also say, by the way, that the folks who are outside of some of these institutions, whether it was outside of companies I worked in, or outside of the governor's office, or outside the civil rights division at [the] DOJ who were pushing for something harder and faster, were without exception helpful to me as a person on the inside— really helpful to me inside. And this is why I keep talking about not making a false choice [between tempered or untempered radicalism]. There are some folks who are much more effective outside pushing and making demands and so on. And having that relationship between the insiders and the outsiders—for me—was incredibly useful on the inside.

He went on to say that part of the question in his mind was *What bits and pieces of this foundation can you chip away at? What good can you do for as many people as you can in the time you have?*

Picking up on his use of the words "bits and pieces," I followed up with a question about whether this implied that incrementalism was his preferred means of change. Here's how he responded:

I want to be careful not to sound too timid, because I don't think it is true that burning it all down never works. It's just not my temperament—and also what I have seen when we start burning stuff is that we burn our stuff. And again, I don't want to be heard to say, "Well, let's go burn somebody else's stuff" [because] that's just not what I believe in. My point is that the "untempered radical"—to use your term—can be, and in my experience has been, incredibly useful for me as the tempered radical inside.

Governor Patrick makes it clear that playing the game versus changing the game is not an "either-or" but a "both-and" proposition. It is also evident that playing the game—or challenging the game, for that matter— does not guarantee that actual change will occur. In their discussion of tempered radicals, Meyerson and Scully admit that they do not focus "on whether the tempered radical ultimately wins the battle for change, but rather on how [they] remain engaged in the dual project of working within the organization and working to change the organization."[15]

And, thus, we turn to the second of the three overlapping pathways: how to engage with the process of *changing* the game, as an individual, a collective, or an institution. The next three chapters will focus on each of those levels of analysis, respectively.

Part III
Changing the Game

Seven

Confronting
Social Injustice

I am no longer accepting the things I cannot change.
I am changing the things I cannot accept.
—Angela Y. Davis

Because the entire system is designed to keep Black people "in their place" and disconnected from a sense of power, Black agency is essential to changing the game. Whereas the last part of the book focused on the dance, this part focuses on the battle—fully recognizing that one can twirl and tussle at the same time, as the Afro-Brazilian martial art capoeira beautifully illustrates.

Resistance can assume many forms, as evidenced by the diverse array of tactics undertaken by fighters such as Dr. Martin Luther King Jr., Nelson Mandela, Rosa Parks, Nat Turner, and Colin Kaepernick. But changing the game does not always require grand gestures that inspire revolutions or social movements. It can also involve seemingly small, mundane acts of advocacy or defiance that, in the aggregate, can produce a substantial impact. Remember my mother's subtle demand for equal representation by requesting a Black salesman at the automobile dealership?

In this chapter, I will focus on individual efforts to change the game by confronting racial abuse and refusing to accept unjust behavior. In the next chapter, I will go beyond individual action to collective action and social movements. In the final chapter of part III, I will discuss specific strategies for eroding the five major pillars of systemic racism: economic, civic, medical, judicial, and educational.

With the phrase "change the game," I am referring to an intentional process rather than an actual outcome. Changing the game is more about a commitment to *challenging* the status quo, regardless of whether that effort produces the intended outcome. The paramount goal is to constantly provide a force of resistance against oppression—which will often result in no win, sometimes yield small wins, and occasionally produce a big win. Some schools of thought posit that racism is a permanent fixture of the American landscape—yet one that should be resisted[1]—while other theoretical perspectives, such as Afropessimism, argue that we must simply accept the reality of our eternally racialized subjugation.[2]

I disagree with both perspectives. I believe that White supremacy is *persistent,* not necessarily permanent. As part of the foundation of this book, I have provided one explanation for its persistence, using the analogy of addiction. Despite the stubborn and formidable nature of this "habit," there is no way of knowing if it will continue indefinitely. Change is possible even if it's not probable. Moreover, I would never champion the notion that the battle should not be fought, and I am overjoyed that our enslaved ancestors were not Afropessimists.

At the same time, I am aware that some form of social hierarchy exists in every society on earth, and I realize that there will *always* be people who prioritize power over justice. Recall my framework from chapter 1 of dolphins, ostriches, and sharks to explain how White supremacy addiction manifests in different ways for different people. Imagining a world where "sharks" don't exist is romantic but not realistic. Imagining a world where they don't always win is definitely worth the struggle. Therefore, we must continue to fight. After all, what is the version of the world *without* this work?

Because changing the game involves a willingness to challenge authority, it also assumes a certain level of risk. Nothing worth having is totally free—though it often doesn't cost as much as we might assume. Nevertheless, confrontation always presents a dilemma, and the decision to confront is guided by both individual and situational factors. The upside is that real power can come from righteous disobedience, even when there are potential consequences for the confrontation. I will share a personal experience of "Flying While Black" to illustrate what I mean.

■ ■ ■

I grabbed my roller bag and headed toward the gate for my flight to North Carolina. During my layover, I had been talking on the phone with my Aunt Mary. We had been engaged in an amusing conversation about the misadventures she had experienced during her first Caribbean cruise. My plane was beginning to board, and I told her I would call her back when I landed.

Mary is one of my "fun" aunts who never fails to make me laugh each time I speak with her. As a youngster, I remember her sometimes wearing leopard-print coats and oversized sunglasses, and she drove a VW Beetle with a large daisy in the dashboard vase. Although she has two adult children and has been married to the same man for over fifty years, she is far from the typical suburban wife and mother. She has always had a vivacious, carefree spirit; an open mind; and an indomitable sense of fun and adventure. As we ended our call on that chilly morning in early spring 2024, she mused about whether the deep sense of tranquility that she experienced during the cruise was due to the beauty of the ocean or the contact high from plumes of marijuana smoke wafting from the neighboring cabin's balcony.

I put away my earbuds and proceeded down the passenger jet bridge. It would be my first time traveling to Greensboro, North Carolina. I had been invited there by a Black family who ran a nonprofit organization that was hosting an antiracism event. As I entered the aircraft—still smiling from my conversation with Aunt Mary—a flight attendant who was a middle-aged White woman with sandy-blond hair headed my way. She let the person ahead of me continue to their seat before nonchalantly raising her palm as an indication for me to stop. No words, no eye contact, just the hand. I immediately halted where I stood, which placed me in the galley area between the cockpit and first class.

She then turned away from me and headed down the aisle toward first class. No big deal. I am a frequent flyer and had seen the routine a million times. As passengers board, the flight attendant in the first-class cabin takes a few drink orders, lets some people walk past, and goes to the galley to pour the drinks before returning to first class to deliver those drinks and take more orders. I was in no hurry, and I glanced at my e-mail while she greeted the first-class passengers, put away their coats and purses, and took their drink orders.

It wasn't until she got to the fourth or fifth row—and I had read and responded to a few e-mails—that I noticed that several minutes had passed and the passengers behind me were growing restless. I turned around and saw a sea of frustrated faces stretching down the entire length of the jet bridge back toward the boarding gate. One of the passengers lined up just outside the plane gave me a shoulder shrug as if to inquire, "What's the holdup?" The passengers standing in the jet bridge looked cold in the frigid morning air.

A couple of minutes passed before another passenger who was standing just outside the airplane door spoke up and asked me what was going on. Was there an ill passenger? Had someone fallen? I signaled with my index finger that I would ask. I turned to the flight attendant and in a soft, polite tone, said: "Hi there, sorry to bother you. I was just wondering if you might be able to tell me how much longer you think it might be before we resume boarding?"

The flight attendant turned to face me. "Sir, you will be able to get through whenever I'm done here," she said. "I will be sure to let you know when that is." Then came the cherry on top: "Patience is a virtue."

I had not been told that since I was in kindergarten. Still in a good mood, I smiled and softly replied, "Yes, patience is a virtue. But an on-time departure is also a virtue."

One of the people in first class let out a light chuckle, which apparently annoyed the flight attendant. With one hand on her hip and a raised tone of voice, she exclaimed: "Don't you worry about an on-time departure! That's my job! We will get there on time, no problem. Like I told you before, we will resume boarding when I say so. Got it? I will let you know when that is. You need to stop being so rude."

"My apologies. I did not mean to come off as rude. Several passengers behind me who can't see into the cabin were just wondering why the line had stalled for this length of time and were asking me for information, since I'm at the front of the line," I explained.

"I don't care who asked what," she responded. "As I said to you before, I'll be done when I'm done. I don't need you telling me how to do my job. I don't tell you how to do your job, so you need to quit being so rude. . . ."

The flight attendant continued to berate me. I tuned out the rest of the vitriol that she was sending my way and decided that I would not offer any further response. I would take it up with the airline.

After she finished her tirade, I simply asked, "What is your name?"

She glared at me before angrily responding, "Don't worry about my name. What is *your* name?"

"Robert Livingston," I said matter-of-factly.

She let out a loud sigh before making a beeline toward me. I turned to the side as she walked past me and into the cockpit. I could not fully make out what she was saying—something about a "rude passenger"—but I could see from her body language that she was quite angry.

A few seconds later she returned to the cabin, pointed down the aisle, and said, "Now you can go to your seat—wherever that is."

"Thank you. But I was still wondering if you could give me your name. Just a first name will do."

She shouted, "It's Karen!" (not her actual name) as she grabbed her name tag with her thumb and index finger and hoisted it in the direction of my face.

"My apologies, Karen. I don't have my glasses on, so I wasn't able to read your name tag. Thank you for telling me."

I then headed to my window seat just beyond the middle of the plane, popped open my laptop, and began drafting a letter to the airline.

Meanwhile, other passengers continued to board the plane, including the gentleman seated in the aisle seat next to me. He gave me a friendly nod before unpacking items from his laptop bag. It took another twenty minutes or so for the remaining passengers to board. Once boarding was complete and everyone was seated, a gate agent in a supervisor's uniform boarded the plane and headed down the aisle.

Once she got to my area of the plane, she looked up at the seat numbers, leaned toward me, and quietly asked: "Are you Robert Livingston?"

"Yes," I responded, somewhat taken aback.

"Would you mind accompanying me to the Jetway?"

"Sure, no problem," I replied as I closed my computer, placed it in my laptop bag, and slipped it under my seat. The man in the aisle seat stood up to let me out.

Once the gate supervisor and I were outside the plane, she declared in her most professional voice: "Unfortunately, the flight attendant has reported that she is uncomfortable with you being on board this aircraft. So, we have booked you on a later flight to Greensboro. It leaves in just under three hours."

I was shocked. "Could you please explain to me what 'uncomfortable' means in this case?" I asked in a calm and inquisitive tone. "Did the flight attendant say I raised my voice, or insulted her, or made some sort of veiled or direct threat? If anything, that is how she behaved toward me. But you don't have to take my word for it. There were at least a dozen people who witnessed the whole encounter. I have no problem with you performing an investigation if you want."

"No, no. She didn't say that you did anything like that. She just said that you made her 'uncomfortable,' and according to new FAA regulations that are aimed at protecting the safety of flight attendants, we have to ask you to exit the aircraft," the supervisor explained.

"I apologize, but that does not work for me, for a whole bunch of reasons," I retorted in a low voice—almost a whisper. "The first is that I have the right to ask a question. The second is that I am flying to North Carolina for an event and there are people waiting for me at the airport right now. And third, there is no safety issue whatsoever. This exchange did not occur in a dark alley. It took place on a very crowded airplane, with dozens of witnesses. As I said before, I would be happy for you to speak with any of the passengers, if you wish."

"I understand, sir. But that is not our protocol. If a flight attendant reports that a passenger has made them uncomfortable, then we have to ask the passenger to leave the plane. Period."

I was stunned. Collecting myself, I replied, "Surely there has to be a higher bar of fairness than that. Otherwise, you open the door to someone's civil rights being violated at will by flight attendants who have a propensity to be 'uncomfortable' around certain types of passengers, regardless of the passenger's actual behavior. As a Black man, I realize that people may feel 'uncomfortable' around me before I even open my mouth."

The gate supervisor remained silent.

To inject some humor, I added in a lighthearted tone: "If I refused to fly whenever I felt 'uncomfortable,' I would never get on a plane. Being confined to a cramped cabin packed with strangers floating thirty thousand feet above the ground with no string attached is not exactly my idea of a good time. But that discomfort doesn't mean that my actual safety is at risk."

The gate supervisor smiled.

I returned to the situation at hand. "Clearly, this is an abuse of power on the part of the flight attendant—and I suspect it might be racially motivated. If so, that's certainly not something I condone. Bottom line, if you can give me some explanation of how I have mistreated or endangered any of the crew or passengers on board, then I will happily grab my stuff and exit this plane. Otherwise, I am going to head back to my seat."

She interjected. "Sir, if you don't voluntarily exit the aircraft, then we will have to deplane everyone and then deal with this issue once we are all back in the airport."

"Unfortunately, I guess that is what you will have to do," I softly replied, with a tone of sincere regret.

I did an about-face and proceeded to reboard the plane—walking past choleric Karen and the gauntlet of puzzled passengers staring up at me, wondering what was causing the delay in takeoff. My neighbor in the aisle saw me coming and stood up to let me in well before I arrived at my row. I slumped into my seat and gazed out the window—apprehensive, exhausted, and unsure of what would happen next.

■ ■ ■

As previously stated, willingness to act is determined by a combination of situational and dispositional factors. It is worth mentioning that my airplane incident took place only a few months before the highly publicized in-flight scandal in the summer of 2024 in which NFL legend Terrell Davis was forcibly removed from a United Airlines flight in handcuffs after asking for a cup of ice. That same month, legendary rapper Sandra Denton from Salt-N-Pepa was ejected from a Southwest Airlines flight and escorted out of the airport by law enforcement for requesting that the additional seat she had purchased to comfortably accommodate her injured leg remain empty. It seems that the behavior of both Black passengers had made people "uncomfortable." (Such incidents are not uncommon. Author Isabel Wilkerson describes in graphic detail in her book *Caste* the abuse that she has received from both passengers and flight attendants while traveling on airplanes.)

Had those high-profile airline incidents occurred *before* my flight, it might have provided some additional "context," leading me to just shut up and take the condescending behavior from the flight attendant. Or, I might have simply exited the aircraft when the gate supervisor instructed me to. On the other hand, perhaps I would have been even more resolute in my decision not to leave the plane, having the ability to cite other well-publicized examples of FWB (Flying While Black) to substantiate what I believed was happening to me on board that day. I might have been further emboldened by my knowledge of the history of the perils of TWB (Traveling While Black) more broadly—a history that brought about the creation of the Green Book and other sources of information to guide Black people away from danger and harassment while traveling. It is difficult to predict in retrospect how I might have responded had I been cognizant of these larger considerations during my own situation. Nevertheless, disposition is another determinant of action—and mine generally compels me to speak up when something doesn't seem right.

As I sat on the plane—for what seemed like an eternity—I noticed that the cabin, despite being completely full, was eerily quiet. Even the comforting hum of the airplane's engine was noticeably absent, as the pilot had shut it off to conserve fuel. About twenty minutes passed before the gate supervisor boarded the plane again and headed down the aisle toward my seat.

"Can you tell me once again how all this started?" she asked.

I briefly reiterated the series of events that had unfolded after I boarded while she listened intently. Once I had finished, she thanked me and headed toward the boarding door. The passenger next to me turned my way and asked in a half whisper, "Do you have any idea what's going on?"

"I'm not exactly sure," I responded, not having the energy to rehash the incident yet again.

Five minutes later, the captain made an announcement.

"Folks, we are just waiting for a change of crew. It shouldn't be too long. We hope to have you in the air in thirty minutes or so. Thanks for your patience."

I saw Karen exit the plane, her face glistening. Her rage and aggression had transformed into crocodile tears in a play for sympathy. About forty minutes later, a different flight attendant came on board.

"Flight attendants, please prepare the cabin for takeoff," the captain announced.

I heaved a huge sigh of relief and dozed off—emotionally spent from the whole ordeal. We arrived in North Carolina about forty-five minutes later than scheduled. Once I exited the airport, I found two smiling Black women in their sixties waiting for me curbside near an SUV. They both gave me a hug and welcomed me to Greensboro. I apologized to them for the delay and told them about the debacle on board that had caused it. They were outraged by the treatment that I had received but seemed proud that I had stood up for myself.

"She will definitely think twice before she does that to another Black person!" one of the women said with a chuckle. They then urged me to put the entire experience behind me and enjoy the evening of Southern hospitality that they had planned. The entire family took me out to dinner at a soul food restaurant in downtown Greensboro. We had a lovely evening, and the conference the next day was uplifting and inspiring. A day later, I headed back to Boston.

On the return trip, I had a layover in the same hub where I had caught the flight to Greensboro. While awaiting my flight, I spotted the gate supervisor who had boarded my outbound flight. I got up to approach her, hoping to obtain some additional insight into what had transpired. As I approached, she recognized me and signaled that she would be with me after helping the gate agents with a few things. I took a seat nearby and waited for her.

I learned several things during our conversation. Apparently, when the gate supervisor had asked Karen what had happened, Karen was not very convincing in her explanation of what exactly made her uncomfortable. The gate supervisor escalated the incident to corporate to receive further guidance on how to handle it. After hearing all the facts, corporate decided to remove the flight attendant from the aircraft and replace her with a different crew member. According to the gate supervisor, this was the first time she had ever seen a flight attendant pulled from a plane. I asked if I should write a letter to the airline, and she told me that it wouldn't hurt, given that there is an investigation anytime a passenger or crew member is removed from a plane.

My letter to the airline was quite long. In it, I not only explained what had happened during the incident, but I did something that may seem surprising: I voiced my support for legislation to protect flight attendants. I was aware of the many high-profile examples of verbal and physical assaults flight attendants have had to deal with in recent years. I made it clear, however, that there also needs to be a change in airline policy to guard against the bullying of passengers by domineering or discriminatory flight attendants. Below are snippets from my longer letter:

> We see examples in the news of people being accused of harassing or threatening others when cellphone video shows just the opposite [an allusion to the Chris Cooper/Amy Cooper Central Park birdwatcher incident, among others]. I never thought I would be the target of this sort of bullying on the grounds of "discomfort." Being threatened is not the same as being annoyed. The two are quite different, and it's important to make a clear distinction. . . .

There is also something to be said about conflict management. Most flight attendants are trained in how to de-escalate a situation. [Karen] did just the opposite. She took a molehill and turned it into a mountain. She also abused her power, in my opinion. And everyone on board paid the price.

Once again, I strongly believe that both company policy and federal law should protect not just the safety of flight attendants (and pilots, gate agents, ticketing staff, ramp crew, etc.) but their dignity as well. That is of paramount importance. At the same time, I feel that it's extremely important that such legislation not be weaponized as a tool of aggression against passengers that flight attendants may disfavor, for whatever reason.

In training, you should establish clearer policies and practices that stipulate when flight attendants can invoke this privilege. "I'm not comfortable with the person" is incredibly subjective and can lead to abuse of power (italics added). Instead, one might ask if there is a more objective basis for reaching this conclusion, especially if the outcome is removing a passenger from a plane. Was there shouting, name-calling, or verbal abuse? A threat of physical abuse? Actual physical abuse? Sexual harassment? Failure to follow safety instructions? Intoxication and boorish behavior? None of these were present during my interaction.

A few days later, a representative of the airline replied with a thoughtful apology. It contained each of the three necessary components of a genuine apology: *recognition* ("I understand what the problem is"), *remorse* ("I feel genuine regret that it occurred"), and *repair* ("I will make you whole and take steps to ensure that it doesn't happen again"). Here is an excerpt from that letter:

On behalf of everyone at [airline], I sincerely apologize for the abrupt manner in which our flight attendant spoke to you. I'm extremely disheartened to read your letter and can only imagine your disappointment when our employee created unnecessary and unpleasant confrontation.

It sounds like she didn't have the most pleasant demeanor, so I can see why this alone was disappointing.

We want you to know that discourtesy is not tolerated within our company. We expect our team members to work professionally, politely and respectfully with everyone on board. While internal handling is confidential, the appropriate departments will thoroughly review your comments and handle [the situation] internally with the employee involved. *We can assure you that appropriate action will be taken through education and training to ensure a similar situation is not repeated* (italics added).

They also credited a significant number of frequent flyer miles to my account as a "repair" gesture. However, what was most gratifying was the acknowledgment that they intended to make systemic changes in education and training to prevent what had happened to me from happening to someone else. That was the "small change" in this game that I was hoping to achieve.

We each have the power, as individuals, to advocate for change. However, there can be costs associated with this advocacy. In the next section, I discuss the research on the pros and cons of confronting racial bias and injustice.

■ ■ ■

There is ample research on the determinants of whether people confront racial bias when they see it, as well as the consequences of doing so. One factor that impacts whether people confront bias or not is whether they prioritize being liked versus being respected.[3] The results of one study revealed that during Black-White interracial interactions, the White interaction partner prioritized being liked by the Black person whereas the Black person prioritized being respected by the White person.[4] Research further shows that people are more likely to prioritize being respected when the need to belong has been satisfied.[5] Going back to St. Martin's

Village, I always felt that I belonged to a strong community. Therefore, my need to be liked by White people was lower than my need to be respected, which, according to research, makes me more likely to speak up when I perceive a transgression.

But every person is different. I remember teaching an advanced course at Harvard Business School (HBS) that brought together leaders and changemakers from all over the country. One of the students was a Black man from Detroit. It was his first time on Harvard's campus, and he had decided to take a walk around. His slender build, boyish face, and casual manner of dress made him appear somewhat younger than his middle-aged peers but significantly older than the typical Harvard undergraduate. While sitting in the Harvard Yard, he was approached by a Harvard police officer who asked him what he was doing on campus. He replied that he was attending a course at HBS. The officer looked skeptical and continued pressing him. Each answer that he gave elicited a new question from the officer. I became increasingly angry as I listened to the man recount the harassment and interrogation that he had endured. "Did you get the officer's name?" I asked. He shook his head. "Why didn't you just tell him you were here for a course and if he had any other questions, he could take it up with the B-school dean? Period." I asked. He looked at me with a blank expression and responded, "I was scared."

At that point, my outrage softened into empathy—and understanding. I could see how the situation would have been terrifying for him. He was from a generation that still remembers the racial violence in Boston during the 1970s. So just being in the city may have been unsettling. Moreover, he was not employed by Harvard but rather was a guest at the school—a guest who may have questioned whether he even "belonged" on campus. Our personal histories were also different. He had grown up in a community where he was often harassed—verbally and physically—by police officers. For all these reasons, and more, he may not have fully realized the power that *he* possessed in this particular situation: being a paying student hosted by HBS. Our life experiences impact how we walk in the world. Individual differences in personality, history, and trauma all play a role in how people respond in these situations.

The willingness to accept the possible consequences of confrontation is also a factor to consider. Both history and social psychological research have shown that the social—and physical—consequences of confronting racism can be dire. Historically, Black people have been brutally murdered for far less. Although the risk of bodily injury continues to exist in the present day, more common are the social and professional risks involved with confronting racism.

Research has demonstrated that Black people who confront bias are seen as "troublemakers" or "complainers" who play the race card—and stunningly, these perceptions still emerged even when there was a 100 percent chance that racial discrimination had actually occurred.[6] This finding suggests that Black people are expected to just shut up and take it, which makes sense given the bulk of our nation's history—when Black folks *did* have to just take it. Some White people today—including elected politicians—have referred to this era as the "good old days."

The important takeaway here is that negative reactions to Black people who confront racism have less to do with the actual legitimacy of the complaint than with the perceived audacity of the complainer. Black people who call out racism exhibit agency that challenges the racial hierarchy by communicating that inappropriate behavior of White people will not be tolerated by Black folks. The fact that Black people are punished for *not* accepting racial abuse is yet another example of know-your-place aggression.[7] Indeed, research has shown that part of the reason that confrontation is disliked by majority group members is that it threatens their status.[8] Confrontation holds people accountable, so that they are no longer able to say or do whatever they want, without consequences or repercussions.

Interestingly, research has shown that confronting racism can literally make someone appear to be Blacker. White people who read about a biracial person who confronted racism attributed more stereotypically Black traits to that person. They also tended to imagine the person as being darker skinned than they actually were! On the other hand, not confronting racial bias made a biracial person appear Whiter and more assimilated.[9] One implication of this finding is that people interested in assimilating into the White mainstream can further their mission by never complaining or confronting when they are the victims of racism or microaggressions.

Not surprisingly, Black people tend to have a very different response to Black people who confront racism. Like the Black women in Greensboro beaming with pride when they heard my airline story, research confirms that Black people who see a Black person stand up to racism evaluate them more favorably than they do Black people who did not stand up to racism.[10]

Black people who reported speaking up when they felt they were mistreated because of their race also tended to have more positive indicators of physical and mental health than Black people who did not. Specifically, research has found that Black people who confront racism have more favorable physiological responses to stress,[11] healthier levels of blood pressure,[12] lower levels of depression,[13] and better overall well-being.[14] One of the reasons for these positive health benefits of confronting racism appears to be a greater sense of personal autonomy,[15] whereas not confronting racism can lead to unhealthy rumination and obsessive thoughts.[16] In short, there are also positive consequences of speaking up, and not simply accepting the indignation and disrespect that can accompany life as a Black person in America.

A simple summary of these findings is that Black people who confront racism tend to have more positive *psychological* outcomes (e.g., well-being, sense of autonomy) but more negative *social* consequences (e.g., more ostracism and hostility from White people). And despite the negative social outcomes, confronting racism can still be effective at producing social change—as it leads to less subsequent racism and a more egalitarian culture.[17] As Robyn Mallett and Margo Monteith state:

When people choose to remain silent in the face of biased behavior, they are safe from interpersonal consequences such as social backlash but face a host of intrapersonal consequences including decreased autonomy and well-being. Moreover, ignoring discrimination conveys acceptance of the behavior and may reduce the strength of egalitarian norms.[18]

I can personally affirm that standing my ground when I felt that I was being mistreated due to my race was extremely empowering. Although doing so resulted in more acute stress in the moment, a more chronic stressor would have been feeling like a helpless victim who is subject to racial hazing whenever I walk onto a plane.

The benefits also extend beyond me personally. The women who hosted me upon my arrival in North Carolina are correct—it is more likely that Karen will think twice before trying to get another Black passenger kicked off a plane. Because people talk, it also sends a *cultural* signal, reducing the likelihood that other flight attendants will go down that road. Confrontation provides an effective option for White allies as well, as research has shown that White people who confront other White people's racism are even more effective at producing change than Black people who do so.[19]

■ ■ ■

Throughout history, there have been many people who have shown the courage to stand up to power and change the things they cannot accept. One prominent example is the source of the quote at the beginning of this chapter—the legendary Angela Y. Davis. I had the good fortune of interviewing her for this book to get her perspectives on the struggle for racial equality and how she presently perceives the prospect of changing the game, after all these years of activism. Our ninety-minute conversation was a profoundly transformational experience for me.

In the next chapter, I will share highlights from my inspiring interview with Dr. Davis, conveying, in her own words, her thoughts on courage, confrontation, and changing the game.

Eight

The Power of We

In addition to the ways in which individuals can confront bias in their efforts to change the game, there is the bigger question of how people can stand together to collectively fight against systemic racism. In December 2024, I had the privilege of interviewing Dr. Angela Y. Davis about a variety of topics, including her views on changing the game.

The profundity of her wisdom, intellect, humility, and humanity is astounding. Rather than diluting the richness of her unique and insightful perspective with my own analysis or interpretation, I have decided to share her brilliance in her own words.[1]

RWL: You're undoubtedly one of the most intrepid and persevering activists of the modern era, now in your seventh decade of social justice advocacy. What is the secret to your courage, persistence, and resilience? Are there ever times when you feel like, or have felt like, throwing in the towel? If so, what gets you through these moments of doubt and despair? And, building on that question, what was it like for you to witness the reelection of Donald J. Trump? What does this signify, if anything, about all the prior decades of struggle and progress? How do we move forward in a moment like this? Do you feel that all your struggle was for naught?

AYD: I don't reflect on my own capacities or lack thereof as an individual. So that question would have to be rephrased for me to consider it, because throughout my life—throughout my political life—I've never been involved in any undertaking that has not been collective. And I can never claim authorship of ideas and of strategies, as an individual. It's always with others. And I think this is something that I learned when I was very young.

I had wonderful teachers. You know, my mother was a teacher. The neighbor across the street was a teacher. My father was a teacher, and I realize now how much they did to prepare us not to imbibe the notions of White supremacy that were everywhere else in our environment. And race was represented, collectively, always. I mean, you saw a photograph of a young Black man in the newspaper who was being charged with some kind of crime, and if you were Black, you felt implicated. You felt a part of that. So that very profound sense of collective identity has remained with me throughout my life.

I suppose that's a way of answering that question—by saying that I've survived precisely because my identity is very much inflected with the work and the consciousness of others. I've never felt weak, even when we've not been able to win, because I've never felt entirely alone. And, of course, because of the fact that my life was saved, literally, by millions of people coming together all over the world—that's a more explicit example of that sense of [my] connectedness with others.

So that's my courage. It is collective courage. It's not individual courage—even, you know, when I was in jail and facing the death penalty three times, not knowing what the outcome of my trial would be. Despite the fact that I, and so many others, knew that I was not guilty, there was no guarantee that I would not be found guilty in the legal process. And so, I often used to imagine what it would be like to walk into the death chamber—because that was a possible future [for me]. And I remember later how different I started to feel when, you know, those thoughts would invade my mind. Then, as the movement became larger, the less scary the whole prospect became. Until at a certain point I realized that if we did lose—because we often lose—and if I were executed, that I would not be alone. I would be with all of the people who were struggling for my freedom. And that made me feel far more powerful than anything else. And those ideas—those invasive ideas—started to go away as a consequence of that.

RWL: Wow.

AYD: And okay, you mentioned Trump. I want to say that we've experienced this before, which we have, but I know this is a very different world. It's not the same world in which Richard Nixon and Ronald Reagan were elected president. And I know that this is a major defeat for people all over the world. But I also know that the struggle is not over. I think that this is one of the reasons why the Black struggle resonates all over the world—because it doesn't end. And even at the most difficult moments, even when it was not clear that slavery would ever end, even when it was not clear that the system of segregation was not going to continue to be the law of the land, Black people still had hope and still fought back.

And I think this is what Black people have offered to the world—that sense of possibility. And you know, I like to point to Mariame Kaba's notion that hope is a discipline. Hope is not just an emotion that is occasioned by what happens in the world. It is a discipline that has to be developed. It has to be created. It has to be produced. It has to be reproduced. I would argue that Donald Trump and his people do not represent the direction of history. This is a moment of defeat, precisely based on the fact that Trump and his people are afraid of the future that we represent. And because they, in a sense, know that it's coming. So they're doing everything they can to prevent it. So, we have to make it through these times, but we also have to recognize that the struggle continues, and we're talking about something that's been in existence for hundreds of years, and that may very well last hundreds of years into the future. So, we owe it to those who came before us and to those who are coming after us to guarantee that "a luta continua" ["the fight continues," in Portuguese].

RWL: Do you think we can ever really change the game? In other words, will we ever be done with the fight for racial equality and finally achieve Dr. King's dream? Or is it the case, as you suggest, that freedom is a constant struggle? That it's not a matter of "winning" the game but rather creating a perpetual force of resistance against this negative force of oppression, like a yin and yang, almost, or a tug-of-war. Because without that, then the bullies and fascists have free rein to do whatever they want.

And if the goal is to provide a constant source of resistance, how do you think most people will feel about that? Because what that means is you're always going to be fighting. There's never really a moment where you can sit back and say, "Okay, we're done. We achieved this thing. We've reached the top of the hill." And so, I'm wondering if thinking of social activism as this perpetual journey, rather than a destination, or seeing it as a process rather than an outcome or solution, is liberating and uplifting—because I see how it could be—or if it's demoralizing and defeatist to say, "Okay, we will constantly have to do this. There may never be a decisive victory."

AYD: Well, I would reframe it, because I think that shifting away from the notion of freedom as a destination to freedom as a journey is very exciting. If one perceives freedom as a destination, it means that once we reach that destination, the struggle is over. So, what is left?

RWL: [chuckles] We rest!

AYD: [smiles] But who wants to rest all the time? I mean, I think that's why it's so important to emphasize that the struggle is not only about challenging oppression, which, you know, is a serious job that people are tired of doing. But I also like to think of the struggle as what has produced so much joy in the world. Black people have always created joy in the context of struggle, and that's one of the reasons why the Black movement resonates with everyone, all over the world. Because it's not been this glum struggle—one in which one has to hide one's desire, you know, for love and joy until one wins the struggle, and *then* we can live and experience joy. No. It's always been about producing joy in the context of struggle. It's not a sense of being separate from the work that is required in order to bring about joy. It's about recognizing that the process itself can give us a sense of what kind of world we want.

And certainly, I see music and art as ways of preparing us for the future that we want, teaching us about the future that we want, allowing us to feel that which we don't yet understand and that which we can't yet put into words. I mean, this is why Black music is so important all over the world, because it's a freedom music. In my opinion, the role that the blues plays, bringing people together, even in difficult times. You know, when women like Ma Rainey and Bessie Smith sang about what it was like to be a washwoman, or being mistreated by a man—the collectivity that's generated by the music, the sense that I am with someone else who has experienced this, creates courage. All this disappears if we say that, okay, there is going to be a time, a specific time, in which we declare the struggle over and we've won everything that we need to win.

Then there's also the question of the knowledge that's generated in the course of the struggle and I guess I would call that the "epistemological value" of engaging in struggle—what we learned that we did not previously know as a consequence of being involved in the struggle.

If one thinks about the way in which the Black movement, for example, has influenced so many other movements. Without the experience of the Black movement, we wouldn't have the feminist movement in the way that we have it today. I doubt very seriously whether we would have learned how to engage in struggles around issues of sexuality, around issues of gender, [or] broader challenges to the binary structure of gender. The very notion of intersectionality comes out of a movement that is constantly opening new vistas and creating new challenges and providing new questions. So that is why I say freedom is a constant struggle. Of course, it comes from an old spiritual [*They say that freedom is a constant struggle / O Lord, we've struggled so long / We must be free*], but I can't see a conclusion because I know that there are other issues that need to be taken up that have not yet. Issues of the environment, which are not nearly as incorporated into other movements. There are food justice issues that we have to take up. Our relationships with animals. You know, there's so much more that has not been included in our agendas of struggle that is yet to come. And then I would say that what excites me is that I know that there are things that I could never possibly imagine now, that will need to be taken up in the future. Who would have ever imagined that we would be talking about pronouns in the context of struggle, right? Nobody could have imagined that. And yet, here we are.

RWL: One question I was going to ask is: What would you say is the biggest misconception about you? But after speaking to you for ninety minutes, I think I already have one answer to that question. I think many people would be surprised to learn that you are a universalist [someone who loves and respects all people and living creatures on the planet], and an optimist.

If you were to ask someone, particularly a White person, what they think of when they hear the name Angela Davis, they might conjure up images of an angry Black woman or someone who is violent and hateful. But you are a humanitarian who continues to show so much love and grace to the world, even after all that you've seen and experienced in your life. It is inspiring.

AYD: [smiles] Let me just say, to echo Antonio Gramsci, that it's pessimism of the intellect combined with optimism of the will. I don't want to see everything through rose-colored glasses. I want to be realistic about what it is we're confronting.

RWL: I love that distinction. I think I would describe myself in the same way. Thank you so much for your time, Dr. Davis. This has been beyond amazing. I hate to do the whole starstruck, groupie thing, but can I get a selfie? You have been a hero of mine for a very, very long time—even more so now.

■ ■ ■

There are several important points to unpack from the sage and powerful words of Dr. Davis. The first is that social change is about people working together as opposed to individuals working in isolation. Even in the face of death, she was thinking about the ways in which her fate was intertwined with that of others. Solidarity was a central and recurring theme throughout our interview, and it is a critical component of any successful social movement. (I will elaborate on this point later in the chapter.)

The second point, which was a bit more surprising and counterintuitive, is that change is not always about actual change. The whole process of changing the game is much more about resistance than about winning. It has more to do with dignity than with victory. It is about honoring our forebears through our engagement in the struggle, and encouraging our descendants to continue the fight. The idea that changing the game is more about actions than about outcomes is liberating, in some respects. The acceptance of a journey attenuates the frustration and disappointment of not having arrived at a specific destination and, somewhat paradoxically, increases the determination to continue the journey.

The third point is that the struggle can be a source of joy, freedom, and artistic expression. We do not have to wait until the fight is over to experience joy. We can experience joy not only during but *because of* the struggle. It brings us closer together and creates a shared sense of humanity and purpose. It also allows us to experience a broad range of emotions that stimulate creativity.

The fourth point is that the struggle can also make us more competent and resilient. There is an apocryphal story of a fourth-grade science class in which the children observed, over time, the metamorphosis of a caterpillar into a butterfly. In the final stage of the transformation, the butterfly struggles to emerge from its cocoon. The eager, well-intentioned students decide to "help" the butterfly by carefully cutting through the tough outer case of the chrysalis. They successfully do so without harming the insect. However, when the butterfly emerges, it is unable to fly. It needed the process of the struggle to strengthen its wings. Without the struggle, it loses its ability to fly, and consequently to live a full and free life.

This parable of the butterfly and the cocoon can be easily applied to real life. Indeed, entire books have been written about the crisis of our youth and their inability to function effectively in the world as the result of not only their dependence on technology[2] but also well-intentioned helicopter parenting and other forms of coddling, overprotection, and hypervigilance.[3] Sure, the playground can be a place of struggle and hard knocks for young children, but it is also a place where mettle is forged and social skills are honed. In *The Anxious Generation: How the Great Rewiring of Childhood Is Causing an Epidemic of Mental Illness,* Jonathan Haidt discusses the benefits of unsupervised play, for example, and how it creates greater coping skills and resilience. In short, there is plenty of evidence, anecdotally and empirically, in support of the benefits of struggle. However, what I had not considered were the hedonic aspects of the struggle—the notion that the process could not only engender fortitude and resilience but also foster fulfillment and enjoyment.

The fifth point is that the struggle creates ripple effects, resulting in downstream consequences that perhaps we never could have foreseen. The whole interview threw me for a loop. Having become fed up and disillusioned by the constant regression to White supremacy in recent years, I was certain going into the interview that Angela Davis—as someone who has been engaged in antiracism for many more decades than I have—would be *really* tired. She's not. I found an upbeat, energetic octogenarian—with a radiant and youthful appearance that belies her age—who is still actively fighting and training the next generation of fighters. The fact that she even agreed to do an interview with me is evidence of that commitment. It dawned on me that activism is not just what she does, it is who she is—an integral part of her identity, being, and purpose.

She is hopeful, but she is in no way blind to the reality of the challenges that lie in front of us—as she herself points out. And although hope is a discipline, and a source of motivation, it is not a strategy. Building a successful, sustainable strategy against oppression requires more than just hope. It requires working together toward a common mission in an intentional way. How might we achieve this? In the sections that follow, I discuss scientific research that echoes some of the points raised by Dr. Davis—about the critical role of shared identity and solidarity, for example—as well as provide an overview of the social science literature that offers guidance on how to create effective and sustainable social movements.

The Significance of Shared Identity

Dr. Davis' observation of the importance of interconnectedness and solidarity, even at our most vulnerable moments, is affirmed by social science. For example, research on crisis and disasters demonstrates that people who find themselves in difficult, dangerous, or unpredictable situations band together and bond around sources of shared identity, rather than becoming more isolated and behaving more selfishly. Social psychologists Jay Van Bavel and Dominic Packer, authors of the book *The Power of Us: Harnessing Our Shared Identities to Improve Performance, Increase Cooperation, and Promote Social Harmony*, analyze research from plane hijackings, train bombings, physical assaults, and many other fraught situations, and ultimately conclude:

> It is often assumed that people look out for themselves in times of danger or threat. . . . But in reality, this rarely happens. A half-century of research on disasters, protests, and crowd behavior has found that dire circumstances often inspire the formation of shared identities that enable groups to coordinate effective responses to major challenges. . . . Shared identities also allow marginalized and disadvantaged groups, along with their allies, to mobilize against injustice and push for social change.[4]

They discuss the difference between what they call "collections of people" and "psychological groups of people." The former just happen to co-exist in the same place at the same time, whereas the latter share a common sense of identity and purpose—often working together to overcome or achieve something bigger than any individual in the group. Van Bavel and Packer's research has found that psychological groups of people share not only common goals and identities but also the same synchronized patterns of neural activation.[5] In addition to being on the same brain wavelength, literally, psychological groups of people also worked more effectively on puzzles, problem-solving activities, and other cognitive exercises—far outperforming collections of people who worked together on similar tasks. Thus, there is something very powerful about having shared identity and connection with others, in both a psychological sense and a practical sense.

Solutions to any major social problems require collective action. Voting means nothing at the individual level. It is only in the aggregate that we see a difference. The same holds true for boycotts. One rider who refuses to board a bus in Montgomery, Alabama, is insignificant. However, an entire community of riders banding together can topple the system. As Marshall Ganz writes in *People, Power, Change,* "There's an account of Dr. King getting up early Monday morning to watch the buses go by—and there was not a single Black face on a single bus. At that moment that community saw itself differently. Powerlessness divides you. But that kind of solidarity empowers."[6] There can never be power without solidarity. Working together in groups also reduces the risk to any given individual.

To be clear, I am not suggesting that individual actions do not matter. They do, as I argued in the last chapter. In fact, too much focus on the collective can lead to a reduction in individual contributions. This is a phenomenon called *social loafing*—where individuals are less motivated to expend effort when they think that everyone else will do the job. However, social loafing can be overcome if individual responsibilities are clear, and individual contributions are visible and recognized.[7]

Nevertheless, individuals may also experience the impulse to defect from the group—preferring to be seen as individuals—particularly those who are members of groups that are viewed negatively by society. This harkens back to the concept of "covering" discussed in chapter 3. Black people, and members of other stigmatized social groups, often try to distance themselves from stereotypes associated with the group. Some individuals may even attempt to disengage from the group altogether, if they are able. Decades of research have documented that in addition to pursuing upward mobility to enhance their own status, some members of low-status social groups will also attempt to dissociate themselves from their low-status group and recategorize themselves into higher-status groups (e.g., "I'm a rich person"; "I'm mixed race, not Black"; "I'm West Indian, not Black").

One famous example is O. J. Simpson, who allegedly said, "I'm not Black, I'm O.J."—the perfect illustration of discarding a shared identity in favor of individualization. Other people may attempt to "trade up," by exchanging their stigmatized social identity for a more socially desirable social identity. For example, Tiger Woods stated on *The Oprah Winfrey Show* many years ago that it "pisses him off" that people often categorize him as Black, because he insists that he is "Cablinasian" instead. But not every high-status Black person seeks an escape hatch from their stigmatized racial identity. Many choose to lean into their shared identity with other Black people.

Fascinating new research by organizational psychologist Tracy Dumas and her colleagues turns this defector trend on its head by investigating Black people who have enough clout and status to "transcend" their race but instead choose to double down by embracing it. The goal of this research was to "study how observers respond when members of low status demographic groups who have transcended their group's lower status (through their achievements, wealth, prominence, etc.) choose to affiliate with and express allegiance to the lower status group rather than downplaying their membership in the lower status group."

This is a process that they term "corrective recategorization" and is reflected in the title of their paper: "Actually, I Am One of Them: Self-Categorization of High-Status African Americans." If a White person attempts to "compliment" a high-status Black person by stating that they "are not like 'other' Black people," the idea is that many elite Blacks will correct the White person by proudly affirming their racial identity and their solidarity with others in the racial group. They give examples of Black folks who could "go mainstream" if they preferred but opt to emphasize their racial identity and engage with the Black community.

They cite people like Robert F. Smith, the Black billionaire who donated over \$34 million to Morehouse College to eliminate student debt for the entire graduating class of 2019. There is also Eddie George, a successful NFL player and entrepreneur who chose to coach at Tennessee State University, an HBCU. Deion Sanders is another football legend who opted to coach at an HBCU. In addition, they cite David A. Thomas, the prominent Harvard professor discussed in chapter 6, who left the Ivy League to become president of Morehouse College. Ruth Simmons—the former president of Brown University who chose to become president of Prairie View A&M, an HBCU—is another example. They also cite Beyoncé and her dedication to racial justice in her music, as well as her homage to the Black Panthers during her 2016 Super Bowl performance. What is the psychological impact that all these individuals have on other Black people?

Although the research is still in its early stages, initial results reveal that exposure to high-status Black people who show strong allegiance to their race led other Black people to also increase their support for the Black community. One way that the researchers measured this was through an increase in the willingness to donate money to Black nonprofit organizations, such as the United Negro College Fund (UNCF). Their observed increase in generosity and Black solidarity was explained by the inspiration and positive leadership perceptions produced by these high-status Black people who showed allegiance to their race. Interestingly, White people also responded more favorably to these high-status Black people who doubled down on their racial identity. Therein lies a paradox. Although defection from stigmatized groups can enhance social status, showing solidarity with one's stigmatized racial group can also increase respect from others. This has parallels to the debate about the "dance" versus the "stance" discussed in chapter 3. Covering can be an effective strategy, but so, too, is authenticity.

Building Social Movements

What are the critical components of building and maintaining a collective force of resistance against the powers that be? Harvard professor Marshall Ganz has spent most of his life addressing this question, as both an academic and an activist. As a young adult, he volunteered with the Student Nonviolent Coordinating Committee (SNCC), working with Bob Moses and other architects of Freedom Summer in Mississippi, as well as spending many subsequent years working with Cesar Chavez and the United Farm Workers (UFW) in California. In *People, Power, Change,* Ganz outlines the steps necessary to build power as a collective and leverage it for social progress. He defines the core mission of social movements as "enabling others to find the courage to lead, to build community, and to enable that community to turn the resources it has into the power it needs to get what it wants."[8]

He draws a clear distinction between "power" and "resources," which, on the surface, may seem quite similar. Power refers to institutional authority and one's position in the social hierarchy. He defines resources not as money, necessarily, but rather as the means and options at one's disposal that can be leveraged to gain power. A resource can be something as simple as feet. Although Black people in Montgomery had no formal authority to change the bus company's egregious policy of relegating Black people to the back of the bus, most Black people had resources (e.g., the ability to walk to where they needed to go) that they could leverage, collectively, to challenge formal authority. Thus, Black people were very "resourceful" even in the absence of formal power, and were therefore able to transform their resources into power.

In their book *Why Civil Resistance Works: The Strategic Logic of Nonviolent Conflict,* political scientist Erica Chenoweth and strategic planner Maria Stephan examined over a century of nonviolent movements and found that they were more than twice as successful as their violent counterparts at achieving their stated goals. To be sure, nonviolent movements were only successful about half (53 percent) of the time—but violent movements had only about a 1 in 4 (26 percent) likelihood of success.[9] The authors provide multiple reasons for the superior success of nonviolent movements, including reasons related to shared values and identities.

Because nonviolent movements appeal to a much broader range of people, nonviolent activists are able to get more citizens to identify with and join their cause. In other words, nonviolent movements created greater *solidarity* with the broader community, which increased their power. Violence against members of these nonviolent movements only increased community support, even among members of military and police forces, who often ended up shifting their loyalties from those in power to the protesters they were ordered to attack. Such a shift marks the beginning of the end for any repressive regime.

So, what are the building blocks of a (nonviolent) social movement? Ganz identifies five key practices of organizing: (1) relationships, (2) storytelling, (3) action, (4) structure/leadership, and (5) strategy.

Relationships Grounded in Respect, Values, and Exchange

Relationships form the foundation of any social movement. Ganz defines a relationship as a connection with another person around a shared purpose and perceived mutual benefit. All relationships begin with respect, a word that is commonly used but often misunderstood. He tells a story about building respect with other freedom fighters in Mississippi, including a Black man named Hollis. Ganz, a Jewish man from the Northeast, asks Hollis for advice on how he can better connect with Black Christians from the South. Hollis' simple response to Ganz was "Respect."

"Sure," Ganz said, a bit too quickly, by his own admission. "I have respect for everyone."

"No," Hollis replied. "Respect is what you do, it's not what you have. First, listen and hear; second, ask and learn; third, show respect, and you will get it; and fourth, don't try to be anyone different from who you are. Be yourself." Ganz states that this advice turned out to be fundamental to every successful relationship he would build in his work for the next sixty years.

In addition to shared purpose and respect, relationships are based on needs and mutual benefits. Each person has a resource that the other person may need. This runs the risk of sounding instrumental and opportunistic rather than authentic, unless we adopt a broader understanding of what a "resource" entails. A resource could be kindness, empathy, companionship, social support, or collaboration. People exchange these resources with each other in the context of a relationship. As Ganz states, "If there's no exchange, there's no relationship—but exchange alone doesn't make a relationship."[10]

Relationships are also built on common values and superordinate goals. Social psychologist Shalom Schwartz defines values simply as what is important to us in life.[11] He is one of the world's preeminent experts on values and has spent decades studying values all around the world and how they shape who we are, what we do, and with whom we choose to form relationships.

Although there exist dozens of distinct values, Schwartz's research reveals that they can be clustered into ten broad values that have a systematic relationship with one another. Values that are next to one another in the circumplex tend to be positively correlated, whereas values that are on opposite sides of the circumplex tend to be negatively correlated. For example, the value of *self-direction* tends to be negatively correlated with the value of *conformity* because the former is concerned with determining one's own path in life while the latter emphasizes changing one's behavior to be consistent with other people's expectations.

Similarly, the value of *power*, defined as the desire for control over people and resources, tends to be negatively correlated with the value of *universalism,* which is about social justice and treating all people and living creatures with equal dignity and respect. Interestingly, research by Kathleen Vohs and her colleagues shows that getting people to think about money can cause them to be less likely to help other people, to sit farther away from other people, and to prefer solo pursuits over group activities.[12]

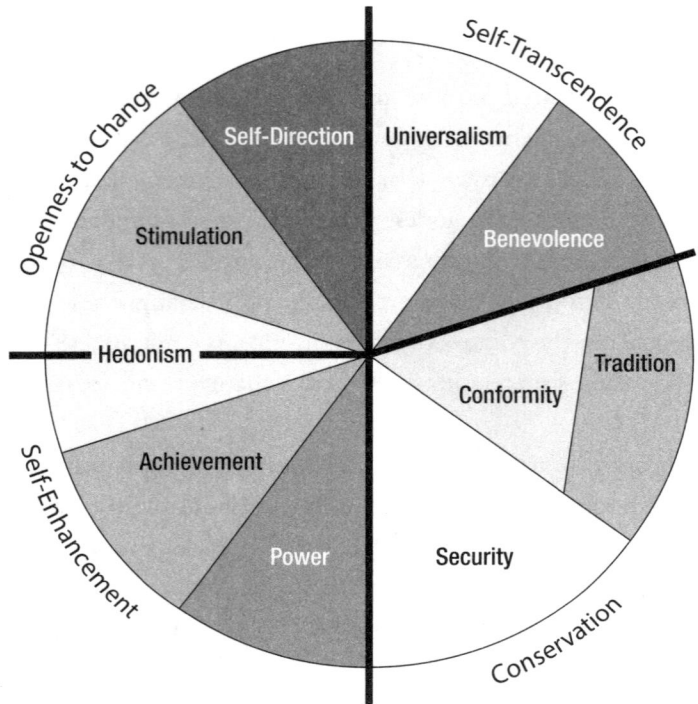

Adapted from "Universals in the Content and Structure of Values: Theoretical Advances and Empirical Tests in 20 Countries" by Shalom H. Schwartz, PhD, *Advances in Experimental Social Psychology,* Volume 25, Elsevier, pp. 1–65.

This is not to suggest that a particular individual could not value both money and relationships. However, they do tend to be negatively related overall.

The main point here is that there are tremendous differences in how people see the world, and these differences predict both our relationships with other people and our actions.[13] It is also not to suggest that power is necessarily a bad thing. Although people often see power as being dirty, it's important to distinguish between valuing power as a means to other things and valuing power as an end unto itself. Dr. Martin Luther King Jr. tried to use his power to bring about universalism, not to obtain wealth or dominate people. Dr. Ganz argues that there is a huge difference between creating power "with" others in the context of social movements and creating power "over" others in the context of oppression.[14]

Stories Are Power

Storytelling is the process of communicating why a particular issue or situation is important and why action must be taken. Part of the function of storytelling is to inspire others to action. Yuval Harari, author of *Sapiens: A Brief History of Humankind,* once commented that "storytelling is our superpower. . . . We are the only species with the ability to use language—not just to describe things we can see, taste, and touch, but also to invent stories about things that don't exist."[15]

Moreover, storytelling serves as a source of not only social engagement and entertainment but also inspiration and cooperation. Stories are an indispensable resource for leaders seeking to rally a population around a common goal. As journalist Carmine Gallo states:

> Reaching the moon was only a figment of people's imagination, and few believed it was possible—until 1961. That's when dreamer John F. Kennedy leveraged the power of words and stories to galvanize massive cooperation.
>
> Kennedy's May 25, 1961, speech to Congress is a masterful example of storytelling techniques. Kennedy relied on metaphors to paint a picture in people's minds. He said space is a "new ocean" to explore, and the country would "set sail" on this new sea to gain new hopes for knowledge and peace.
>
> Kennedy's passion, vision, and storytelling skills—his superpower—galvanized the country's collective imagination and inspired 400,000 people to support Kennedy's "adventure."[16]

As Black people, we have many stories to tell—both stories of the past and stories of our imagined future. The Kingdom of Dahomey is our story. The Middle Passage is our story. Juneteenth is our story. "I Have a Dream" is our story. We tell thousands of stories, not only of past suffering but of a vision of a brighter future, through music, literature, art, and film. Angela Davis referenced the power of our story and art, not just for our struggle but for the world. And as she astutely observed, this power is threatening to those who seek to oppress us. Some states have passed legislation in an effort to prevent our stories from being told. There is a logical reason for this: Stories can create not just understanding and solidarity but action.

Action Requires Structure and Strategy

Resistance is more about action than about motivation. It is about behavior, not courage. As Audre Lorde has asserted, people can act even when they are afraid. Dr. Davis acknowledged this during my interview:

> I love Audre Lorde and the way in which she always encourages us to do that which is seemingly contradictory to the way that we're feeling. You know, so that you can feel silence and at the same time you can speak, you can feel scared to death and at the same time you can fight back.

But action requires direction and discipline. It also requires structure and leadership. The critical challenge of any social movement is getting people to realize that they have resources, and then enabling them to transform those individual resources into collective power to effect social change. Structuring establishes the rules and procedures necessary for organizing. However, this does not imply dominance by leaders or policies.

Ganz states, "We distinguish leadership from authority in that leadership enables rather than commands. The reality is that no one person can really do [everything], yet many think they can. Some people react by abandoning the idea of authoritative leadership entirely for a structure in which everyone leads. Neither structure lends itself to effective organizing."[17]

Contrary to some people's assumptions, there is no such thing as an entirely leaderless group. Political scientist Jo Freeman argues that "the absence of a transparent formal structure only disguises opaque, informal, personalistic, and unaccountable structure which ensures its dysfunction." This is what she calls the "tyranny of structurelessness."[18] To be sure, leadership does not necessarily entail the work of a single person. Rather, leadership refers to the roles and actions of a group of individuals who have taken on the commitment and responsibility of effecting social change. Organizing is a particular form of leadership that involves bringing people together with a common goal and mobilizing them to take action.

Finally, strategizing is about creating *specific* plans of action to achieve a desired goal. The first step of strategizing is having a clear understanding of what the problem is. Ambiguity is the enemy of strategy. Because a concept like systemic racism can seem abstract, making it more concrete can facilitate strategizing around ways to combat it. I find that it helps to break systemic racism down into discrete domains or components such as economic disparities or bias in the criminal justice system. The second step is devising a clear plan for how to address the specific problem or situation that has been identified.

In the last chapter of part III, I will conclude our exploration of changing the game with an examination of real-world strategies that have been employed to weaken the foundation of systemic racism.

Nine

Eroding the Pillars of Systemic Racism

The elimination of systemic racism is a noble aspiration, but it is far too abstract to be a realistic plan of action. Any strategy—regardless of how far-fetched and quixotic it might be—first requires specifying and concretizing the problem in need of a solution. There is nothing concrete about the concept of systemic racism.

Because the notion of systemic racism can seem vague, even mysterious, it is helpful to identify core components, which can be more easily recognized and measured. As I first discussed in my previous book, *The Conversation,* I believe that there are five domains that encapsulate the bulk of systemic racism:

- **Economic**—this refers to racial disparities in wealth and professional opportunity, including hiring discrimination, income disparities, living wage employment and unemployment, access to lending and venture capital, access to state and federal benefits and assistance, and redlining/housing discrimination.

- **Civic**—this refers to disparate access to and participation in local, state, and federal political systems. It includes both process variables (e.g., voter registration, suppression, and disenfranchisement), legislative representation (e.g., gerrymandering), and legislative outcomes (e.g., laws, policies).

- **Health**—this refers to disparities in physical and mental health outcomes such as life expectancy, infant mortality, maternal health, malnutrition and food deserts, access to health insurance, medication affordability, healthcare quality, and environmental racism.

- **Justice**—this refers to racial disparities in the criminal justice system, including both over-policing and lack of police access, police brutality, disparate prosecution and conviction rates, criminal sentencing disparities, access to legal representation, bail policies, plea bargaining, and capital punishment.

- **Education**—this refers to systemic differences in access to and quality of public K–12 education as well as preparation for and access to higher education. Some specific disparities are school district funding, student tracking, disciplinary procedures, teacher quality, access to counseling and mental health services, college exam preparation, and college funding.

To be clear, it is the relative specificity of a goal or strategy, not the perceived feasibility, that is most important. As discussed in the last chapter, getting to the moon once seemed impossible. But in addition to being a lofty—and seemingly impossible—aspiration, it was also a relatively concrete goal. We knew what the moon looked like, how big it was, where it was located, and how far away it was. Beyond being seemingly impossible, a goal such as exploring the entire universe is also much more abstract and immeasurable than the goal of getting to the moon. Therefore, it is difficult to devise a strategy around exploring the universe. However, moonshots are fair game.

When broken down into concrete components, systemic racism becomes much more tangible and amenable to viable solutions. This chapter provides an overview of the efforts of individuals and organizations to address some of these pillars of systemic racism. Because the first two pillars of systemic racism—economic and civic—are direct causes of or contributors to the last three pillars, I focus my attention on strategies aimed at reducing economic disparities and those aimed at producing more democratic civic engagement.

■ ■ ■

The United States is one of the most economically disparate countries in the industrialized world. Inequality is a fraught and complicated topic, with many variables contributing to its rise in recent decades, including the decline of labor unions, increases in financialization and globalization, less progressive tax policies, and legislation around the minimum wage.

Some argue that one of the biggest drivers of economic inequality in the United States is the specific way in which the system of capitalism is, and always has been, structured in this country. The invocation of "capitalism" in America is often used to defend unfair and exploitative labor practices. This "low-road" capitalism, as it has been labeled by sociologist Joel Rogers, is modeled on the plantation slave economy, and is designed to create wealth for relatively few at the expense of many. Sociologist Matthew Desmond elaborates on this idea in his book *Poverty, by America*. He also authored an article in *The New York Times Magazine* titled "In Order to Understand the Brutality of American Capitalism, You Have to Start on the Plantation." In this article, he states:

> If today America promotes a particular kind of low-road capitalism— a union-busting capitalism of poverty wages, gig jobs and normalized insecurity; a winner-take-all capitalism of stunning disparities not only permitting but awarding financial rule-bending; a racist capitalism that ignores the fact that slavery didn't just deny black freedom but built white fortunes, originating the black-white wealth gap that annually grows wider—one reason is that American capitalism was founded on the lowest road there is [i.e., slavery].[1]

One of the modern consequences of this low-road tradition is setting a minimum wage that fails to come anywhere close to a living wage. Many companies are reluctant to raise wages because increased financialization means that there is a higher priority placed on shareholder value than on the well-being of workers. Therefore, one strategy to increase economic and racial justice centers around the question of how to put more money in the pockets of hardworking employees.

Fortunately, higher wages and higher profits are not mutually exclusive. In her book *The Case for Good Jobs: How Great Companies Bring Dignity, Pay, and Meaning to Everyone's Work,* MIT professor Zeynep Ton argues that seeing employees as a cost to be minimized, rather than as an asset to be invested in, can lead to higher operating costs and lower profits. She states "the costs of low pay . . . ended up being greater than all the benefits that could come from raising pay to a living wage."[2]

The reality is that many millions of Americans live paycheck to paycheck, particularly in communities of color. In fact, in 2020 a survey from the Board of Governors of the Federal Reserve System found that over a third of Americans (37 percent) would struggle to cover an unexpected expense of $400.[3] According to Ton, the number of working Americans whose earnings are below a living wage is greater than the *total* number of people living in the nations of Canada and Portugal combined. She writes:

> Even before the pandemic, 53 million people—44 percent of the workforce—worked in jobs for which the median annual pay was just $17,950. Black and Hispanic Americans are disproportionately represented in these low-wage jobs; economic and racial justice are, as Martin Luther King Jr. reminded us, inexorably linked. . . . Even among those who have succeeded most in the system, there are corporate leaders who believe that capitalism is broken.[4]

Although it is true that higher skills and qualifications command a higher salary, Ton makes the case that the inverse is true as well—that a higher salary can actually lead to higher performance. She cites a study in India that randomized the timing of when workers got paid and showed that on the days when workers had more money in their pocket, they were more productive and made fewer mistakes.[5]

Consistent with Ton's arguments, many companies are shifting away from low pay and high turnover toward what she calls the "Good Jobs" strategy. As director of the Good Jobs Institute at MIT, she assists corporations in making structural and operational changes that enable them to create not only higher employee pay and satisfaction but also more satisfied customers, shareholders, and investors.

It is difficult to make the case that good jobs can reduce the racial wealth gap if Black people do not get those jobs. We know from numerous studies that Black people are less likely to be hired than equally qualified White candidates. For example, one study found that applicants with the name Lakeisha or Jamal were far less likely to be hired than applicants with the name Emily or Greg, despite having the same education and experience.[6]

Fortunately, this problem can be addressed through a number of strategies. Some are legislative. I interviewed prominent legal scholar Kimberlé Crenshaw about the role that the law has played in reducing employment discrimination and the racial wealth gap. She points to the transformative effect of Affirmative Action, saying it "literally changed the game" as we know it. Affirmative Action is commonly misrepresented—often intentionally—in the current discourse. Here's how Crenshaw explained it:

> I think people have forgotten that when we were growing up in the late '60s and the '70s, basic civil service jobs like being a firefighter were not accessible to Black people. It was clear that the way these jobs were distributed created an exclusive pipeline that led to the overrepresentation of White people.
>
> The need to create clear benchmarks for workforce utilization was what created the impetus for Affirmative Action. How do people get access to the information about these jobs? How does the hiring process work? How do people actually move up the ranks? The impetus was to really rethink how concrete material opportunities are distributed, and whether the criteria for hiring are actually rational or is it just because we have always done it this way.
>
> So, when some people say that Affirmative Action only benefited

the middle class, I say, "No, it created it." And it created the middle class not just for Black people but for many groups who were historically excluded from workforce opportunities to obtain good jobs to raise families and all that kind of stuff.

It had a ripple effect as well. In discipline after discipline, and industry after industry, the question was raised about why we look the way we do. And when you ask the question, you begin to realize that the standard of what counts [as fitting the job] was established during a time when Black people weren't there. I'm a law professor because one Black man said, "Hell, yeah, we have to rethink what the pipelines look like and who gets in them and I'm going to create this alternative pipeline that helps us redefine what a law professor looks like." It is precisely because strategies like Affirmative Action have changed the game that the right wing has gone after them so hard and tried to discredit them. Somebody once said, "Dogs don't bark at parked cars." People don't go after strategies that don't work.

Today, as it often does with progressive policies, the right wing has effectively rebranded Affirmative Action not as an antidote to White male mediocrity, cronyism, and overrepresentation—and a portal for highly qualified Black talent (like Kimberlé Crenshaw) to enter spaces where they had traditionally been excluded—but rather as a license for hiring unqualified Black people (which is often code for *all* Black people).

This same political constituency is rebranding DEI as MEI (merit, excellence, and intelligence), as if those standards were equally applied to White candidates. One reason these re-brandings are so effective is not the genius of the message but rather the widespread propensity to accept any message that paints White people as inherently worthy and exceptional and Black people as unqualified and undeserving. Even White people who don't buy into these messages can often understand how "other" White people can believe them—because on some level even progressive White people believe them too. It is all a symptom of the White supremacy addiction discussed in chapter 1.

Because of this current backlash against DEI, the game has changed.

Consequently, strategies for promoting racial equity in the workplace have evolved too. Gone are the days of sympathy toward groups that have been historically excluded. It's the return of White entitlement, without compunction or apology. This shifts the ways in which pro-justice policies and initiatives must be framed and implemented.

In a brilliant *Harvard Business Review* article titled "DEI Is Under Attack. Here's How Companies Can Mitigate the Legal Risks," law professors Kenji Yoshino and David Glasgow address the challenge of how to sustain DEI efforts in the face of right-wing legal assaults, such as the Supreme Court's *Students for Fair Admissions* (*SFFA*) case in June 2023, which "effectively ended race-based Affirmative Action in higher education." They advocate moving away from hiring quotas, tie-breaker decisions (if choosing between equally strong Black and White candidates, go with the Black candidate to raise diversity), race-specific internships and fellowships, and tying manager compensation or bonuses to diversity hiring. They describe these as "risky" strategies because they confer palpable benefits (e.g., jobs, fellowships) to people based on their membership in protected groups (e.g., race, gender).

The solution, ironically, is to avoid focusing benefits on the groups that federal laws were designed to protect. Instead, the attention should be focused on interests, experiences, and goals. Here are a few examples that they give:

- **Leveling Versus Lifting**—this strategy shifts the goal from uplifting groups that are legally protected against discrimination, based on a history of bias, to the goal of leveling the playing field so that all groups are equally represented. Because the playing field is already tilted, it essentially produces the same outcome as the lifting. But this subtle shift in framing makes all the difference in the world. One example would be systematically reviewing employee pay to ensure that there are no racial or gender gaps in compensation, which will almost certainly lead to a raise for Black folks, particularly Black women. In theory, however, these efforts "level" the playing field for everybody rather than "lift" the salary of underpaid minorities.

- **Content Versus Cohorts**—this strategy shifts the focus of programs or fellowships from racial groups to *topics* that are of interest to these groups. Instead of creating a fellowship for Black students, you create a fellowship for applicants with a demonstrated commitment to racial equity, for example. According to Yoshino and Glasgow, "Three major law firms were sued for diversity fellowship programs that limited eligibility to members of underrepresented groups. As soon as the firms changed the eligibility criteria to include anyone with a demonstrated commitment to diversity and inclusion, the lawsuits were dropped."[7] It is also legal to design and deliver educational content that focuses on bias, allyship, or the benefits of DEI.

- **Narratives Versus Numbers**—this strategy shifts the focus from someone's racial category to someone's individual story. In the *SFFA* decision, the Supreme Court explicitly stated that universities could consider "an applicant's discussion of how race affected his or her life, be it through discrimination, inspiration, or otherwise." Colleges and universities can assess this through essays, for example. Likewise, instead of hiring someone based on their race, employers can opt to consider the hardships candidates have endured that have produced tenacity, resilience, grit, determination, and other factors indicative of desirable leadership qualities. With regard to hardship, universities and employers can even consider socioeconomic status *directly* and categorically (rather than individually), given that it is not a protected characteristic under federal anti-discrimination law—as long as it is not used as a proxy for protected characteristics, such as race.

- **Sourcing Versus Selecting**—this strategy is about deliberately recruiting from a pool that represents racial diversity rather than hiring a specific individual based on their race. It is perfectly legal to establish recruitment plans that target Historically Black Colleges and Universities, for example. It is also legal to specify interview criteria similar to that of the Rooney Rule, which requires that any job search contain a racially diverse array of interviewees. In addition, it is legal to fund organizations with an antiracist mission. For example, corporations can provide philanthropic support to nonprofit or community organizations that focus on racial equity or DEI.

Finally, Yoshino and Glasgow argue that organizations are free to develop a *culture* that is supportive of inclusion, even if it offends some people in the organization. One example is all-gender bathrooms (leveling). Another way to level the playing field is upskilling, which rewards talent and potential while reducing the biases created by differences in access to higher education. A nonprofit organization that builds on this strategy of upskilling as a way to reduce racial and economic disparities is OneTen. The organization derives its name from its ambitious goal of hiring, promoting, and advancing *one* million Black Americans in good-paying, family-sustaining jobs over the next *ten* years.

OneTen: An Organization Committed to Equal Prosperity

The mission of OneTen is to level the economic playing field by "changing the way America hires to advance skilled talent without four-year degrees at every stage of their career."[8] Due to a long history of structural and economic discrimination in the United States, there is unequal access to employment and educational opportunities, as well as a staggering gap in income and wealth between Black and White households. By some estimates, the median net worth of a White household is roughly ten times that of the median Black household.[9] In Boston, those differences are even greater, with the median wealth of a White household being $247,000 compared with the median wealth of a Black household being $8.[10] As stated by Black entrepreneur and retired Harvard Business School professor Steve Rogers, "The only real cure for America is the elimination of the [racial] wealth gap, which would make the Black community as healthy, safe, and self-sufficient as the White community."[11]

OneTen founders Ken Chenault, former CEO of American Express, and Ken Frazier, former CEO of Merck, came to understand that helping companies focus on hiring for skills, rather than higher education, would open higher-paying jobs to well-deserving and talented individuals. Doing this at scale could narrow the racial wealth gap.

One observation they made is that companies often rely too heavily on hiring and promotion practices that do not accurately reflect talent. A typical barrier to entry for good-paying jobs is a four-year college degree. Although many guilds, such as medicine and law, require college and postgraduate degrees to enter their profession, the assumption underlying OneTen's mission is that there are millions of good-paying jobs that do *not* require a college diploma or professional degree to be done effectively. Hiring based on skill (and potential) rather than higher education requirements enables companies to vastly expand the hiring pool without sacrificing quality. In fact, according to OneTen's website, hiring skills-first is five times more predictive of future performance than a candidate's education and two and a half times more predictive than hiring based on experience.

Together, OneTen and management consulting firm Bain & Company identified the three key stakeholders: Black talent, large employers, and talent developers such as community colleges and training organizations like Year Up and NPower. The founders of OneTen assembled a coalition of CEOs of more than sixty large corporate employers, including Airbnb, Allstate, Bank of America, Deloitte, Humana, IBM, Merck, and Nike. Collectively, these companies have made a strong commitment to hiring, upskilling, reskilling, and promoting one million Black individuals over the next ten years. OneTen found that their member corporations required a four-year college degree for roughly 88 percent of their middle-skill jobs. However, when they examined the underlying skills needed to perform the job, they found that a college degree was necessary in far less than 88 percent of those jobs. The challenge resided in convincing these corporations to strike the degree from the job requirements, while also providing Black professionals the opportunity to acquire the skills they needed, through talent developers or the organizations themselves, to succeed.

This approach was not undertaken blindly. In addition to the expertise and wisdom garnered from the decades of high-level corporate experience of their CEO founders, OneTen partnered with Bain to conduct research to inform their approach. They analyzed where OneTen's target demographic tended to live, and overlaid employer data to understand where there was opportunity. They established employee working groups in those areas to get them talking about skills-first hiring, and to hear their reactions. All this led the Bain teams to conclude that a "skills-based" approach was indeed the correct framing. They also hosted a CEO forum and focus groups with chief human resources officers, which confirmed that the degree requirement could be overcome if talent developers and training partners could certify job candidates.

Bain also helped OneTen launch a tech platform to support virtual job matching, activate hiring on the ground in key markets like Philadelphia and Dallas, and establish employee working groups to train the employers on skills-first hiring. After those first markets proved successful, OneTen began rolling it out across the rest of the country. In addition to working with organizations to remove the four-year college degree barrier and provide strategic guidance on skills-first practices in hiring and promotion, OneTen also serves as a conduit through which Black talent can connect to talent developers (over a hundred talent developers have joined the coalition). Finally, OneTen helps to build and ensure an ecosystem that provides the right conditions for success (e.g., inclusion, mentorship) so that diverse talent can thrive at these organizations.

OneTen's model seems to be working and gaining momentum. The nonprofit has reduced exclusionary hiring practices, helped companies identify tens of thousands of talented individuals, and offered people new education paths that lead to family-sustaining careers. After only two years, it has created over fifty thousand new hires in good-paying jobs. In addition, it has produced nearly twenty thousand promotions in existing jobs—promotions that likely would not have happened if they were based strictly on formal educational requirements rather than skill. There are currently more than 360 locations across the United States with OneTen job opportunities.

■ ■ ■

There are at least three lessons for all corporate employers, based on Zeynep Ton's findings and the results of OneTen. The first is to widen the net. Focusing too narrowly on formal job qualifications can unnecessarily narrow the pool of professional talent. The second is to invest resources in training and development. Employers aren't just scouts, but coaches. The third is to pay people well. Being penny-wise but pound-foolish can lead to costly reductions in morale and productivity.

There are many other organizations and individuals working tirelessly to narrow the racial wealth gap. In fact, *Time* magazine published an issue during Black History Month in 2024 that featured over a dozen examples of people who were working to close the racial wealth gap. Among those profiled were John Hope Bryant, whose organization, Operation Hope, founded in 1992, has been providing financial literacy education, counseling, and coaching to communities across one thousand locations in the United States.[12] John Rogers, the billionaire founder of Ariel Investments, has done similar work through his school—founded in Chicago in 1996 to teach kids from under-resourced neighborhoods financial literacy through stocks. In an article for *Black Enterprise* magazine, Rogers stated, "To me, financial literacy is not just about saving, credit cards, retirement, and home mortgages. All those things are important. But equally important is understanding how to invest in the equities market and compound money. Long-term stock market returns have substantially outperformed the returns on savings accounts."[13]

In addition to good jobs and financial literacy, a bold legislative appeal for reducing the racial wealth gap is through reparations. The book *From Here to Equality: Reparations for Black Americans in the Twenty-First Century,* written by Duke economist William A. Darity and A. Kirsten Mullen, makes a strong case for reparations while also addressing the economic and legal specifics around who would be eligible and how much money would be distributed. Based on numerous factors such as back pay and interest, wrongful death liability, stolen property, and institutionalized discrimination (e.g., redlining), the compensation for each living descendant of enslaved African Americans would be roughly $400,000. Moreover, Darity and Mullen suggest that reparations are the only viable way to erase the racial wealth gap. Their mission is not totally wishful thinking, as they cite multiple surveys indicating a more favorable shift in attitudes toward reparations over the past few decades.

Moreover, Darity and one of his former PhD students, Professor Darrick Hamilton—founder of the Institute on Race, Power and Political Economy at the New School—have been successful in implementing a reparations-based idea conceived by Hamilton when he studied under Darity. It was the idea of establishing government-funded trust accounts for kids. The logic was that there would be greater legislative and public support for financial initiatives aimed at helping children. As Darity told *Time* magazine, "Nobody could claim that the infants were responsible in any way for the financial position of their family. So it was kind of an innocence argument or strategy."[14] That strategy worked. According to journalist Janell Ross, "In July 2023, Connecticut deposited $3,200 into an account for a newborn creating the nation's first ever baby bond. Over the next 18 to 30 years, the effects of time and compounding interest will give that baby up to $24,000 to pay for college, make a down payment on a home, start a business, or do other things that will shape her life and build wealth."[15]

Finally, Black entrepreneurship is seen as another pathway for narrowing the racial wealth gap. I will discuss entrepreneurship in greater depth in the next chapter. In the meantime, I will switch gears to talk about another important pillar of systemic racism: voter rights and representation.

The Importance of Democratic Civic Engagement

One of the most foundational manifestations of White supremacy in the United States is the legislative apparatus itself. Our system of government was deliberately designed in a way that allowed only wealthy White men to have a voice in who got to represent all Americans, which laws were passed, and how public funds could be spent. It is the ultimate form of power and control—one that was never meant to be pluralistic or truly democratic.

In the article "Vote. That's Just What They Don't Want You to Do," the Editorial Board of *The New York Times* contends that "keeping people from voting has been an American tradition from the nation's earliest days, when the franchise was restricted to white male landowners. It took a civil war, constitutional amendments, violently suppressed activism against discrimination and a federal act enforcing the guarantees of those amendments to extend this basic right to every adult." Therefore, changing the game and wresting power from the hands of an elite few requires strategies for increasing voter registration and participation among socially marginalized populations.

Vot-ER: A Strategy for Broadening Voter Representation

When Alister Martin began Harvard Medical School in 2010, he was full of idealistic hope. As he moved through clinical rotations, he became increasingly aware of the harsh realities of the healthcare system. His initial excitement began to wane as he witnessed firsthand the deleterious impact of not just physical illnesses but also the ways in which the system perpetuated social and economic disparities. For example, a patient without health insurance could be charged double for a simple procedure because they do not benefit from the bargaining power of insurance companies. Vulnerable and under-resourced communities also receive different treatment. As Martin painfully observed: "It became clear [to me] that this was a world where money and privilege often outweighed compassion . . . that our healthcare system, as it stands, can perpetuate harm as much as it provides healing."

Due to his disillusionment, Martin decided to take a break while he sought to understand whether there could be a more synergistic relationship between healthcare and social justice. After studying at the Harvard Kennedy School, he landed a job working in state government and became convinced of the power of people's voices to influence legislation. "Policy, I discovered, could be a powerful tool for improving health outcomes on a grander scale." He returned to medicine with the hope of bridging the worlds of healthcare and public policy to find ways to help people beyond the walls of the hospital.

His inspiration for how he could change the game came one winter night when a woman carrying her two young children—all three shivering from the bitter cold—was rushed into the ER. After fleeing their home state to escape her abusive partner, she and her children had been sleeping in her car for two days. They were exhausted and scared and had nowhere else to go. But without proof of Massachusetts residency, they didn't qualify for the state housing program that had been created to help families like theirs. Because they lacked this residency status, they now faced the threat of being separated from one another and forced into different shelters. However, a social worker at the hospital suggested a solution. If they registered the woman to vote, it would count as residency proof under the Motor Voter Act, given that she was a U.S. citizen. This ultimately allowed the mother and children to stay together.

In that moment, something clicked for Dr. Martin. He realized that voter registration was a tangible way for the healthcare system to impact patients' lives beyond the emergency room. This led to the creation of A Healthier Democracy—a nonprofit organization that he founded to tackle upstream problems facing vulnerable communities in the healthcare system. He argues that about 80 percent of a patient's health outcomes are due to factors that lie outside of the clinical healthcare setting—things such as housing insecurity, food insecurity, and various political determinants of health. The mission of the organization is to address those upstream determinants of poor healthcare, including voting and poverty.

The Vot-ER initiative was founded on the idea that healthcare systems across the country could facilitate voter registration—much like the Department of Motor Vehicles had been doing since 1993. Hospitals became a gateway to voter registration, reaching people where they were—often in a moment of crisis—and helping them engage in the democratic process to shape the policies that were impacting their health and livelihood.

Historically, political power was maintained by disenfranchising entire populations who were unable to register to vote. Vot-ER turns the undemocratic practice of voter disenfranchisement on its head by enfranchising some of the more than 72 million voter-eligible unregistered voters in the United States—a staggering number that exceeds the entire national populations of Spain and Sweden combined.

The way that Vot-ER facilitates voter registration is simple. Healthcare providers volunteer to wear a badge that bears the question "Ready to Vote?" and a QR code that patients can scan with their phone. All voter registrations are completed directly via Secretary of State websites, and every patient must meet their state's eligibility requirement. Vot-ER is nonpartisan, and its advisory council includes former Secretaries of State who represent both the Democratic (Miles Rapoport–CT) and Republican (Trey Grayson–KY) parties. More than fifty thousand healthcare professionals are now participating in the Vot-ER program, and more than seven hundred hospitals across the country are Vot-ER partnering sites and see voter registration as part of patient care.

Since the organization was founded in 2019, Vot-ER has successfully helped more than three hundred thousand people vote on election day across all fifty states. This includes populations—young people, people of color, and low-income individuals—who are often underrepresented in voting booths. In today's political landscape, politicians tend to be much more focused on swing or undecided voters, with no one accounting for *unregistered* voters in their political calculations. Democracy is strengthened when voters reflect the entire population of a nation.

In addition to mobilizing at the grassroots level, the momentum needs to be pushed to the top so that the system can capture and freeze that change. To make a real and lasting impact, those at Vote-ER knew that they also had to mobilize at the "grasstops" level. So, they lobbied to make the case that civic health/engagement is another important facet of patients' health that clinicians and health systems should support. Their efforts were rewarded in 2022, when the American Medical Association (AMA) formally recognized voting as a social determinant of health. This resolution acknowledged that health disparities were not just individual issues but also symptoms of broader social injustices. Indeed, voting can lead to greater investments in economic opportunity, education, housing, and healthcare.

This was a powerful validation of Vot-ER's efforts. With the AMA's endorsement, a hospital or clinic can integrate civic engagement into patient care, promoting voter registration as both a metric-driven initiative and an act of empowerment. This means that healthcare providers are not just healers but agents of broader societal and cultural change. This dual approach of grassroots and "grasstops" mobilization, which engages both individual clinicians and large institutions, has a higher likelihood of producing deep, crystallized change.

Recognizing that civic engagement is tied to economic solvency, Dr. Martin also created the Link Health initiative, which links patients to economic opportunity. As he puts it: "In my patients' lives, money is often medicine. Poverty is the real crisis they face, impacting their health far more than a single diagnosis." Link Health has connected patients to over $80 billion in unused federal and public benefits. These funds can be used to pay rent, cover utilities, and buy groceries. Since its inception in 2022, Link Health has helped nearly three thousand individuals obtain over $3 million in financial assistance, giving patients greater access to nutrition, digital connectivity, and energy assistance—and greater opportunity for civic engagement. He summarized the collective effort by explaining, "These financial supports address immediate, acute needs, giving patients the stability they need to begin thinking about longer-term issues, like civic engagement. With their most pressing needs met, patients can think beyond survival. A few months down the line, we bring up voting. We talk about the power they hold to impact policies that shape their communities. By linking economic security with civic empowerment, we're creating a pathway for patients to reclaim their agency." As mentioned at the outset, the five pillars of systemic racism are all inextricably interconnected. By addressing economic deprivation, Link Health puts patients in a better position to engage in civic participation.

■ ■ ■

The takeaway of this chapter is that it is possible to change the game in important ways by devising concrete strategies to erode the pillars of systemic racism. OneTen and Vot-ER are only two examples of the many organizations that are disrupting the status quo in bold and creative ways. Given the abundance of apathy, at best, or outright oppression from the mainstream toward communities of color, there is something to be said for the power to create our own rules and communities. In the final part of the book, I will focus on the third pathway of "leaving the game." Specifically, I will discuss the three E's—entrepreneurship, enclaves, and exodus—respectively, in the next three chapters.

Part IV
Leaving the Game

Ten

Entrepreneurship: The Path to Professional Autonomy

Should you consider "leaving the game"? And if so, how would you go about it? These are big questions with complicated answers. In many ways, the dilemma facing Black people is the same as for anyone who is entangled in a dysfunctional relationship. What do we do when conversation and counseling fail to substantially improve our circumstances? Do we seek a divorce?

African Americans have been in a four-hundred-year abusive relationship with a domestic cohabitant who has been unwilling to change in any profound way. If we no longer wish to invest the energy and effort required to conform to, or reform, the current condition, then how do we create an environment that is relatively disconnected from their madness—one that fulfills our basic needs for safety, autonomy, and tranquility?

The word "relatively" is important when describing the intention to disconnect from the game. In our conversation, Angela Davis professed skepticism that we could ever fully leave the game:

> I don't think it is possible to entirely leave the game because no matter where we go, we're influenced by the tentacles of a system that is grounded in slavery and colonialism. To exit the game entirely would be death. And in so many ways, the struggle itself has been life-giving. But this isn't to say that we don't desire, and need, rest sometimes. So I would say that, strategically, it may be important for people to rest and to reflect. That kind of reflection oftentimes leads

us to insight that is required to move forward. Sometimes it can be helpful to try to imagine ourselves outside [the game], even if we can never truly be outside.

While I agree with Dr. Davis' assessment that the only absolute exit from the game is death, I nevertheless believe that it is possible to leave the game, relatively speaking. By that, I mean we can distance ourselves from the game in ways that can allow us to make our own rules of engagement and/or mitigate our exposure to White supremacy.

In the next three chapters, I will discuss what I call the "three E's" of leaving the game—entrepreneurship, enclaves, and exodus—as pathways that Black people can follow to achieve some level of separation from the burdens of mainstream culture. Let's begin, however, by exploring the fundamental question of whether we *should* leave the game—versus playing it or challenging it.

To Leave or Not to Leave?

When is the right time to walk away from something, and what are the factors that can impact one's decision to do so? A classic 1970 book explores this question from an economist's perspective. In *Exit, Voice, and Loyalty: Responses to Decline in Firms, Organizations, and States,* Albert Hirschman addresses the question of what it takes for people to turn their back on organizations or nations when those entities fall short of their obligations to treat their stakeholders appropriately. In Hirschman's telling, whether someone exits a faltering organization or other institution depends on two factors: the degree to which they believe they have a "voice" in producing change, and the degree of loyalty that they feel.

When people "resort to voice, rather than exit," Hirschman writes, it reflects "an attempt at changing the practices, policies, and outputs" of an organization. "If [people] are sufficiently convinced that voice will be effective, then they may well *postpone* exit." Exiting, Hirschman concludes, is sometimes "a reaction of *last resort* after voice has failed."[1] The second factor is whether people feel a high level of "loyalty" to a firm or other entity. If so, they may be willing to stay despite the dissatisfaction they experience, or the firm's (un)deservingness of their loyalty.

These two factors—voice and loyalty—interact in complex ways to determine whether people stay or go. In addition to loyalty, Hirschman acknowledges that not everyone has the *ability* to exit. In these cases, people tend to make even greater use of their voices whenever unsatisfactory situations arise. Many Black people may feel unable to leave the game, whether through entrepreneurship, enclaves, or exodus, and some may feel fervently committed to remaining, out of "loyalty" to an individual, institution, nation, or ancestral tie. These individuals will be more likely to remain committed to changing (or playing) the game, versus leaving the game.

Optimism may also impact people's decision to leave the game. That is, if one feels they can genuinely change the game by exercising voice, then leaving the game will seem unnecessary. However, if White supremacy is akin to an addiction, then the words of Dr. Andrew Proulx may be worth hearing: "In order to stop ourselves from being drawn into the chaotic action-reaction cycle—where the addict acts and we react—we can employ the simple technique of detachment. . . . Detachment isn't about being cold-hearted; we're detaching ourselves from the addiction, not from the person."[2] In the case of addiction, exit is often a sensible option.

Finally, pride may affect the decision to leave the game. People may be reluctant to exit because they do not want to be perceived as quitters or as "losing" to the other side. However, the decision to leave the game does not necessarily reflect resignation or defeat. On the contrary, it can serve as a demonstration of agency and self-determination. It can also signal a rational decision to seek rest and relief during difficult moments—as Angela Davis suggested—or simply a decision to direct one's energy toward more productive pursuits.

Assuming there is the personal desire or motivation, as well as the economic or legal possibility, to leave the game, the next logical question is *how*. In this chapter, I will focus on ways to gain some degree of separation from the game through entrepreneurship, while the following two chapters will discuss the ways in which enclaves and exodus can provide shelter from the game.

The Power of Entrepreneurship

When you hear the word "entrepreneurship," your mind may leap to the idea of an economic enterprise aimed at maximizing profit or output production. That is what many people think of—developing business plans, raising capital, creating a viable product, and trying to make the numbers work. But there are other—and I would argue, more profound—components to entrepreneurship apart from the purely commercial aspects: Entrepreneurship can also mean achieving greater personal and professional autonomy in a domain that is aligned with your passion and expertise. Entrepreneurship is about channeling your unique talents, skills, and interests into work, products, and/or services that create prosperity and purpose for you and value for others. Although there is a certain level of risk involved with any entrepreneurial endeavor, there is also the potential of high reward and professional freedom.

Of the three E's, entrepreneurship is perhaps the one that is most deeply embedded in the framework of the larger game. In starting business ventures, there is always the chance of replicating the very systems of exploitation that one is trying to escape. And many contemporary scholars are quite skeptical of capitalism, as mentioned in chapter 9. For instance, sociologist Matthew Desmond, author of *Poverty, by America,* deeply criticizes "low-road" capitalism, which tends to characterize much of the American system of enterprise. Because it emulates the plantation business model, it tends to produce "bad jobs" that demand maximum output for minimum benefit, rather than the "good jobs" discussed in the last chapter. Other scholars, including Angela Davis, share Desmond's suspicion of capitalism, while also recognizing that there is a difference between a business owner and a "capitalist." In her view, "Capitalism is a system that requires exploitation. Exploitation is at the very heart of capitalism. Now, I'm not saying that every Black businessperson is a capitalist."

Retired Harvard entrepreneurship professor Steven Rogers makes an even stronger distinction between businesspeople who participate in the capitalist economy and people who are "low-road" capitalists. In his book *A Letter to My White Friends and Colleagues: What You Can Do Right Now to Help the Black Community,* he discusses his involvement in helping Black residents on the South Side of Chicago fight a Fortune 500 company—Norfolk Southern—that had threatened to take legal action via eminent domain if the homeowners did not agree to sell their homes voluntarily. The corporation wanted to purchase the homes so that they could expand their freight yard.

However, many of the homeowners had seen their homes passed down through multiple generations and did not want to sell at all, or certainly not for the $20,000 to $80,000 that Norfolk Southern was offering in 2011. During a board meeting, one executive asked Steven Rogers why he, "a business school professor who believes in capitalism," was engaged in a fight against a corporation.

Rogers' response was "I am a race man, always interested in helping the Black community. I believe in capitalism but not the 'low-road' capitalism that has the objective of growing at all costs and abusing the powerless." Rogers is a businessman and successful entrepreneur who believes in many of the principals of capitalism. However, he is not a capitalist.

Rogers redoubled his efforts to help the Black residents get a better offer from the capitalist giant, and ultimately succeeded. In the book, he wrote: "This was the kind of capitalism used to enslave Black people from 1619 to 1865, and I saw remnants of it being practiced by Norfolk Southern." Over the course of a decade of work, Rogers reported that thirty-five of the original thirty-nine members of the coalition settled with the railroad "for prices that ranged from $120,000 to $538,000," which amounted to "200–400% more than was originally offered."[3]

In short, there are lots of ways to do business. The beauty of entrepreneurship is that, to a large extent, you get to make your own rules. If a company wants to be exploitative, it can be. But there are also companies for which the happiness of employees forms the core foundation of their business model, as discussed in chapter 9. The same spectrum of choices is open to individual entrepreneurs. For example, if you own residential properties, you can be a slumlord. Or you can be someone who beautifies the community and provides tenants with a safe, well-maintained place to live at an affordable price. You have the power to express your values and priorities through your entrepreneurial actions.

Although the tried-and-true path of a salaried employee offers the benefits of stability and a steady paycheck, the act of forging your own path is where true power and prosperity lie. Ken Chenault, the first Black CEO of American Express (from 2001 to 2018), talked to me about his belief in the power of entrepreneurship as a mechanism for wealth creation, particularly in the modern era:

> What has changed dramatically in the last fifty years is that the way to substantial wealth creation has not been from working at a company. It's been from founding a company. The growth of private equity and venture capital has changed the paradigm in a fundamental way. Most people are on the old pathway, which is, you know, if I go to college and then medical school, then I can become a doctor. It used to be that a doctor would do pretty well. Now it can be challenging. . . . So, I think what's happening is that the pathways to success are evolving at a very rapid pace. And most people are behind. And so that means Black people are way behind. There has to be more of a connection to where the markets are going, and what are the wealth creation opportunities. At the same time, obviously, you always need growth of a stable middle class.

Nine-to-five jobs will always serve as a viable path to economic security for most people. For that reason, Chenault co-founded OneTen—the organization with the mission of creating "good jobs" for individuals without a college degree. At the same time, he also believes that we must create entrepreneurial opportunities. He currently serves as the CEO of General Catalyst—a venture capital firm that describes itself as a "global investment and transformation company that partners with the world's most ambitious entrepreneurs."

Venture capital (VC) has always been hard to come by for any aspiring entrepreneur with a great idea, but it is particularly challenging for someone who is not a White male. A 2019 report from the Harvard Kennedy School's Women and Public Policy Program revealed that a mere 2.4 percent of VC funding went to women of *any* race.[4] And only a tiny fraction of that went to women of color. For this reason, Arian Simone and Ayana Parsons founded Fearless Fund—a VC fund that invests exclusively in retail, consumer, and tech-based companies owned by women of color, as explained by Janell Ross in her *Time* magazine article "The Fearless Fund Is Investing in Women of Color—and Fighting in Court."[5] According to Ross, the Fearless Fund has invested "over $27 million in 44 companies including the restaurant chain Slutty Vegan, the cosmetics company the Lip Bar, and the digital platform COMMUNITYx. Still, this is a drop in the bucket in the VC world, which is dominated by white men who tend to fund white men."

One of my former Harvard students, Adah Ojile, found a clever way to get around this stumbling block of limited funding. He was inspired by the story of Tope Awotona, who emigrated to the United States as a teen with his mother and siblings, after his father was tragically killed during a carjacking in Lagos, Nigeria. After graduating from the University of Georgia with a degree in management information systems, Awotona moved through a series of corporate jobs, including positions at IBM, Dell, and the start-up Perceptive Software—where he was exposed to the functions and operations of a software company. After becoming frustrated one day with how difficult it was to schedule a meeting, he decided to start his own scheduling automation software company. Because of the lack of readily available venture capital, he cashed in his savings and 401(k), took out loans, and flew to Ukraine to hire engineers more economically. The result: Calendly, launched in 2013, which now serves over 20 million users and is valued at more than $3 billion. In 2022, Awotona, who is reported to be worth about $1.4 billion, was featured on the cover of *Forbes* magazine. He did not wait for the system to recognize him. He took a bet on his own talent, resources, and creativity to build his business.

Ojile, also a Nigerian immigrant, and a U.S. Air Force Academy aeronautical engineering graduate with degrees from Cornell and Harvard, launched a couple of early-stage start-ups and held several corporate roles before becoming chief information officer at File & ServeXpress, following its divestiture from LexisNexis. He later served as global head of platforms at MoneyGram International, leading digital transformation across both digital and retail operations, and then served as executive director at JPMorgan Chase, heading up a team of three hundred engineers modernizing credit-risk technology across the investment bank, commercial bank, and wealth management divisions.

Despite his high level of mastery and performance, he noticed that corporate America did not fully appreciate Black talent. He told me: "In many rooms, you're not expected to be the architect behind the innovation—even when you are. So, you learn to let your performance speak louder than the assumptions." In 2022, he came across a McKinsey article on fintech in Africa that painted a picture of a continent on the cusp of a digital leap, and a young population hungry for opportunity. He decided he didn't want to just read about global opportunity, he wanted to create it.

Ojile left JPMorgan and launched several projects, including VentureCore, a venture incubation company committed to leveraging talent from Africa and emerging markets to build transformational products for the world—including an agentic AI project-execution intelligence ecosystem designed to accelerate innovation and scale project delivery. His ultimate aspiration is to build human-machine collaborative intelligence to solve the world's toughest business challenges and social problems. Like Awotona's, the beauty of Ojile's clever business model is that he doesn't have to outspend Silicon Valley. In many ways, he has gone around the game and created a new set of rules by leveraging top African talent rather than Stanford graduates to build his business.

As he puts it, "You have to find a way to overcome the fundraising disadvantages that come with being an outsider, and turn disadvantage to advantage by going where others hesitate to look. Seven hundred thousand dollars in pre-seed funding might get you three engineers in the United States. It gets me forty-five world-class engineers and data scientists in Nigeria."

This approach has enabled him to create jobs and pay a generous salary (by Nigerian metrics), which enables his employees to maintain a comfortable standard of living. He has also built a transatlantic partnership between an African university and a Historically Black College in the United States to co-develop a system to transform patient triaging and referral processes, reducing long emergency room wait times that have often led to preventable deaths.

Entrepreneurship can be a powerful path to wealth creation because it involves leveraging your own talent and skills in a way that makes *you* the primary beneficiary. In many respects, Black entrepreneurship is the antithesis of slavery—providing a way for Black people to directly reap the fruits of their labor as opposed to someone else profiting from their hard work.

One could argue that Tope Awotona and Adah Ojile played the game to leave the game. They both spent quite a bit of time in corporate America gaining experience and competence (i.e., mastery, as discussed in chapter 4), expanding their social networks, and learning the inner workings of businesses in their industries and how they operated. Armed with this arsenal of expertise, they then made the bold decision to strike out on their own. For both individuals, the result has been socially impactful and financially rewarding.

■ ■ ■

If done right, entrepreneurship benefits not just the entrepreneur but an entire community. Steven Rogers writes, "Businesses are usually more than just places that offer goods and services. Black entrepreneurs are the largest private employers of Black people in the country."[6] According to Erin Horne McKinney, director of Howard University's National Center for Entrepreneurship, "Research shows that entrepreneurship is really the way we will close the wealth gap in this country."[7]

Given that entrepreneurship can be a path to autonomy, freedom, and social equality, it is no surprise that there has been a long history of White backlash against successful Black entrepreneurship. It is one of the reasons

Black Wall Street—the prosperous and independent commercial center of the all-Black Greenwood community of Tulsa, Oklahoma—was destroyed, along with the residential community, by a White mob in 1921. As mentioned in chapter 4, there is even research data showing that competent Black entrepreneurs are not funded *because* they are so competent. Their competence threatened the self-esteem of White evaluators.[8]

Nevertheless, there are many people—from all races—who strongly champion high-potential Black businesses and entrepreneurs. Professor Rogers and his co-authors have compiled a gold mine of resources available for aspiring Black entrepreneurs in a Harvard Business School case titled "Sources of Capital for Black Entrepreneurs."[9] It is a must-read for anyone interested in mega-entrepreneurship. However, as mentioned at the outset of the chapter, you don't have to build a massive company or create hundreds of new jobs to be an entrepreneur. In the next section, I will discuss ways in which the average person can explore paths to entrepreneurship.

The Everyday Entrepreneur

There are many ways to be an entrepreneur. You don't have to create a hedge fund, tech company, or billion-dollar firm to be one. I titled this section "The Everyday Entrepreneur" because I wanted to emphasize the ways in which ordinary people could embark on paths to entrepreneurship and autonomy. If, as I do, you define entrepreneurship as the process of creating autonomy and translating your talent and passion into value, then by this definition, artists are entrepreneurs. So are writers. A wise person once told me: Do what you were born to do, and the money will come.

There are at least three pathways for the everyday entrepreneur: (1) the side hustle, (2) the real estate game, and (3) the professional pivot. The side hustle has always been around, and has even served as the primary stream of revenue for several Fortune 500 companies, including Avon and Mary Kay. Therefore, one common model for the side hustle is becoming an independent salesperson for an existing product that has a profit-sharing or compensation structure. In addition to the two aforementioned Fortune 500 companies, Tupperware parties were all the rage in the 1970s. Cutco knives were all the rage in the 1980s (as a teenager, I sold them to friends, family, and neighbors).

A variation of this corporate-sponsored, sales-based side hustle is creating your own product to sell. The classic example would be a lemonade stand, or selling homemade baked goods, such as pies, cakes, or cookies. This is how Wally Amos started his business, which began as a side hustle but ended up becoming a multimillion-dollar company: Famous Amos cookies. Amos' main gig was working as a talent scout at the William Morris Agency in New York City—he was the first Black person to ever occupy this position. He began baking cookies as a hobby to relieve stress, using his aunt's recipe. During his meetings with people in the record and movie industries, he would offer some of his home-baked cookies. They became such a hit that people would look forward to meeting with him just to get the treats. In time, Amos was able to secure the support of famous investors, such as Marvin Gaye and Helen Reddy, which enabled him to open a cookie store on Sunset Boulevard in 1975. By the early 1980s, his business had grown to an annual revenue of over $12 million.

Amos' story demonstrates the importance of finding untapped markets and fresh opportunities. I discovered an untapped market as a sixteen-year-old—in candy, not cookies. I was working part-time at Kmart, and every so often, they would run big sales on premium candy bars at four for $1 (this was 1987), or Charms Blow Pops (lollipops with bubble gum in the middle) at ten for $1.

I would buy up lots of candy, take it to school, and sell it out of my locker or under my desk during class. The high demand and lack of supply (on school grounds, at least) meant I could sell the candy bars for 50¢ each (which was the price in any convenience store or gas station) and Blow-Pops for 25¢. Although my business was subject to very strict regulation—namely, seizure and temporary confiscation of merchandise whenever I got caught—I could still easily make $50 to $75 per week.

The main point here is that you can make a side hustle out of anything. What do you like to do? What is the demand for that product or service?

Is there a (legal) opportunity that has not yet been tapped into? One contemporary cornucopia of side hustle opportunities is digital media and the internet. Thousands of people are making big bucks on TikTok, Instagram, Facebook, Twitch, and other platforms. There is no shortage of influencers and/or content creators who have managed to turn a hobby into a lucrative enterprise. Some of the most successful are Druski, Kai Cenat, IShowSpeed, and Duke Dennis. In the twenty-first century, even kids are getting paid millions of dollars to do what every kid wants to do—play with toys. Ryan Kaji of Ryan's World is one example. Apart from these megastars, everyday people are making a few hundred to several thousand dollars a month through ads and content creation. In my field, there are many scholars and experts who have created side businesses through podcasts and paid newsletters on Substack and other platforms.

The antithesis of the virtual world is bricks, mortar, and land. Owning property has long been a path to prosperity in the United States. As it turns out, Black people have always been drawn to owning buildings and land—even as early as the seventeenth century. The very first Black property owner in America was Anthony Johnson, an ex-slave who purchased 250 acres of land in Virginia in 1651.[10] To this day, owning property remains one of the best ways that ordinary people can build wealth.

The Real Estate Game

When it comes to real estate, and entrepreneurship more broadly, I was fortunate to have good role models and mentors. My mother was a successful entrepreneur who owned both residential and commercial property. My paternal grandfather was also an entrepreneur, and owned several rental properties. My mother's brother—my Uncle Virgil—is the owner of multiple properties, too, and is the person who most strongly inspired and encouraged me to get into real estate.

I caught the real estate bug when I was fifteen. That year, in 1986, my Uncle Virgil and Aunt Peggy bought a large, run-down Victorian house near downtown Lexington for $30,000. At that time, the inner city was blighted, and many people, Black and White, were choosing to live in the suburbs. My aunt was a programmer at IBM—a company that was instrumental in growing the Black middle class in Lexington, as discussed in chapter 2—and my uncle worked for General Electric. They had purchased a house in Green Acres—one of the recently constructed all-Black middle-class subdivisions in Lexington—in the 1970s.

They had also saved money and had started buying rental properties. However, this dilapidated Victorian house was one that they hoped to live in. For the life of me, I couldn't understand why. It was full of dust, cobwebs, peeling paint, and dead rodents. There may have even been a ghost or two lingering in the decrepit hallways. They had a beautiful home in Green Acres with modern appliances, not to mention electricity and plumbing that actually worked. Why would they want to move to this dump? When I asked my uncle what he was thinking, he would smile and lift up the corner of the carpet to show me the herringbone hardwood floors underneath—something the fifteen-year-old me couldn't yet appreciate. Working nights and weekends, and with the help of several family members, my aunt and uncle transformed the haunted house into a stunning showpiece. Years later, their house was even featured on the HGTV show *If Walls Could Talk*.

Seeing such a dramatic transformation during my teens left a lasting impression on me. Real estate design and development became an avocation and a relaxing creative outlet for me—much as chocolate chip cookies were for Wally Amos. I would spend hours in Lowe's, tile stores, and kitchen showrooms. I began to discern the differences between granite, marble, travertine, soapstone, and onyx. I would go to open houses on the weekend and try to guess how much the home I had viewed would actually sell for. Eventually, I developed a sixth sense for real estate value and potential—ugly properties that could be transformed into something spectacular.

It began as a hobby but evolved into a side hustle. In the decades since I first caught the bug, I've bought and sold over thirty homes in seven states and three countries. People at my day job came to know me as a real estate guru, and I became the person they would ask for advice when they wanted to buy, sell, or remodel a house. As I mentioned in chapter 5, one of my professor colleagues even approached me with a partnership opportunity—and a big chunk of cash—to make a joint real estate investment.

I've been in the real estate game so long that I can't help but see houses through an investor's lens. Even my primary residence in Cambridge, Massachusetts, was an investment property! When I first moved to Boston in 2015, it was nearly impossible to buy a home. I put in offers on six or seven homes and lost them all in bidding wars involving multiple offers. Many of the offers were cash with no contingencies. Because I needed a mortgage—and wanted a home inspection—my offer was less attractive.

Finally, I found a tired, unprepossessing Edwardian house in a stellar location near Harvard Square. It was such a mess that it was challenging, even for me, to decide how to transform it into a place where anyone would want to live. Convinced that I would come up with something, I put in an offer and included a personal letter to the sellers. My offer was accepted. Because of my previous real estate experience, I had the confidence and competence to complete the necessary gut remodel, taking the walls down to the studs. I was able to create a beautiful two-family home with a garage and parking. I decided to live in half of the house and rent out the other half.

The rent that I received covered most of my mortgage, which allowed me to invest what I would have spent on rent or mortgage payments. I had had the same tenants for years—a mellow retired couple who did the gardening and landscaping, even raking the leaves and taking out the trash and recycling on pickup day. They insisted that they enjoyed it and it gave them something to do. In return, I promised never to increase their rent while I owned the property, given that they were on a fixed budget and the low interest rate on my mortgage would not increase.

My Uncle Virgil and Aunt Peggy are still in the real estate game. Long retired from IBM and GE, they have become full-time landlords. Although they have pensions and 401(k) plans, their primary source of revenue is rental income from the half-dozen properties they own. Because they bought the properties long ago—in the 1970s and '80s—they do not have a good sense of rental values in the 2020s. Although they could raise the rent on all their properties by 30 percent or more and still fall well below market value, they feel blessed to have enough income to live on and don't mind giving someone else a break. And because my uncle sees it as a hobby, and a way to interact with people, he doesn't mind the work that it takes to maintain the properties. The tenants receive an attentive landlord in beautiful properties in what are now prime locations—for below-market rent. My uncle and aunt receive more than enough money to subsist, as well as a capital investment that continues to appreciate over time. It's a win-win for everybody. In contrast to "low-road" capitalism, they engage in entrepreneurship in a way that creates value for both themselves and the community.

Don't Be Afraid to Pivot

Sometimes disaster can open doors. In fact, the Chinese word for crisis (危機) is formed by combining characters that mean both "danger"/ "precarious" and "opportunity"/"change." I experienced this odd juxtaposition firsthand once when I was unexpectedly fired from a job. Just two weeks earlier, I had been congratulated and informed that I was being promoted—only to have the committee's overwhelming consensus reversed by a single individual. I was both shocked and devastated. I felt a profound sense of loss and confusion, combined with shame and humiliation. I was also afraid, as I didn't have another job lined up and wondered how I would support myself. Our profession can form a big part of our identity and purpose, and when we lose a job, we can feel that we have lost a piece of ourselves.

I was angry, too, due to the profound sense of injustice I was experiencing. In this particular case, the dismissal was due, in part, to a deeply insecure, immature, and devious White person who shares many other unflattering personality traits with Donald Trump. Because the entire situation was fueled by politics and personal animus rather than any real substance, this put me in the catbird seat in terms of what I wanted to do. Did

I want to stay? Did I want to go? My soul was telling me that it was not a healthy place for me. So I decided it was best to leave. Because the circumstances surrounding the termination were highly unusual and unorthodox, I ended up leaving with a healthy severance package—everything I asked for. Still, I harbored unresolved feelings of injustice and a loss of dignity.

As previously mentioned, when one door closes, another door opens. And the second door often leads to us to a better destination. Many Black people have encountered ordeals in their careers that have precipitated the pivot to a different path—one that ultimately led to a more successful and fulfilling outcome. One notable example is that of Vanessa L. Williams, the first Black Miss America, crowned in 1983. She was later forced to resign her crown amid a scandal produced by the unauthorized publication of nude photos of her in *Penthouse* magazine. In an interview, Williams recalls feeling "a tremendous amount of onus, pressure, shame, [and] judgment. It was global. You can fail quietly, but that was a worldwide fail." Oprah has interviewed Williams about the ordeal and asked how she got through it. Williams stated that Black women have "been surviving for hundreds of years" and she had no doubt that she would get through that difficult moment in her life. Oprah later stated that one of the universal spiritual laws that she has observed is that everything happens to bring people to their higher good, and asked Williams whether she believed that. She responded, "I think so. Nothing can faze me now." Williams also commented, "I am finally getting a chance to do what I like [to do]."

The last sentence is critically important. Although the world saw her as being an incredibly beautiful woman, she saw herself as someone with brains and talent, and had always dreamed of singing and acting. In this interview, she mentioned that during casting calls people would not take her talent seriously due to the Miss America title. The scandal allowed her to pivot to an R&B singing career, and eventually Broadway and big-screen acting. In short, her crisis led to opportunity, and success, because it created the space for her to focus on what she was born to do.

I experienced a similar transition, although in a different field under very different conditions. My crisis created a journey to understand myself and what I wanted to do in life. For the first time in a long time, I became closer to God. I began to read the Bible for guidance, and it actually made sense to me in a way that it never had in my younger years. I read more philosophical and spiritual texts as well, such as *A New Earth* by Eckhart Tolle. These readings that focused on letting go of the ego also made sense to me in a way that they wouldn't have even two years earlier.

The day the firing took place, I voluntarily left the office early—skipping out on a meeting I was supposed to attend with everyone in the organization. My Aunt Patricia just happened call me right as I got into my car. After listening to the story, and hearing how upset I was, she said in a soft voice, using a nickname she hadn't called me since I was a little boy, "Beeno, I want you to do a favor for me if you can. I want you to turn the car around, drive back, and walk into that meeting with your head held high. You don't have to stay long. Just make an appearance and show them who you are." And that's what I did. Even at my lowest point, I was getting in touch with myself, my people, my strength, and my power. Williams was right. Black people have been surviving for hundreds of years. In no way does a title or career define who we are as human beings.

As time passed, the fear, sadness, anger, and shame gradually dissipated. I realized that God had a plan, even though I wasn't sure what it was. I was certain, however, that the real me was more than a job or professional identity. There was an unbreakable fortitude deep inside me that my ancestors had been cultivating for centuries.

I landed another job that was more exciting and challenging than the previous one. It was also more lucrative and gave me more formal authority and informal influence. Many friends and colleagues who visited me were bragging to others that I was the big boss "running things" at this place. And in many ways, I was. But with that power came a lot of institutional duties and responsibilities that I didn't welcome. On paper, I had everything I was supposed to want, yet I felt uninspired and unfulfilled. I was still chasing titles, money, status, and reactions like the one from friends who were bragging about me. I had yet to get in touch with *my* true purpose.

Around that time, while on a consulting gig, I had dinner with the president of a large university who confessed to me, after a few glasses of wine, that he wished he had never accepted the president's job. I asked him to elaborate, and he did.

"You know, when I was dean of the school, I got to interact with the students and the faculty. I could attend research seminars and help shape the teaching curriculum. I really enjoyed all that. Now I have little contact with research faculty and almost no contact with the students. I spend more time with donors than anybody else," he said.

"Why do you think you accepted the job?" I asked in earnest. "Were you unsure what the duties would be?"

He paused, then stated: "I guess I took it because that's what you're supposed to do, right? It was a big promotion. More money, more prestige, more respect from family, friends, and colleagues."

Something clicked for me. Here was someone who, despite his ostensible "success," was miserable in his current job—and longed for the previous, less prestigious one. It occurred to me that we don't know what success, or even power, really looks like. We all just follow roads that are paved by someone else to lead us to a destination that society thinks we should want to travel to. The destination usually includes a big salary or lofty title that sounds impressive to others at a cocktail party. But 99.9 percent of our life is not a cocktail party. The only thing that makes a job truly meaningful is the actual *work* that you're doing. And it is in this meaningful work that you find real power.

Writer Gary Zukav defines "authentic" power as our ability to align who we are—our personalities, talents, and values—with work that reflects our soul's intention and purpose.[11] Power based on status, position, authority, or possessions—what he calls "external power"—is an illusion. It exists only to make us appear more impressive to others, or to make us feel less afraid or more in control.

The actual work that the university president was doing was not as closely aligned with his passion, talent, or purpose as the work that he had been doing in the dean's position. So, despite his more prestigious title, he was not in touch with his power. And the look on his face at that dinner showed it. I will never forget that meeting.

A year later, I found myself in the position of weighing a number of different job offers, including two very different offers from Harvard. One was a tenure-track academic position at Harvard Business School (HBS), whereas the other was a non-tenure-track practitioner position at the Harvard Kennedy School (HKS). The salary of the HBS job was nearly double the salary of the HKS job. The job title and institutional prestige were, arguably, also higher with the HBS job. In fact, many friends and colleagues did not understand why the decision was so difficult.

For me, it came down to the actual work that I would be doing at each school. HBS was a well-oiled machine. It was efficient but rigid—having what is known in the academic literature as a "tight" culture.[12] It was a very strict and regimented environment where even veteran professors taught courses in which all the readings, cases, and course materials were preselected by the dean's office. Moreover, I was told that all the people teaching a core course would have to meet weekly to coordinate their teaching. There was little room to be creative in what I taught due to the institutional-level governance and control imposed on the curriculum.

In contrast, HKS was the Wild West. The John F. Kennedy School of Government's programs covered many of the same topics as those in the business school—leadership, management, negotiation, organizational diversity—but focused on the public sector rather than the private sector. Many of the students were people aspiring to make a difference, either through government, nonprofit, or some other public-facing endeavor. Unlike at the business school, the culture at HKS was relatively "loose," which would afford me a lot of freedom.

The dean who'd offered me the job at HKS described the school as a "holding company of entrepreneurs," which piqued my interest. He went on to say, "We don't care what you do, or how you do it, as long as you do it well and it makes a positive contribution to the world." I would have a blank slate to decide how I wanted to impact the world, with the full support of a world-class institution. That was exciting! I was also told I could design my own courses from scratch, call them what I wanted, and include any readings or materials that I wanted to. In fact, just this year, HKS gave me approval to create an Executive Education course based on this book—a move that surprised many people, including me, given the current anti-DEI climate. That is yet another example of the entrepreneurial freedom offered by a "loose" culture. In short, the mission seemed more closely aligned with who I was and the type of work that I wanted to do.

Initially, many of my academic colleagues were surprised that I had accepted the HKS offer. I remember the HBS senior associate dean for faculty development, Frances Frei, telling me, "You are a full professor. If you step off the tenured ladder and take a practitioner position, you will have a hard time getting back on it at a top university. Are you sure you want to do this?" I wasn't sure, because of everything I had been socialized to believe about title and success. But accepting the HKS offer felt right, so I did it. I made a bet on myself.

More than ten years later, I can honestly say that joining HKS was one of the best decisions I've ever made. I pivoted to essentially become a writer, speaker, advocate, and consultant, rather than a traditional academic burdened with committee duties, institutional obligations, and other activities that I do not enjoy. To echo Vanessa Williams, I am finally getting to do what I like to do. To achieve this, I had to leave the game, in a certain manner.

Some have a slightly different interpretation. When I asked a colleague at Berkeley whether she thought I was an example of "leaving the game," she gave me the following lighthearted reply: "You didn't leave the game. You were able to *subvert* the game. You put yourself in a position to leverage resources and networks in an autonomous and advantageous way— separating the wheat from the chaff—in a manner that met your goals and allowed you to create something better than what the system offered. How do I be like you when I grow up?!" My colleague was essentially making a distinction between utilizing the master's tools and being dependent on the master's tools, as discussed in chapter 6. She saw me as someone who had created a situation in which I had full access to the master's tools to build whatever I want, without being controlled by the master providing those tools. She is correct in the sense that entrepreneurial ventures are not about leaving the game as much as they are about creating a certain level of freedom and autonomy within the game.

In summary, the point of this chapter is to help you see that entrepreneurship is about you. They can take away your job, your network, your status, but not your talent. Not your knowledge and expertise. I now profoundly understand what Zach Hubert, a formerly enslaved Black man, meant when he told his children, "Get your education, it's the only thing they can't take away." And while you possess that knowledge and talent, and align them with your purpose, you will always have authentic power.

I am doing exactly what I was born to do. And consistent with what the wise person once told me (i.e., Do what you were born to do, and the money will come), I have prospered beyond what I could have imagined. Most important, I have freedom—freedom to focus on work that is meaningful for me, without feeling that I am shirking duties, responsibilities, or obligations to someone else. And through that meaningful work, I am able to create impact and value for others. Passion, purpose, freedom, value, and impact are what entrepreneurship is all about. What is the entrepreneurial journey that you have yet to discover?

Eleven

Enclaves: Incubation Is Not Segregation

In addition to entrepreneurship, another way to leave the game, relatively speaking, is to seek refuge in ethnic enclaves that provide shelter from the racial stressors that can be prevalent in mainstream environments. Growing up in St. Martin's Village was the epitome of that experience—a residential enclave that allowed Black youth to flourish. In this chapter, I will go beyond residential enclaves to discuss the psychological, social, and professional benefits of educational and organizational enclaves.

Let's begin by clarifying some terms. There is an important difference between what we might call *incubation* (or cocooning) and *segregation*. An incubator, or cocoon, is a safe, supportive, and hospitable space that offers protection against the toxins that are present in the broader environment. Segregation, on the other hand, is an effort to preserve racial hierarchy and status. Even today, Black spaces are about creating contexts in which Black people are welcome, in light of the fact that they are not fully welcome in many integrated environments. In contrast, the creation of White spaces (e.g., all-White country clubs) is more about safeguarding racial exclusivity and privilege. These are two very different motivations for what appear, on the surface, to be similar actions—racial separation. These distinct underlying motives make any direct comparison between so-called Black separatism and White separatism highly problematic.[1]

As discussed in chapter 2, St. Martin's Village was created because Black people were not *allowed* to live in White neighborhoods. In addition, many Black people may *choose* to live in Black neighborhoods to avoid the microaggressions, and more virulent forms of racial hostility, that often exist in White neighborhoods. As mentioned in chapter 3, integrated environments pressure people of color to "cover" or assimilate in multiple ways. Civil rights activist Stokely Carmichael (aka Kwame Ture) went as far as to say that "integration is a euphemism for White supremacy," raising the question of whose culture is being preserved or respected—and whose is being co-opted, devalued, or altogether erased—when integration occurs. In *The Devil You Know,* Charles Blow wrote:

> I must confess that at a certain point, I simply believe that it is spiritually healthier to be in spaces, to create spaces, where you are wanted, honored, and loved, rather than ones where you are simply tolerated at best, or, worse yet, despised. Integration has its virtues, but it can also inflict spiritual and psychological violence. Nine experiences may be lovely, or at least tolerable, but the tenth is terrible. The mind settles on that tenth, using an extraordinary amount of energy to anticipate it, confront it, and overcome it. The unfortunate fraction becomes a consuming detriment.[2]

Ethnic enclaves have been utilized for decades to address both the social alienation of integration and the challenges presented by legal segregation. One of the most prominent historical products of such challenges in the United States are Historically Black Colleges and Universities (HBCUs). For younger people of color, the decision to attend an HBCU may be their first significant brush with the idea of "leaving the game." But as we'll see, rather than setting them apart from society, there is strong evidence that HBCUs produce graduates who are better adapted to and invested in society, while also being better equipped to "change the game."

Similar to my childhood neighborhood, HBCUs were created because Black students were not *allowed* to attend White universities. And just as my childhood residential enclave served as a cocoon for my personal and social development, educational enclaves—such as HBCUs—provide a space where Black youth can escape the racial ostracism that is often experienced in Predominantly White Institutions (PWIs). It is a place where they can develop relationships, community, self-confidence, and a sense of purpose during one of the most critical periods of adult development.

In her brilliant book *The Power of Black Excellence: HBCUs and the Fight for American Democracy,* Duke professor Deondra Rose reports the results of a large-scale study in which she examined differences between the campus experiences of Black students attending HBCUs and those attending PWIs. Based on her data, she concludes that "Black HBCU students overwhelmingly reported feeling safe on their campuses, protected from racism, and fully included in the joyful social life on their campuses."[3]

She further argues that HBCUs have played a critical role in not just educating Black people and preparing them for the workplace but also in the "holistic development and empowerment of [Black] citizens, which has had important implications for American democracy."[4] In the next section, I will take a closer look at the benefits, and challenges, of HBCUs.

A Different World

The vast majority of HBCUs are located in the South, and most of these (75 percent) were built during the Reconstruction Era, between 1865 and 1877. Author Steven Rogers further observes that the greatest number of these HBCUs were founded in 1867, four years after the Emancipation Proclamation. Prior to 1965, Black colleges were seen as independent, disconnected institutions of higher education embedded within the more general landscape of American colleges and universities. It was the Higher Education Act (HEA), signed by President Lyndon B. Johnson in 1965, that created the framework for Black colleges to be seen as a coherent category of institutions of higher education with an overarching mission and an interconnected set of goals.

This legislation also introduced the term "HBCU" as a means of identifying institutions with this mission. Rose argues that "by historicizing Black colleges and emphasizing their shared mission of promoting Black advancement through education, the HEA has played an important role in shaping how we think of Black colleges and their relationship with government."[5] Throughout the 1960s, the federal government provided financial support and a formal classification for institutions whose goal was the formation and advancement of Black students. Scholar and DEI expert Autumn A. Arnett has argued that, in many respects, HBCUs are the closest thing to reparations provided to Black Americans since the eradication of slavery.[6]

According to the Thurgood Marshall College Fund, there are approximately a hundred HBCUs, serving over 325,000 college students across twenty-one states, districts, and territories, including the District of Columbia and the U.S. Virgin Islands. Alabama has the largest number of HBCUs, whereas North Carolina has the largest number of undergraduate students enrolled in HBCUs. HBCUs serve non-Black students as well. In fact, some HBCUs, such as West Virginia State University— where the famous rocket scientist Katherine Johnson, whose life was portrayed in the movie *Hidden Figures,* was educated—are now predominantly White. Today, approximately 9 percent of all Black college students in the United States are enrolled in HBCUs. Prior to 1964, that number was about 90 percent, whereas in 1980, approximately 17 percent of all Black college students in the United States were enrolled in HBCUs.

Rose found that one of the biggest factors associated with Black students' decisions to attend HBCUs was their experience with racial discrimination—which is consistent with the notion that Black enclaves provide a refuge from White supremacy. Another factor that predicted HBCU attendance was having a family background that promoted high levels of racial awareness. A third factor was the legacy effect. Her findings show that about 42 percent of Black respondents who attended an HBCU had at least one parent who also attended an HBCU. In contrast, only 15.4 percent of Black respondents who attended a PWI had a parent who attended an HBCU.

Black students who attended an HBCU describe the experience as one that was both inspiring and empowering. Even Dr. Martin Luther King Jr. spoke of the positive impact that his HBCU experience had on him:

> There was a free atmosphere at Morehouse, and it was there that I had my first frank discussion on race. The professors were not caught

up in the clutches of state funds and could teach what they wanted with academic freedom. They encouraged us in a positive quest for a solution to racial ills. I realized that nobody there was afraid. Important people came in to discuss the race problem rationally with us.[7]

The intellectually inspiring and politically energizing effect of an HBCU education is not limited to Dr. King. The pathways of other prominent Black leaders were paved at HBCUs as well. For example, in 1957, Kwame Nkrumah became the first prime minister of the newly independent Ghana after having been exposed to the Black struggle in the United States while studying at Lincoln University in Pennsylvania. This motivated him to fight against colonialism back home, which resulted in Ghana's becoming the first colonized sub-Saharan country to gain independence. His success set in motion a ripple effect that led other Black leaders across Africa to resist colonialism and establish independent nations.

The empowering impact of HBCUs on Black political engagement in America is also evident. Rose's data reveals that a significantly higher proportion of HBCU students than of Black students attending PWIs are engaged with national politics, including volunteering for political candidates, voting in presidential elections, writing to government officials, contributing money to political candidates, and participating in marches and protests. They are also more likely to run for political office. Rose finds that Black HBCU graduates are 67 percent more likely to consider running for office, and a stunning 400 percent more likely to *actually* run for office, than Black graduates of PWIs.

However, the freethinking and the political activation produced by HBCUs can also lead to misperceptions. One is that ethnic enclaves, such as HBCUs, make Black people more insular, closed-minded, and antagonistic toward other racial groups. Nevertheless, Rose's survey found that Black students at HBCUs were a whopping 40 percent more likely to study abroad than Black students at PWIs. Similarly, my own experience growing up in a residential ethnic enclave made me *more* open to exploring the world, whether it was South America, Africa, Europe, or Asia. I believe that the confidence and security provided by ethnic enclaves can make Black people more open to contact with other ethnic and cultural groups. This is consistent with research in developmental psychology showing that children with a "secure base" are more willing, rather than less willing, to roam and explore new environments.[8]

This openness extends to social and political attitudes, too. Black people who attended HBCUs love America just as much as Black people who attended PWIs. In fact, Rose's data shows that Black HBCU attendees were slightly more likely to report feeling "proud to be an American" than Black PWI attendees. Black HBCU attendees also reported feeling as warmly toward White people as Black people who attended PWIs—even though they reported feeling warmer toward Black people than Black PWI attendees did.[9] In short, there is no evidence that enclaves make Black people more antagonistic toward White people and mainstream society. In fact, the data suggests that ethnic enclaves do just the opposite, perhaps because Black people enter mainstream environments with less racial trauma.

During my interview with Charles Blow, he described how growing up in a Black neighborhood and how attending an HBCU gave him a sort of "Black privilege":

> I got a Black privilege that was comparable to a White privilege— and that truly was beneficial. I emerged from my developmental years with none of the racial battle scars [that many Black people have]. I didn't know how important and valuable that was until I ran into [Black] people, many of them much more credentialed than me, who were covered in racial battle scars. And that led to all sorts of negative behaviors, as I saw it, from them that were kind of self-destructive. The constant doubting of themselves, the constant need to prove themselves and prove their worth to people around them, to prove their right to belong. And I had none of that.

Knowing one's own worth is a recurring theme of HBCU graduates. Rose provides several examples of HBCU graduates who not only survive but thrive in the broader world as a result of the experience they had at

HBCUs. She describes one such person: "For Chanté, the confidence that she gained as an undergraduate at Spelman College created a strong foundation for pursuing a law degree at the University of Texas." Chanté herself says, "I felt strong and sure of myself when I left [Spelman]. And so, I really liked the University of Texas. I wasn't sure how I was going to feel about it, but I loved it. It was a great time—I made a lot of great connections and learned a lot. It was awesome. But a lot of that came from being sure of myself. I wasn't insecure about how I looked. I wasn't insecure about my academic ability.... [Spelman] really hammered home and drilled into us that we were capable, that we were enough, and honestly, that we were the best."[10]

The idea that HBCU graduates are better positioned to thrive in mainstream environments is something that some people might find counterintuitive. After all, shouldn't the mainstream itself better prepare people from marginalized groups for life in the mainstream? Perhaps the answer is "no" if the mainstream is rife with messages to Black people that they are not worthy or able. This would only undermine the ability to thrive there. My colleague Naisha Bradley, who is an HBCU alumna, contends that "White supremacy is only able to exist to the extent that *we* agree with White people's perceptions of who we are. HBCUs provide a space outside of that gaze."

Similar to what St. Martin's Village did for me, HBCUs help Black people fully understand and appreciate who we are and what we are capable of—rather than allowing the White gaze, which is omnipresent in mainstream environments, to distort Black people's perceptions of who we are. In the next section, I take a closer look at the hypothesis that Black enclaves, such as HBCUs, better prepare Black people for life outside the cocoon.

Cultivating Black Excellence

The question of whether HBCUs effectively prepare students for mainstream society can be evaluated both subjectively and objectively. In Deondra Rose's study, she asked students to rate the statement "My college or university prepared me well for life outside of college." Contrary to the notion that HBCUs do not sufficiently prepare students for the real world, the number of Black people who strongly agreed with this statement was 50 percent higher for those who had attended HBCUs than for those who had attended PWIs. Specifically, 39 percent of HBCU graduates strongly agreed that their college prepared them for the outside world, whereas 26 percent of Black graduates of PWIs agreed with this statement.

More objective indicators of the ability to competently function in the broader society confirm these subjective assessments from HBCU graduates. Rose cites data from the Thurgood Marshall College Fund that indicates that "HBCUs have educated a stunningly high percentage of Black political elites. For example, a full 40 percent of Black members of Congress were educated at HBCUs, as were 50 percent of Black lawyers and a whopping 80 percent of Black judges."[11]

In addition, 13 percent of Black CEOs, 40 percent of Black engineers, and 50 percent of Black professors teaching at PWIs also attended HBCUs. In fact, Steven Rogers cites data showing that Howard University alone has produced almost as many doctoral graduates in the sciences as the top PWI universities combined. He states that, looking at Black undergraduates between 2002 and 2011 who went on to get PhDs, "Howard University produced 220 STEM doctorates, while Stanford, Harvard, MIT, and Yale combined to produce 221 such Black PhDs."[12] HBCUs can also serve as a refuge not just for its Black students, but for its Black faculty as well. In recent years, several top Black academics, including Ta-Nehisi Coates, Nikole Hannah-Jones, and Ibram X. Kendi, have made the deliberate decision to work at HBCUs—in some cases, due to the hassle, disrespect, or abuse experienced at PWIs.[13]

Echoing the previous chapter, HBCUs may also create a higher percentage of Black entrepreneurs. Former Morehouse president David A. Thomas has stated: "Even on the business side—we have done some research—a higher proportion of Black men who go to Morehouse go [on to] create their own businesses than Black men who go to predominantly White, Ivy League institutions. And part of going out to create your own business—as a Black person who *can* survive materially in the master's house and do well—is a sense of [the fact that] excellence is not defined by the master's house *and* my sole source of support in not the master's house."

The list of Black luminaries and success stories among HBCU alumni is astounding. In addition to politicians such as Kamala Harris, Keisha Lance Bottoms, and Stacey Abrams, notable graduates of HBCUs include TV hosts Oprah Winfrey and Michael Strahan; famous authors such as Alex Haley, Langston Hughes, Toni Morrison, and Alice Walker; the first Black Supreme Court Justice, Thurgood Marshall; activists such as Jesse Jackson and Marian Wright Edelman; eminent journalists and writers such as Ta-Nehisi Coates and Charles Blow; recording artists Erykah Badu, Toni Braxton, and Lionel Richie; and Hollywood director/actors Spike Lee, Taraji P. Henson, Phylicia Rashad, and Samuel L. Jackson.

Beyond the confidence and strong sense of self that HBCUs provide, many also have exceptionally high academic standards. Throughout my twenty-plus-year career, I have mentored Black students from both HBCUs and PWIs. Many of my most outstanding students have been HBCU graduates. Some students have expressed to me the belief that PWIs have lower expectations of Black students than HBCUs—where professors demand nothing but the best. This sentiment was reflected in Deondra Rose's book. According to one student she interviewed, "Faculty members' willingness to invest heavily in students was widespread, but it came with one simple condition: students needed to demonstrate that they were taking their work seriously. . . . Specifically at Howard, mediocrity was really looked down upon. It was like, mediocrity was horrible when I was there. That was something that was very clear. If you wanted a professor to stop investing in you . . . seem as if you accepted mediocrity."[14]

However, all is not rosy at HBCUs. Many are financially strained and administratively challenged. Although Howard University has an endowment of about $693 million, the average endowment of an HBCU is a meager $12 million.[15]

In Rose's study, many respondents commented on the lack of resources as well as aging infrastructure and administrative challenges. In one conversation, Rose talks about a young woman whose father showed significant hesitation about leaving her on campus right before her first year, citing the dilapidated conditions of some of the buildings.[16]

Other respondents discussed the challenges and frustrations of trying to register for classes, pay outstanding bills, or even obtain the necessary paperwork to graduate. However, she emphasizes that HBCU attendees did not see many of these factors as detracting from the quality of their educational experience. In fact, many saw the tribulations that they faced as building character and resilience. For example, one respondent said, "The fact that everything wasn't perfect on campus really helped me to better prepare for the real world, because nothing ever goes [according] to plan."[17]

Black Enclaves Within White Organizations and Industries

While Black neighborhoods and HBCUs are examples of entirely or predominantly Black institutions set apart from the broader society, it is also possible to create ethnic enclaves within predominantly White institutions and organizations. Research has shown, for example, that the presence of ethnic enclaves within PWIs not only increases feelings of belonging and community but also improves academic performance and retention.

The Posse Foundation was started in 1989 because one student said, "I never would've dropped out of college if I'd had my posse with me." The foundation works to place individual students of color into a "posse" of ten students from similar backgrounds at the same university. The foundation's research has found that having this small group of people the students can identify with and draw support from makes a big difference in terms of academic outcomes.

The Posse Program has well over five thousand alumni and boasts an impressive graduation rate of 90 percent. However, roughly a third of the Posse Program alumni seriously considered dropping out of college at some point. When asked what kept them going, roughly 70 percent pointed to their posse as one "important" or "very important" element that helped them stay on track. When asked how their posse was important to them in college, 61.5 percent reported "academic support" and a hefty 87.2 percent reported "social support."[18]

Within PWIs—and HBCUs—Black fraternities and sororities also serve as a source of support, service, and inspiration for Black college students. The documentary *Twenty Pearls: The Story of Alpha Kappa Alpha Sorority, Incorporated* chronicles the history of the first Black sorority in the United States, founded at Howard University in 1908, two years after the first Black fraternity—Alpha Phi Alpha—was founded at Cornell University. The second Black sorority, Delta Sigma Theta, was founded at Howard in 1913 due to disagreements over the size of the role that public service and women's issues should play in sorority life. Today, all Black sororities and fraternities (known as the "Divine Nine")—including Kappa Alpha Psi, Omega Psi Phi, Zeta Phi Beta, Phi Beta Sigma, Sigma Gamma Rho, and Iota Phi Theta—hold public service as being central to their mission.[19]

Similar benefits of ethnic enclaves can be seen in the predominantly White workplace. A study based on data from a large organization showed that employees of color who were members of one of the company's employee resource groups (ERGs) reported lower motivation and intention to leave the company compared to employees of color who had not joined an ERG (also called an "affinity group," "networking group," or "business resource group").[20] Another study analyzed a survey of members of the National Black MBA Association and found that ERGs were associated with higher career optimism and that this was due to the fact that membership in an ERG provided greater access to mentorship and a Black professional network.[21]

According to organizational scholar Ray Friedman, ERGs originated in the early 1970s at Xerox due to then CEO Peter McColough's strong commitment to Affirmative Action. At the time, Black managers at Xerox were often assigned to smaller accounts by their superiors and felt culturally isolated in the White male world of sales and management, with few people to turn to for advice or support. In response, Black employees formed their own internal networking groups to address many of these challenges. Friedman writes:

Black managerial employees at Xerox began to look to each other for advice and support and as a mechanism to inform top management about the problems they faced. In Washington, DC, a group was formed that called itself the "Corporate Few." They encouraged Xerox to openly post managerial job openings so that Black employees would know about those jobs and could apply for them. In San Francisco, the "Bay Area Black Employees" helped resolve the problem of how salespeople were assigned to clients. Around the country, Black salespeople formed groups that met at night and on weekends to practice sales techniques and get advice from those who were more experienced. In all, seven separate support groups formed that helped make Xerox one of the best companies in the country for Black employees. By 1980, there were 22 Black vice presidents at Xerox.[22]

Given the positive impact on morale, performance, and promotion, the concept of the ERG spread to other organizations. In spite of their multiple benefits for people of color, ERGs can also produce backlash from White employees. For example, one CEO reported to Friedman that "assimilation of minority groups into the mainstream is preferable to continual 'Balkanization' of the country into so many groups. Network groups, he believed, were a source of separation and division."[23]

This type of thinking reveals a problematic paradox. On the one hand, ERGs exist because ethnic minorities feel excluded from mainstream White organizations. On the other hand, the very existence of these enclaves leads White employees to feel excluded—perhaps due to a strong sense of entitlement, rather than actual exclusion. Consistent with this notion, Friedman writes, "Some [Whites] will feel that any group to which they could not belong should not exist."[24]

One could take the argument even further by proposing that any assembly of Black people, whether it is official and formalized or unofficial and purely social, is apt to create some level of discomfort among White people. Recall, in chapter 3, the unspoken pressure to avoid creating even "informal" enclaves—by merely socializing with each other in the office—

Black people felt in predominantly White organizations. Psychologist Beverly Daniel Tatum wrote a superb book titled *Why Are All the Black Kids Sitting Together in the Cafeteria?* to describe the need for affiliation, identity, and safety that Black people of all ages experience.

We should bear in mind that these enclaves—both formal and informal—are often born of a need to create safe or hospitable spaces. Therefore, it is ironic that the creation of these spaces is subsequently viewed by White people as a personal slight or unwelcome "Balkanization." This paradox was brilliantly captured in a LinkedIn post by DEI expert and consultant Paul Ladipo. In it, he included the following cartoon from artist and author Alex Norris:

Courtesy of Alex Norris

Alongside the cartoon, Ladipo wrote:

> ERGs are not about segregation, they are about providing psychological safety to marginalized groups. . . . ERGs aren't about segregation.

They are about allowing employees to bond over shared experiences. This encourages marginalized folks to be their authentic selves because everyone else can relate to their experiences. It's not that SWM [straight White males] don't belong. It's that they've always belonged, and because of this, they had (and still have) the privilege of setting standards the rest of us try to live up to.

Most ERGs have always been open to members of any racial group, because the ultimate goal is to provide a safe environment, not a racially exclusive environment. To the extent that individuals from outside the ethnic group genuinely support the ERG's mission, they are generally welcomed with open arms. Unfortunately, however, integrated environments often result in what you see in the last frame of the cartoon.

The fact that these safe spaces for people of color are cited as evidence of "reverse racism" is ironic, and even offensive, in light of their function as a sanctuary from White supremacy. It is possible that what we are seeing is a perverse form of projection. That is, White people are nervous about ethnic enclaves because they believe that Black people are out to do to them what they did to Black people. They assume that what Black people really want is not safety, comfort, and autonomy—or a society that is just and equitable—but rather to subvert the existing racial hierarchy to put Black people on top and White people at the bottom.

I've been privy to thousands of conversations among Black people in private settings and never once have I heard a Black person express the desire, directly or indirectly, to enslave or otherwise oppress or dominate White people. In fact, White people often do not even factor into the consciousness or concern of Black people at all. James Baldwin wisely summed it up many decades ago when he stated:

I do not know many Negroes who are eager to be "accepted" by white people, still less to be loved by them; they, the blacks, simply don't wish to be beaten over the head by the whites every instant of our brief passage on this planet.

On the other hand, White people do not know how to relate to Black people outside of the context of power differences—whether it's the White oppressor or the White savior. In her masterful book *Yurugu: An African-Centered Critique of European Cultural Thought and Behavior,* Marimba Ani takes a deep dive into the underpinnings of European ethnocentrism and colonialism. It is an extraordinarily profound and brilliant work with many nuances and complexities. In it, she writes:

> The African world-view, and the world-views of other people who are not of European origin, all appear to have certain themes in common. The universe to which they relate is sacred in origin, is organic, and is a true "cosmos." Human beings are part of the cosmos, and, as such, relate intimately with other cosmic beings. . . . Rob the universe of its richness, deny the significance of the symbolic, simplify phenomena until it becomes mere object, and you have a knowable quantity. Here begins and ends the European epistemological mode. What happened within embryonic Europe that was to eventually generate such a radically different world-view?[25]

Ani spends the remaining 500+ pages of the book providing the answer, positing that European thought tends to view human beings (or at least, humans of European descent) as being distinct and disconnected from nature, rather than as one component of a universal whole. The more troubling implication of this detachment is that it creates a "taker" mentality in which the people and resources of the world exist only to serve one's own sense of uniqueness and grandiosity. In many respects, Europeans define "civilization" itself in terms of this disconnection from and dominance over "lesser" others and the natural environment.

She argues that this form of cultural thought—separation and domination—is uniquely European. Because this way of thinking is fundamentally different from how non-Europeans see the world, it produces an asymmetry in the centrality of dominance as a guiding principle. Succinctly stated, Black people simply do not have the desire to conquer and exploit the universe and all its resources and inhabitants for the sake of ego enhancement. What is more important is harmony and interconnectedness with the universe and other people (e.g., Ubuntu). I will return to these themes in the epilogue.

■ ■ ■

Enclaves provide a source of respite from the constant beating over the head from mainstream society that James Baldwin alluded to. Far from being crucibles of hatred against White people, they are bastions of love, support, learning, and growth for Black people. It is also worth mentioning that the need to "leave the game" and retreat to enclaves always increases with heightened hostility from the dominant group. HBCUs only exist because White people refused to allow Black people to study with them. Many Black people fled the South during the Great Migration at the height of the violence of Jim Crow. The Back-to-Africa Movement also reached its apex during this time. As a consequence of White supremacy, there have been waves of Black migration both domestically and internationally. In the final chapter, I will examine the idea of exodus—of leaving the game in a more physically and geographically decisive way in order to create a new life in a different location, either here at home or abroad.

Twelve
Exodus: In Search of Wakanda

n the previous chapter, we touched on the fact that Black spaces—such as HBCUs—tend to be under-resourced. The same is true for many Black school districts and neighborhoods. Although public education is federally funded almost everywhere else in the world, it is primarily funded locally in this country—in part, to ensure that tax dollars remain as racially segregated as the neighborhoods they come from and the schools they fund. The economic deprivation of Black communities is not inadvertent or incidental—it is a very intentional outcome. Indeed, research has shown that in the United States, you need only imply that a policy benefits Black people to create widespread opposition from White people—even if the policy also benefits White people.[1]

Let's imagine a different reality. What if there were abundance and prosperity in Black schools and communities? Microcosms of Black excellence have existed for over a hundred years. The most notable example is the aforementioned Greenwood neighborhood in Tulsa, also known as Black Wall Street—a thriving community of Black businesses and residences. It was also home to several Black millionaires, including J. B. Stradford and O. W. Gurley. Other prominent historical Black communities include Rosewood in Florida, Bronzeville in Chicago, Freedmen's Town in Houston, and, of course, Harlem in New York City—the epicenter of a vibrant intellectual, artistic, and cultural movement during the 1920s and '30s known as the Harlem Renaissance.

What if these microcosms of Black autonomy, excellence, enterprise, and solidarity could exist on a much larger scale, perhaps at the level of an entire state or nation? Musings of a Black utopia—whether within the geographical boundaries of the United States or elsewhere—have existed for quite some time. It has been portrayed in both cinema—as the mythical nation of Wakanda in Marvel's *Black Panther* franchise—and literary fiction, as in the book *Fire on the Mountain* by Terry Bisson.

But is Wakanda confined to fiction? In this chapter, I will discuss movements from the past and present to create Black spaces of abundance and excellence in reality, in both in the United States and abroad. I will also discuss challenges facing this dream of a Black utopia and what can be done to overcome those obstacles.

Pan-Africanism and Black Solidarity

Even before slavery was abolished, there were settlements in Africa of formerly enslaved Black North Americans who were freed after the American Revolutionary War, which ended in 1783. In the late 1700s, the British transported Black loyalists from the United States and Nova Scotia, Canada—where many Black Americans had resettled only to find that racism also existed north of the border—to a settlement in present-day Sierra Leone.

The population of free Blacks in the United States grew steadily from around 50,000 people in the late 1700s (out of roughly 750,000 Blacks living in the United States during that time) to around 300,000 free Black people in 1830. In 1816, the American Colonization Society was founded to deal with the so-called dilemma presented by the increasingly large free Black population that many Whites did not want to integrate into American society.

Among those in support of the return of freed Africans to their motherland were Quakers and abolitionists, as well as slave owners—evidence that neither "dolphins" nor "sharks" wanted to have free Black people living in the United States. There was the fear from many White Southern slaveholders that free Black people would be rabble-rousers and advocates for the freedom of the enslaved Blacks, who were critical to the maintenance of their wealth. Added to this motley crew of supporters of Black expatriation were some members of the free Black population who were looking to escape the oppression of the racial caste system in America.

In the early 1800s, Paul Cuffe—a free Black/Native American Massachusetts-based whaler and shipping merchant of considerable wealth—began transporting free Black people to Sierra Leone and Liberia. However, there was a high mortality rate—as high as 60 percent—among Black North Americans who had returned to Africa stemming from tropical diseases against which they had lost their immunity. This accelerated the abolitionist movement in North America, and led to controversy and debate around the best option for free Blacks in North America.

In the wake of the Civil War, with an even larger free Black population, the Back-to-Africa Movement began to gain steam once again—and garnered increasing support from the Black population amid the intensification of Jim Crow laws. One of the most prominent leaders of the movement was Marcus Garvey, an impassioned Black nationalist and the founder of the Universal Negro Improvement Association (UNIA). Garvey was born in Jamaica in 1887 to a middle-class Black family, and in 1910 traveled to Costa Rica to work on banana plantations owned by the United Fruit Company. He began his activism in Costa Rica, publishing a bilingual newspaper that criticized the deplorable working conditions on the plantations, angering many prominent White-identifying locals.

Garvey ultimately decided to return to Jamaica, where he founded the UNIA in 1914. Inspired by the work of the Black educator Booker T. Washington in the United States, Garvey sought the betterment, or "uplift," of the Black population in his native Jamaica, and made plans for the establishment of educational and industrial colleges for Black people—a Jamaican version of Tuskegee University, so to speak. Interestingly, the plan attracted broad support from prominent White citizens, including the mayor of Kingston, but was met with indifference and even some opposition from within the Black population. In his book, *Black Moses: The Story of Marcus Garvey and the Universal Negro Improvement Association*, historian David Cronon describes the situation in the following way:

The blacks, the chief beneficiaries of the scheme, were indifferent, however, and the [UNIA] was actively opposed by the mulatto group.... They could not understand why any man with talent would concern himself with improving the lot of the lower-class blacks.... Obstructed by hostile mulattoes and ignored by unimpressed blacks, Garvey soon came to the ironic conclusion that the chief support for Negro betterment in Jamaica must depend upon public-spirited members of the white group.[2]

It is worth mentioning that in Jamaica, and in many other nations in the West Indies and South America, race does not operate according to the notion of hypodescent, or the "one-drop rule," as it does in the United States.[3] In Brazil, for example, a Black person (preto) was historically defined as someone with no White ancestry, as opposed to someone with any Black ancestry.[4] The strong assimilationist tendencies of the mixed-race population of Jamaica created antagonism rather than solidarity among two groups that would both be considered Black in the United States.

A few years later, Garvey moved to the United States, where he established a branch of the UNIA in New York City in 1917. He arrived at the height of Jim Crow. The racist propaganda film *The Birth of a Nation* had been released in 1915, and the country was smoldering with racism. The magnitude of racial hostility made Garvey's message of pride and solidarity among Black people across the Diaspora resonate strongly with the African American public. Cronon argues that the enthusiastic reception of Garvey's Black pride and Pan-Africanist messages were due to the fact that "he told listeners what they most wanted to hear—that a [*sic*] black skin was not a badge of shame but rather a glorious symbol of national greatness. He promised a Negro nation in the African homeland that would be the marvel of the modern world."[5]

The relative solidarity between people of African ancestry in the United States, compared to Garvey's experience of a fractured Black population in Jamaica, is an important historical detail. The fact that light-skinned Black people in the United States have largely viewed themselves as Black has been instrumental to the struggle for racial equality in this country. Even today, many multiracial people of African ancestry see themselves as Black. In his HBO documentary *1000% Me: Growing Up Mixed,* Kamau Bell asked a young girl with one Black parent and one White parent what she would say to anyone who wonders what it means to be biracial. Her response was "I want people to know that being both doesn't make us less of either."

Notwithstanding this relative solidarity among people of African descent with different skin tones, colorism—prejudice among people of the same race with different complexions—certainly does exist in the United States, as well as in Africa, Asia, and South America.[6]

And despite this relative solidarity, there are also political disagreements within the African American population. One important one during the World War I era centered around the question of showing "loyalty" to American society (versus exercising voice or exiting). Cronon notes that "on the whole, American Negroes responded loyally to the call to arms" even though some leaders such as A. Philip Randolph and Chandler Owen "cynically questioned the advisability of dying for a country that denied all of its citizens equal treatment." However, Cronon describes people such as Randolph and Owen as representing "a very tiny, though vociferous, minority. The overwhelming majority of the Negro people wanted to prove their patriotic loyalty and supported the war effort in every way possible."[7] Consistent with this sentiment, prominent African American scholar W. E. B. Du Bois published an article in 1918 urging Black Americans to "forget their special grievances and stand shoulder to shoulder with their white fellow citizens in the fight for democracy."[8]

Garvey strongly disagreed with Du Bois' stance, and the two developed an acrimonious relationship. In contrast to Du Bois, Garvey did not believe that Black Americans should risk their lives for a nation that insisted on relegating them to second-class citizenship. Rather, he felt that "the first dying that is to be done by the black man in the future will be done to make himself free."[9] This thinly veiled intimation that the Black man should be fighting *against* the White man rather than fighting *for* the White man was "sufficiently frightening to white legislators in New York that it was cited in the report on radicalism and sedition in that state."[10]

Continuing Garvey's practice of journalism and publication, the UNIA published *Negro World,* a weekly newspaper that reached tens of thousands of Black people in over forty countries. *Negro World* carried advertisements for the Black Star Line—Garvey's ambitious shipping company launched in 1919 that aspired to transport goods across the African Diaspora, as well as to eventually transport Black Americans to Africa. Many Black people purchased stock in the company, and naysayers were surprised when the company bought its first ship, the *Yarmouth.* The sale of stock was limited to Black people, and no one person could purchase more than two hundred shares. In 1922, Garvey was charged with mail fraud for having advertised the sale of stock for a ship that the Black Star Line had not yet purchased. He was eventually convicted and spent a couple of years in prison, before returning to his native Jamaica, where he continued the work of the UNIA on the island and abroad.

Many African Americans—particularly those from the middle class—viewed both Garvey's entrepreneurial undertakings and the Back-to-Africa Movement with suspicion. The fact that the Ku Klux Klan viewed Garvey's movement as a good thing was sufficient reason for them to conclude that it was a bad thing for Black people.

This does not mean, however, that African Americans did not view the African motherland with reverence and romanticism. Notwithstanding the many historical and cultural differences between old-world and new-world Black people, there has always been a certain level of transatlantic solidarity, community, and exchange. In the last chapter, I discussed the way in which Kwame Nkrumah, the first president of Ghana, was inspired by the African American experience while studying at Lincoln University. In turn, Nkrumah invited W. E. B. Du Bois to relocate to Ghana. Given Du Bois' long-standing support for racial integration and his contention with Garvey over Black nationalism and the Back-to-Africa Movement, there is some irony in the fact that Du Bois spent the final years of his life in Ghana—without an American passport—and was ultimately buried there.

In 2019, Ghana established the "Year of Return" campaign, which commemorated the four hundredth anniversary of the arrival of the first enslaved Africans in Virginia. Ghana also established a "Right of Abode" program that allows people of African descent from the Diaspora to return to Ghana to live indefinitely. And many people are doing so. Ghana has one of the largest expat African American communities in Africa—one that continues to grow.

In 2024, HBO Max launched a series titled *Coming from America,* which follows the lives of four Black families who move to Africa to escape White supremacy and pursue new opportunities. At the end of the series, a couple of the families weigh the pros and cons of returning to the United States versus staying in Ghana, but ultimately all four families decide to remain in Africa due, in part, to their heightened sense of belonging and the relative absence of racism.

However, the effort to escape White supremacy does not necessarily entail moving abroad. There are those who have proposed the establishment of a Black homeland within the United States.

Here Is Where We Belong

In contrast to the notion of foreign exodus, some African Americans have favored the idea of creating their own independent state within the United States. Many Black people view the South, in particular, as a region that they helped to build and therefore have the right of ownership to. Because of the essential, but unrecognized, contribution that Black people have made in building the nation, the idea of a Black homeland is often tied to the concept of reparations. Historically speaking, the U.S. government has long understood the merit of "reparations" and the debt owed to enslaved Africans and their descendants.

The first and only attempt at creating such a path of restitution is Field Order No. 15. It was passed in 1865, four days after a meeting between Union general William Tecumseh Sherman and numerous leaders of formerly enslaved Black people in a pivotal moment at the end of the Civil War.[11] The deeper story underlying this turn of events was a choice about whether the formerly enslaved wanted to be integrated into White society or live independent of it. The story, as recounted by Steven Rogers in *A*

Letter to My White Friends and Colleagues, and as previously alluded to on page 35 of this book, goes as follows:

> In the winter of 1865, as the Union Army was defeating the Con-
> federates, many formerly enslaved people began marching with and
> following Union soldiers. They were taking refuge. Union Army
> leaders did not know what to do with this group, estimated to be
> upwards of 17,000 people. They told President Lincon about their
> dilemma. In return he sent the following question via messenger
> from Washington, D.C., to General William Tecumseh Sherman in
> Savannah, Georgia, "What do these Negros want?"[12]

To get an answer, Sherman met with a group of Black religious leaders
who ranged in age from twenty-six to seventy-two years old, including
Garrison Frazier, who had purchased his freedom and that of his wife for
$1,000 in gold and silver:

> Frazier told Sherman that he defined slavery as one person "receiv-
> ing by irresistible power the work of another man, and not by his
> consent" and went on to tell Sherman that freedom meant "placing
> us where we could reap the fruit of our own labor, and take care of
> ourselves." The best way to accomplish this was "to have land, and
> turn it and till it by our own labor." Sherman asked the group if they
> would rather integrate into the general society or live separately. The
> youngest member of the group, 26-year-old James Lynch, who was
> free born, voiced his support for the former. The other 19 men voted
> for the latter with their full support of Frazier, who responded, "I
> would prefer to live by ourselves, for there is a prejudice against us in
> the South that will take years to get over."[13]

This wise and prescient statement by Frazier was made in 1865. Little
did he know just how true his prediction about White people's prejudice
against Black people taking "years to get over" actually was. Here we are,

more than 150 years after his statement, still facing many of the racial prej-
udices that plagued the newly emancipated.

What is also interesting about Field Order No. 15 is that it did not
represent reparations in the strictest sense of the word. Rather, Black people would be given the option to *buy* the land seized from the Confeder-
acy, with the price of the land to be fixed at $1.25 per acre, with 40 percent
due up front.[14] However, less than three months after Field Order No. 15
was enacted, Lincoln was assassinated. Therefore, even the option to buy
the land was rescinded and the formerly enslaved never realized their
dreams of autonomy and independence.

Notwithstanding, the idea of reparations in the form of land in the
South would resurface more than a century later, with the founding of the
Republic of New Afrika in the wake of the bloody Detroit Rebellion of
1967—in which forty-three people died and over a thousand were injured. The founders of the Provisional Government of the Republic of
New Afrika—which included Robert F. Williams, a former branch president of the NAACP living in exile in China; attorney Milton Henry; civil
rights activist Audley "Queen Mother" Moore; Black nationalist Imari
Obadele; and Betty Shabazz, the widow of Malcolm X—drafted their
own Declaration of Independence. The document designated five states in
the cotton belt of the United States (Louisiana, Mississippi, Alabama,
Georgia, and South Carolina) as the site of the homeland of New Afrika.
The mission and core values of the Republic of New Afrika (RNA) centered around pride in Black history and culture, resistance to White
supremacy, the establishment of collective prosperity ("We" would be
capitalized while "i" would be lowercase), landownership, autonomous
governance, and self-defense.

The ultimate goal was the establishment of an independent, Black-
majority country whose geographical boundaries spanned from Louisiana
to South Carolina, and the procurement of billions of dollars in reparations
for the Black citizens of New Afrika as remuneration for damages caused
by slavery, Jim Crow, and other institutional harms to Black people. The
U.S. government would then issue a referendum to all its citizens of Afri-

can descent assessing whether they wished to remain citizens of the United States of America, or become citizens of New Afrika.

While the aspirations of the Republic of New Afrika were never realized, they inspired fictional works such as the 1988 novel *Fire on the Mountain* by Terry Bisson. The story takes place in "Nova Africa," a utopian socialist community that was created after John Brown succeeded, with the help of Harriet Tubman, at creating a victorious slave revolt at Harpers Ferry. The result is a futuristic, Wakanda-like world that is far more advanced and egalitarian than our actual world.

■ ■ ■

The founding of the Republic of New Afrika also corresponds, chronologically, with another historical event whose effects, in the decades since, have become profound: the reverse migration of Blacks to the South. This return to the South began in the 1970s due to a number of "push-and-pull" factors, such as the deindustrialization and loss of jobs, rioting, and White flight and crumbling urban infrastructure in the North versus the lower cost of living, stronger familial ties, and better climate in the South. The movement South has continued to this day, and has been identified by Charles Blow as a ripe opportunity for Blacks to gain political power not only in the South but in the nation as a whole.

In his documentary *South to Black Power,* Blow questions the wisdom of appealing to White people for racial justice by asking: "What if we could skip over all of the pleading, and the begging, and the marching, and the shouting, and go straight to the power?"

Instead, he proposes a path to Black political power that does not require the participation, or even approval, of White people. Blow's strategy relies on the resettlement of Black people to targeted states in the South where there is the highest likelihood of establishing an electoral majority and taking democratic control of political institutions. He identifies states in the South with the largest Black populations—such as Georgia, North Carolina, Mississippi, and Maryland rather than Arkansas, Tennessee, or

Kentucky—where there is the greatest likelihood of achieving a Black majority large enough to seize the political reins of the state legislatures and upend the oppressive systems currently in place. Another advantage of having a Black majority at the state level is the ability to elect senators and presidents that truly represent the interests of Black people. In his book *The Devil You Know,* Blow argues that until now, all the Black representation in the Senate or Oval Office has been sanctioned by White people:[15]

> Black people have never popularly elected a senator on their own or been the majority of a coalition that did so. There have been only ten African-American senators, and they have all been either appointed or elected by white people. This is not problematic in theory, but as is the case with all politics, politicians are most beholden to the electorate that installs them.[16]

Being beholden to an electorate that is afflicted with an addiction to White supremacy runs the risk of restricting the ability of popularly elected Black politicians to promote racial progress. As mentioned in chapter 6, many have argued that Barack Obama, the first and only Black president of the United States, was too dovish in his approach to Black empowerment out of fear of offending White people—even those who voted for him. In contrast, his successor, Donald Trump, was, and is, very hawkish in his promotion of White supremacy. Thus, it is both paradoxical—and conceptually consistent—that many of the same White people voted for both Obama and Trump. Each candidate behaved in ways that were consistent with mainstream societal prescriptions: toning down Black advocacy and ramping up White advocacy.

Blow's plan is not entirely quixotic. In the past, targeted relocation has been employed as an effective tool of political revolution. In the early 1970s, journalist Richard Pollak wrote an article in *Playboy* magazine urging all the hippies to go to Vermont—not to march, protest, or stage sit-ins, but rather to establish permanent residency and register to vote. The next step would be to take over the state in what he referred to as the "approved American way—by ballot." The plan worked. This clarion call essentially transformed Vermont from a red state to a blue state, as Blow argues in his documentary.

Charles Blow has issued a similar call for descendants of the Great Migration to return to the land of their African American ancestors. He rejects the notion that people should be reluctant to return to the South out of fear of encountering more racism. In *The Devil You Know,* he writes that "Black people fled the horrors of the racist South for so-called liberal cities of the North and West, trading the devil they knew for the devil they didn't, only to come to the painful realization that the devil is the devil."[17] He even suggests that, in some respects, racism in the North can be worse than racism in the South:

> I often think of racism as having developmental cycles. In the South, it's an old man. There, racism hasn't vanished (far from it), but it has come to terms with itself. In the North, particularly in destination cities, racism is a teenage boy, acting out as the old man did years ago.[18]

If Black people do not encounter more racism by moving south but gain tremendous political power at the state and national level by doing so, then it is a rational move from a group-based or community standpoint. Whether individuals see living in the South as more exciting or desirable from a quality-of-life perspective is a different question. In the documentary, Blow himself admits to being reluctant to leave his comfortable life in New York to move to Atlanta but ultimately concludes that "this is what we must do as Black people. . . . There are some things in life that are bigger than you [as an individual]." All social movements require group solidarity and a certain degree of individual sacrifice and inconvenience (e.g., walking to work during the Montgomery bus boycott) to uplift the community as a whole.

Although it is a viable strategy on paper, there are at least two practical challenges when it comes to the implementation of Blow's strategy for Black empowerment. The first challenge lies in the fact that Black people are not a monolith. There are myriad fault lines and features that could serve as a basis for fracturing the Black community—color, class, ethnicity, region, religion, ideology, or even personality. As Black folks, we have all had the experience of being thrown under the bus by another Black individual, particularly in a professional setting. Most of us have also witnessed tension between Black subgroups as well. One common basis from intragroup conflict where I live, on the East Coast, is ethnicity.

Research has shown that increasing levels of Black immigration from the West Indies and Africa over the last sixty years has shifted the meaning of Black identity in the United States.[19] For example, more than 25 percent of New York City's Black population is of African or West Indian descent, hailing from places that have very different conceptualizations of race than the United States.[20] Some social scientists have argued that many of these immigrants were never "Black" in their majority-Black homeland, and only experience becoming Black once they arrive in the United States,[21] due to the fact that they are often categorized and subject to much of the racism that affects African Americans. Due to a host of factors, including economic migration, Black immigrants (or their descendants) make up a disproportionately large percentage of the Black student population at highly selective colleges and universities.[22] In fact, at Harvard a whopping 67 percent of the Black student population is of West Indian or African descent.[23]

In the book *Crosscurrents: West Indian Immigrants and Race,* sociologist Milton Vickerman writes:

> The attitudes exhibited by West Indian immigrants in [the United States] derive from the conflict between a strong desire for upward mobility that is implied in the immigrant ethos, and the existence of an entrenched ethnic hierarchy which tends to tightly constrain individuals of African ancestry.[24]

One consequence of this conflict is that West Indians (and Africans) themselves often hold negative stereotypes toward African Americans as being lazy, uneducated, or otherwise deficient, without taking context into account. It is important to understand that, given their immigration status, Black immigrants in the United States are not a cross section of the population of their countries of origin. Princeton professor Eddie Glaude spoke to me about this subject when I interviewed him:

> My wife is Jamaican, and I'm always having these conversations with my in-laws as they talk about, you know, poor African Americans who are lazy. And I say to them, you're making the wrong comparison. Y'all had the ability to leave, right? You're economic migrants. Why don't you compare the folks back in Kingston [Jamaica] to the [poor, lazy] folks that you're talking about in Liberty [neighborhood in Miami]? So, what does it mean to be mindful of your ability to leave—to leave the game—and how this affects where you then end up, and how you then orient yourself wherever you land. That's really important—so you don't reproduce the same inequalities.

Despite the enormous diversity within race, and the potential threats to solidarity created by this diversity, there is ample evidence that *enough* of the Black community (80 to 95 percent) are on the same page to constitute a solid voting bloc. Therefore, reverse migration is still a viable strategy for increasing Black legislative power. There is also empirical evidence that indicates that an effective way to increase solidarity among Black people, and all people of color, is to highlight the one thing that we all share: the burden of confronting racism.[25]

The second big challenge of Blow's proposal is getting enough Black people living comfortably in the North, West, and Midwest to move South to make it work. In his documentary, several prominent Black people scoffed at Blow's idea, including Ford Foundation president Darren Walker, as well as some of Blow's own Black colleagues at *The New York Times*. Even grassroots activists in places like Chicago—who supported his overall plan of Black power—were highly reluctant to move to the South.

I asked Angela Davis for her views on the viability of the reverse migration strategy. Her response was thoughtful and nuanced. Although she offered support for the idea, she also expressed some skepticism due to the heterogeneity of Black people, as well as the regional rather than global focus:

> I know that we use the term "Black people," and I know what we intend when we use these conceptual shortcuts. But, in reality, Black people are very heterogeneous in terms of politics, especially now, as we're learning. And so my response would be that we have to think about the ways in which the concepts with which we work often don't reflect the realities that they are meant to reflect. I mean, I want to sympathize with Charles Blow's assumption. I'm from the South. I don't know whether I would actually want to live in the South, but I get it. I understand the sentiment.
>
> The world is so complicated—and our tendency is often to become more intimate, to become smaller, to retreat, you know, rather than to think about a global citizenship and our responsibilities to those who are in Palestine, for example, or those who are fighting in the Sudan, or in Haiti. My sense has always been to become larger, more global. To become world citizens, and to carry some of the ethics that come from the struggles that are grounded in places like the South with us wherever we go. So, yeah, I'll say right on to my brother Charles. But I think that we don't have to move in order to do the work that's necessary to change the world. We have to not only change our backyard; we have to change the globe.

I had a conversation about the viability of the reverse-migration strategy with my colleague Tracy Dumas. Although she supports the idea in theory, she admits that she herself would not be keen on moving to the South for one practical reason: her sense of responsibility to her aging parents, who are located in Chicago. However, she offered a few suggestions on how to get more Black people to the South en masse:

1. Church planting: Enlist Black megachurches in Northern/ Western cities to "plant" new congregations in strategic Southern states. Usually a church plant is "seeded" with a few

hundred members from the "mother" church who move to the location of the plant. Megachurches in Chicago, New York, Detroit, Houston, Dallas, and Los Angeles combined could send a few thousand folks.

2.   Campaign to target (and assist) current remote workers who can easily move without having to search for a new job in the South. Incentivize them by pointing out all the extra money they could possibly have by earning an "East/West Coast" salary in a place with lower state taxes and a lower cost of living.

3.   Encourage Northern/Western Black-owned companies to move offices or employees to a Southern state. Large firms like Ariel Capital might be good candidates for this campaign.

4.   Build a network of "sponsors" able to offer financial support to young folks who are willing to move South but don't have the funds to do so. Young people, who can be fruitful and multiply, will be essential for sustaining power long term.

5.   Partner with Stacey Abrams' voter registration apparatus to ensure that reverse migrants can easily navigate voter registration in their new states. If they move but don't vote, the whole strategy becomes useless.

As stated throughout the book, playing the game, changing the game, and leaving the game are not mutually exclusive, but rather synergistic. Charles Blow's strategy involves elements of all three pathways: leaving the game by moving from one location to another; playing the game by using the rules, institutions, and systems already in place to achieve one's goal; and changing the game by relying on an electoral majority to alter the game. I find the combination of playing, changing, and leaving the game embedded in Blow's strategy of reverse migration to be one of the most promising prospects for obtaining enduring and sustainable Black political power on a national level that currently exists.

■ ▧ ▩

I wrote this book as a way to shift from focusing exclusively on grievance and protest to also allocating attention on agency and empowerment. A very important point, in closing, is that we must allow people to be who they are, and contribute to the community in the way that best suits them. There is no one right pathway, and we can all make a difference, regardless of whether we are playing, changing, or leaving the game. The key to uniting all these pathways is solidarity. We must always support one another. My primary goal has been to raise our awareness of our agency and the various pathways for managing the burden of White supremacy. As you will have surmised, there are no perfect solutions. Indeed, there are costs involved with playing, changing, and leaving the game. However, real change requires the courage to take risks, as well as the willingness to imagine possibilities that are not currently present. It also demands a lucid understanding of why we're in the game and what it means to win. That is where I turn my attention in the final chapter of the book. In the epilogue, I expand the focus from how to navigate the game to the bigger question of how we navigate life.

Epilogue

Our Obligation to Lead a Good Life

The fact that I was able to write this book is a testament to the power of my ancestors. I experience both awe and gratitude when I think of their strength and resilience. From their resolute determination to survive the unimaginable horror of the Middle Passage, to their tireless tenacity in abiding the indignities of slavery, to their unrelenting fight for full citizenship and representation—our ancestors have endured and overcome so much.

It is incumbent upon us to continue their struggle by utilizing the pathways explored in this book to achieve the equality and prosperity that we deserve. Above all, as we honor our obligation to carry on with their fight, we must never lose sight of our forebears' ultimate desire for future generations: to have a good life. It is our duty to live well.

But what does it mean to lead a good life? It's a hoary question that humans have spent millennia trying to answer, in both philosophical and practical ways. It's a question that is integrally relevant to the core themes discussed throughout the book—from White people's attachment to their presumed superiority, to Black people's strategies of engagement with "the game." What are we looking for? What do we all hope to achieve? In many respects, psychologist Abraham Maslow mapped it out long ago in a hierarchy of needs—ranging from sustenance and safety to self-esteem and self-actualization. But how does all this translate into a good life, and what we must do to obtain it?

The notion of what a good life entails varies across geography, ethnicity, and culture. Having spent many years living abroad, I've even observed significant differences between people in Spain and England—two relatively similar empire nations within Europe—when it comes to how the game is defined and what it means to win it. Spain is a more collectivist culture, where people place a high premium on relationships and community. England is a more individualistic society, where ambition and self-interest are high priorities.

When I lived in England, I didn't know the names of any of my neighbors. People kept to themselves and minded their own business. In Spain, I knew the names of everyone in my building within a month. My neighbors made a point of introducing themselves and, at times, even got in my business a little.

Back when I was a smoker, I would sometimes conduct an informal field study while out at a restaurant, bar, or nightclub in Spain or England. I would offer someone a pound or euro for a cigarette. About eight times out of ten in England, they would accept the coin and hand me a cigarette. In Spain, about eight times out of ten they would give me the cigarette and tell me to keep the money. This difference in public generosity wasn't driven by the monetary value of a pound versus a euro, or differences in the cost of cigarettes in each country. Even if I offered more than a euro or asked for two cigarettes, the people in Spain would just give them to me. And if I asked without offering money, I would most often be given a cigarette in Spain but receive a polite excuse (e.g., "Sorry, mate, I'm all out") in England.

Borrowing the metaphors from chapter 1, one might describe Spain as more of a "dolphin" culture—centered around the pod, or community—whereas England is more of an "ostrich" culture, focused squarely on self-interest. On the other hand, the United States is more of a "shark" culture, characterized by the creation of "winners" and "losers" as a way to define what it means to triumph in the game of life.[1]

The whole notion of the loser—in the way that we mean it in the United States—is something that is difficult for Spaniards to comprehend. There is not even a direct translation of the word, with the same connotation. My good friend Javier—whom I met thirty-five years ago when I studied abroad in Spain during my junior year of college—is amused by the word "loser" in English. "Oye tío, eres un perdedor!" he chuckles, while shrugging his shoulders at how ridiculous the translation sounds in Castilian Spanish.

In fact, he would argue that people see "winning" in the exact opposite way in Spain. Javi is a successful entrepreneur who owns a hospitality company with restaurants, hotels, and vineyards all over Spain, and in North America and South America. The company started in 1989 with just one modest roadside restaurant with amazing food. When we met in 1991, they still had only the one restaurant in the small town where he grew up. He left college and has spent the last three decades expanding to dozens of restaurants, as well as establishing two wine labels and various hotels. In the United States—which is where he happened to spend his junior year of high school, in 1985—he would be heralded as a success story—a "winner."

In Spain, however, he's viewed as being a bit of an enigma—perhaps even a fool. Despite his "success" in an economic sense, no one can understand why he would want to "complicarse la vida"—or complicate his life. He was making a good living with one or two restaurants. Why build two dozen and create the headache of managing them all? Most people in Spain (and Italy, Portugal, Greece, etc.) prioritize quality time with family and friends. The focus is on having *enough* to be comfortable, not creating stress and hassle in one's life for the sake of constantly chasing more and more financial wealth. In the United States, that's the whole point—to be number one. Go big or go home, as they say. "Greed is good," according to cultural icon Gordon Gekko, played by Michael Douglas in the 1987 movie *Wall Street*.

They are playing a different game in Spain. While Spaniards certainly value financial security, what is missing is the obsession with monetary wealth and lofty job titles as life goals. They don't need to be number one, and don't tend to evaluate other people based on the size of their home, car, or bank account. In fact, Javi might even be considered the "loser" to them, if they had a word for it, because he does not embody what they view as being most important in life.

In the United States, on the other hand, there is a clear cultural sense of what it means to be a "winner," and as I discussed in chapter 1, it is strongly tied to *relative* position—as defined by both (low-road) capitalism and racial caste. Examples of it are everywhere, even in popular culture.

In a scene from the popular HBO series *The White Lotus,* Mark Mossbacher—played by actor Steve Zahn—responds to the indignation of his White progressive daughter and her friend. Her friend is a woman of color who was offended by a dinnertime show in which her Native Hawaiian "vacation boyfriend" performed a ceremonial fire dance for an affluent White crowd staying at the resort. Adding insult to injury, her lover performed the dance on land stolen from his family to build the resort. After hearing this information, Mark scoffs:

> Look, obviously imperialism was bad. Shouldn't kill people, steal their land, and then make them dance. Everybody knows that. But it's humanity. Welcome to history. Welcome to America. I mean, what are we gonna do, huh? Nobody cedes their privilege. That's absurd. It goes against human nature. We're all just trying to win the game of life.
>
> How are we gonna make it right, hmm? Should we give away all our money? Would you like that, Liv? [he asks his progressive daughter, as she looks at him sheepishly]. Yeah, that's what I thought [he gloats in response]. Mm-hmm. [Or] maybe we should just feel shitty about ourselves all the time for the crimes of the past. Wear a hair shirt and not go on vacation?

In many respects, this scene reflects the inherent dilemma of White supremacy addiction. Mark admits that it's bad if you do the drug (i.e., imperialism/White supremacy), but you also miss out if you don't do the drug (i.e., no privilege). So why not just do it, enjoy the high—in both senses of the word—and don't waste your time feeling guilty about it? Like a typical dolphin, his progressive daughter seems to both comprehend and acquiesce, albeit begrudgingly.

Let's consider two of his statements in isolation: "Welcome to America" and "We're all just trying to win the game of life." Exactly what "game" is he playing, and how is the "win" being defined? And what relevance does "America" play in this whole game? As explained in chapter 1, many scholars and social scientists have theorized about the unique ways in which "success" was defined in a land of European immigrants desperately searching for freedom and self-made glory—both of which required White subjugation of people of color. To borrow another theme from *The White Lotus* (season 3), they were the "LBH," or "losers back home," who traveled to a new place so that they could feel like winners.[2] However, the "win" has always been tied to the oppression of others as a means of overcoming an inferiority complex. The "up-and-coming" have always had to try a lot harder than the patricians.

Economist Albert Hirschman has offered a related argument to those I proposed in chapter 1. He maintains that White Americans have developed a fervent chauvinism and blind belief in the ideal of America as the land of freedom in part because they fled from countries where they were not free. This makes the whole idea of freedom in America an unassailable "fact" and the idea of exit utterly unthinkable. He writes:

> In retrospect, the "old country" will appear more abominable than ever while the new country will be declared to be the greatest, "the last best hope of mankind," and all manner of other superlatives. . . . To most of its citizens—with the important exception of those whose forefathers came as slaves—exit from the country has long been peculiarly unthinkable.[3]

This hyper-attachment to land that was never theirs, paired with a fragile sense of freedom conditioned on the subjugation of Black, Native, and other non-White peoples, breeds a profound sense of nationalism and entitlement. White Americans have internalized on a deep psychic level the notion that they are uniquely American,[4] and that prosperity—achieving "self-made" status—is their birthright. Because "success" is construed in *relative* terms, White poverty in the face of Black prosperity egregiously violates the covenant. Therefore, outrage is the unavoidable outcome if White people are perceived as struggling while a Black person prospers. However, the inverse scenario creates a sense of comfort and faith that the system is working the way it was intended to.

As we explored in chapter 10, the more unavailable the "exit" option is, the more aggressive and unrestrained people will be in making their voices heard. We witnessed a particularly egregious and unbridled form of "voice" on January 6, 2021, during the attack on the Capitol and the violent assault of those defending it. Perhaps what the rioters were heeding was Trump's admonition "If you don't fight like hell, you're not going to have a country anymore"—that "country" being an America defined by White supremacy and the subjugation of people of color.

During my interview with historian Carol Anderson, she brought up an op-ed that she had written four years prior to the January 6 attack that she thought was consistent with my addiction hypothesis. This article, published in *The Guardian* in 2017, explored the reasons we were witnessing so many mind-boggling political transgressions—actions that made many people scratch their heads and wonder how such events could transpire in America. She described how the "reality-warping drug" of White supremacy led to the normalization of behaviors that would have seemed "lunatic" when viewed through sober eyes. In her op-ed, she wrote:

> None of this makes sense. Unless, that is, we come to grips with the reality that we are seeing the effects of far too many Americans strung out on the most pervasive, devastating, reality-warping drug to ever hit the United States: white supremacy. . . . Trump is, in fact, only a symptom. All of his racist rants would have dropped him on the outskirts of the lunatic fringe if it hadn't been for the way that a major political party had spent decades making white supremacy the Republican party's drug of choice.[5]

Anderson was delighted to learn that I had independently reached a similar conclusion concerning the nature of White supremacy in the

United States—that it functions like an addiction—as were others with whom I spoke, including Ibram X. Kendi and Janai Nelson, who had pondered similar ideas.

To be sure, none of this is to imply that racism, White supremacy, or even White supremacy addiction do not exist in other Western nations. They certainly exist in every nation that I have visited—including Spain and England. However, addiction has a much deeper connotation than habitual or recreational use. It means being so strung out on a substance that you just can't let it go, even if it destroys you and everything that is dear to you (e.g., democracy). That level of fervent commitment to White supremacy, no matter what, does not exist to the same degree everywhere. There are differences between nations.

What's interesting is that these cultural/structural differences emerge even when we compare three Western nations with imperialist histories (the United States, the United Kingdom, and Spain).[6] The differences are even further magnified as the comparisons become more culturally and geographically diverse (e.g., the United States vs. Tibet). To people in traditional societies, greed means stealing from yourself, because you are an integral part of the land and the community—not separate from it.

If, as Marimba Ani suggests in her book *Yurugu,* "success" for White Americans is defined in terms of separation and domination, then a big part of what "winning" means for White people is to be better than people of color. Indeed, that was the *only* thing that "winning" meant to indigent White Southerners in the antebellum era.

But what does "winning" the game mean for Black folks? What does it mean for us to lead a good life? We must each answer that question for ourselves, because the answer has strong implications for how we define not only success but happiness.

I believe there are five goals that form the foundation of a good life and define the "wins" of the game:

1. Physical health

2. Mental health

3.   Loving relationships

4.   Financial security

5.   Purpose (personal, professional, and spiritual)

It would take another book to fully unpack these five goals and how they specifically relate to the Black community. Perhaps I will write that book someday. For now, I simply want to name those goals in an effort to demystify the building blocks of a good life.

Separation and domination represent such a misguided way to live one's best life. This is not so much a judgment as an assertion of fact. Researchers have long investigated what makes people happy, and it's neither wealth nor power.[7] It's people. It's experiences. It's purpose. Money also plays a role—which is why "financial security" is on the list. However, you don't need tons of money.

In 2010, the late Nobel laureate Daniel Kahneman found that the relationship between money and happiness reaches a plateau around $75,000 (about $110,000 in 2025). In other words, having more money does correlate with being happier, but only until you make about $110,000 per year. After that, it doesn't matter if you make $110,000 or $110,000,000—your level of happiness is about the same.

If that's the case, then why would someone who's already financially secure be willing to lie, cheat, steal, or kill just to get more money? Being greedy and power-hungry might have been justifiable, from a purely utilitarian standpoint, if it actually led to something worth having, like happiness and fulfillment. It doesn't. All it does is feed the ego—which has a voracious appetite that can never be truly sated.[8] It is the same with all addictions, and power is a potent drug. But like any addiction, it produces short-term gratification without long-term satisfaction. Moreover, oppression can be soul-crushing, not just for the oppressed but for the oppressor too.[9] Too much money can actually impede happiness. Research has found that money can, ironically, create distance and separation from one of the biggest contributors of happiness—people.[10]

Unabashed joy while surrounded by my people.

I am grateful for the wonderful people in my life, and the sacrifices of all those who came before me. I view my wholehearted embrace of the good life as a tribute to my ancestors. My prosperity is their dream. My joy is their triumph. And my voice—to say what they could not—is their vindication. May we all endeavor to continue the legacy of those who preceded us, being mindful of the fact that a good life does not require greed, oppression, wealth, or power. It simply demands that we understand the game that we want to play, and what it means to win. True victory is the power to create your own goals—and even your own rules—regardless of whether you are playing, changing, or leaving the game.

Author's Note

To avoid bogging down the introduction, and your journey, with onerous explanations and excessive throat clearing, I decided to put the "author's note" at the end of the book, to provide any additional clarification that might be needed. As you may have noticed, I excluded the conjunction "or" in the title *Play the Game. Change the Game. Leave the Game.* to signify that the three paths are not mutually exclusive. I also declined to insert "and" to communicate the fact that you do not *have* to do all three. There is also no sequence implied by either the title or the subtitle. In other words, it is not necessary to play the game before changing the game or changing the game before leaving the game. And empowerment is not a prerequisite for prosperity or joy. Joy or prosperity could just as easily facilitate empowerment.

I speak of "Black" empowerment nonexclusively. That is, although this book is primarily written for a Black audience, there was no intent to exclude other populations of color. I am very much a universalist, and feel a strong sense of affinity and solidarity not only with all marginalized peoples—but with all people on the planet.

So why focus on Black empowerment? For many of the same reasons historians focus on a particular state, region, or country. It is difficult to boil the ocean. My decision to focus on Black people is as much a pragmatic one as it is a personal one. Just as historians write books about the history of France, for example, or even the history of the Basque region of France, without intent to slight the rest of the world, so, too, can race scholars focus on a particular group in a particular region without seeking to offend any other group.

Although this book focuses on Black people in the United States, I am keenly aware of the enormous diversity within the category "Black people" and the vast cultural, historical, and political variability within the United States. Thus, even with my circumscribed focus on Black people in America, I still have not done justice to all the diversity (and conflict) that exists within that racial/ethnic category.

I capitalize both "Black" and "White" to signal the absence of a racial default. Blackness and Whiteness are equally racialized and dialectically intertwined. I also use upper-case racial signifiers to avoid linguistic confusion. For example, a white church is a building whose exterior is painted white regardless of the racial composition of the congregation, whereas a White church refers to a church with a congregation of White people. Many elderly people have white hair (e.g., a "silver fox"), regardless of their race, whereas people of European descent have White hair (straight hair), regardless of its color.

Unlike my previous book, *The Conversation,* which was very science-based and cited nearly one thousand studies, the current book is more wisdom-based than science-based. I focus much more strongly on personal anecdotes, lived experience, community wisdom, and historical events than empirical studies. Nevertheless, I have included a great number of citations in this book (I couldn't help it!).

However, I want to be clear that my goal was not to be comprehensive and exhaustive in my integration of the scientific literature. Thus, there might exist books, studies, and experiments that are relevant to a given phenomenon but are not cited. Again, the goal was not to create a scholarly book or one that provided definitive answers. Rather, my goal was to write a book that is thought-provoking and stimulating while also being accessible and engaging to a broad swath of the Black community—including high school students or working adults who did not attend college.

Because this is not an academic work, the manner of citation and attribution varies throughout the book. Sometimes the words or ideas of others are indicated using quotes, particularly when embedded within paragraphs. At other times, the words or ideas of others are demarcated by means of indentation. Finally, the words or ideas of others are acknowledged through a label or verbal description, particularly in the case of interviews that alternate back and forth between speakers. I take pride in celebrating the brilliance of my heroes and colleagues, and have taken great pains to ensure that proper credit is given. A team of editors and copyeditors have also focused attention on ensuring that the work from others is recognized and acknowledged, if not with quotations, then via one of the other means indicated above.

After the publication of *The Conversation,* I discovered three or four typographical errors in a book comprised of about ninety thousand words. These typos managed to slip through the cracks, despite careful reading of the book multiple times by highly qualified individuals, including professional proofreaders. I say this, not as a slight to the proofreaders, my editors, myself, or any of the other dozen highly intelligent people who know how to spell. Rather, the appearance of a handful of typographical errors in the final version of the book is a testament to the implausibility of human perfection. Despite all this meticulous effort and attention that went into the creation of *Play the Game,* it is possible that there will also be a few typographical errors. It is also possible that we may have inadvertently overlooked a couple of attributions. If this is the case, then I apologize in advance and want to emphasize that it was not due to any nefarious intent or gross incompetence, but rather the inevitability of human error.

Finally, there are topics that did not make the final version of the book. One important topic that merits deep discussion is the nature of conflict among Black people. In earlier versions, there was an entire chapter on this issue. However, it did not seem to squarely fit into the play, change, or leave theme, nor did it fit the spirit of the book, which was as much about inspiration as information. Undoubtedly, other themes of interest to the readership have been omitted as well. Hopefully, there was enough substance across a large variety of topics to satisfy readers' curiosity. My hope is that you found the stroll down the many paths of this book to be meaningful, engaging, and ultimately uplifting and empowering. I am truly grateful for your willingness to accompany me on this journey.

Acknowledgments

I wish to extend my heartfelt gratitude to the countless individuals who contributed to this project, including the phenomenal people who were gracious enough to be interviewed for this book: Carol Anderson, Charles Blow, Kenneth Chenault, Kimberlé Crenshaw, William "Sandy" Darity Jr., Angela Y. Davis, Anthony Foxx, Eddie Glaude Jr., Herminia Ibarra, L. Duane Jackson, Ibram X. Kendi, Alister Martin, Deval Patrick, Steven S. Rogers, Lumumba Seegers, Patrick Tannock, David A. Thomas, and Kenji Yoshino. I am thankful for your willingness to take time out of your busy schedules to share your astounding wisdom and brilliance.

I also want to send a special thanks to the team at Crown, particularly my extraordinary editors Paul Whitlatch and Katie Berry, who went above and beyond the call of duty—investing not only time but remarkable dedication to this project. I am also grateful to the many guest editors who furnished invaluable feedback on earlier drafts of the book: Naisha Bradley, Marilynn Brewer, Tracy Dumas, Robin Ely, SaMee Harden, Antony Haynes, Leticia Smith-Evans Haynes, Sa-Kiera Hudson, Patricia Ledesma, Onjale Scott Price, and Emiliano Void. Your input has undoubtedly enhanced the quality of the final product.

Kudos to many others who have provided support behind the scenes, including Tara Gilbride, Gwyneth Stansfield, and everyone at PRH who gave me support throughout this grueling process, as well as my agent, Jim Levine, and the staff at LGR, and my amazing assistant, Louie Mitchell, who has been an unwavering source of support for many years.

Of course, I want to acknowledge various members of my biological family, as well as the members of my chosen family—friends, mentors, and colleagues whom I love deeply. The fact that stories involving so many of you are sprinkled throughout this book is a testament to the profound and indelible impact that you have had on my life. You have all been a tremendous blessing to me. Please know that I appreciate you more than I often have the opportunity to express.

Last but not least, I salute all the readers who have taken this journey with me. I recognize the pain and disappointment that we all feel, as a nation and a community, in light of these latest attacks on our freedom, dignity, and humanity. Rest assured we will persevere and overcome, as we always do.

Notes

Introduction:
From Antiracism to Black Empowerment

1. Telford, "As DEI Gets More Divisive."
2. *NBC Nightly News*, "John Deere Pulls Back."
3. *Chronicle of Higher Education*, "DEI Legislation Tracker."
4. Proulx, *Understanding and Helping an Addict*.
5. Wilderson, *Afropessimism*.
6. Bell, "Racism Is Here to Stay."

Chapter One:
White Supremacy and Other Drugs

1. Kang et al., "Whitened Résumés."
2. DiAngelo, *Nice Racism;* see also Danbold and Unzueta, "Drawing the Diversity Line."
3. Hacker, *Two Nations*.
4. For further discussion of how motivations interact with cognitions, see Bruner and Postman, "On the Perception of Incongruity"; Greenberg and Pyszczynski, "The Effect of an Overheard Ethnic Slur on Evaluations of the Target"; McGinnies, "Emotionality and Perceptual Defense"; and Kunda, "Case for Motivated Reasoning." And for further information about how motivations impact racism, see Sinclair and Kunda, "Reactions to a Black Professional," and Fein and Spencer, "Prejudice as Self-Image Maintenance."
5. Mobasseri et al., "Racial Inequality in Organizations."
6. Morrison, "Pain of Being Black."
7. This claim is likely to be a source of debate, with many arguing that White supremacy is just as strong in Europe and that other forms of intergroup conflict are just as prevalent around the world. It is a controversy without a definitive resolution because it ultimately boils down to one's own definition of what it means for a situation to be "different" or "similar." It is akin to debating whether racism in the North and South of the United States is different or similar. The answer is both, and evidence can be mustered to support either perspective. My belief is that the brand of racism in the United States—and particularly the presence of White supremacy addiction—is different from that in any other place, while acknowledging similarities across context. I also acknowledge that there are many other "-isms" all over the world, even in Africa.

The Rwandan genocide is but one example. However, what makes it fall short of an addiction is that Rwandans were, and are, willing to move forward. Addiction is being so committed to something that you simply can't let it go, no matter what the harm may be. Rwandans have taken an entirely different approach, and have not seen a "relapse" in over thirty years. Other nations such as South Africa have undergone a "rehabilitation" process (e.g., a truth and reconciliation). The United States has never seen such a process. The addiction is still very much active—not in remission or recovery.

8.   I am aware that a systems-level addiction analogy challenges the common tendency among White people to individualize racism. Although there can be considerable individual differences in how White supremacy addiction is manifested and expressed (which will be discussed later in this chapter), I want to make clear that it is primarily a systems-based process that afflicts almost every White person born in the United States. Indeed, addressing the problem as an individual-based phenomenon is what has held up progress.

   I also argue that White supremacy addiction does not afflict Black people because the psychological *needs* are different from those of White people. It's absurd to think that Black people *need* to believe in White supremacy in order to feel better about themselves. Although internalized racism exists among some Black people, the *need* for White supremacy is simply not there. There is no way to argue that the dismantling of White supremacy is as frightening to Black people as it is to White people—many of whom struggle to imagine what a world without White supremacy might look like.

   Finally, I do not believe that the need to feel superior is entirely symmetrical between Black and White people. As James Baldwin and others, including Marimba Ani, have argued, Black people do not need to feel superior to White people. Baldwin insists—and I agree—that we just want to be left alone. And as Ani argues in her book *Yurugu*, "separation" and "domination" are more characteristic of European thought than African, Asian, or Indigenous thought. I discuss these ideas further in chapter 11.

   In short, the self-esteem of Black people is not contingent on relative positions of power vis-à-vis other people. Indeed, research has shown that Black people have higher self-esteem than White people, despite our lower social position in society, precisely *because* we do not define our self-worth by wealth and power. See Crocker et al., "Collective Self-Esteem"; Crocker and Wolfe, "Contingencies of Self-Worth"; Twenge and Crocker, "Race and Self-Esteem."

9.   In most cases, the message is tacit and indirect. Children might observe the fear on their parents' faces as they drive through Black neighborhoods, even though the adults tell the children that everyone is the same. Children can also get messages through social surroundings—via films, cartoons, books, media, and other children. The messages are so pervasive that they can be "absorbed" from the environment even without direct or deliberate socialization from parents. Hughes et al., "Growing Up, Learning Race."

10.   DiAngelo, *Nice Racism.*

11.   Varley and Wilkerson, "Embracing the Uphill Struggle."

12.   Consistent with the idea that much of the polarization is driven by perceptions of racial progress, Hochschild points out that polarization is due to people moving right,

not left. Specifically, she writes: "The [ideological] split has widened because the right has moved right, not because the left has moved left. Republican presidents Eisenhower, Nixon, and Ford all supported the Equal Rights Amendment. In 1960, the GOP platform embraced 'free collective bargaining' between management and labor. Republicans boasted of 'extending the minimum wage to several million more workers.' . . . A founder of the organization [Planned Parenthood] was Peggy Goldwater, wife of the 1968 conservative Republican candidate for president Barry Goldwater" (7). In short, it is the right wing that has moved much further right, due largely to politics of racial resentment—which formed the foundation of Donald Trump's campaign.

13. Darity, "Review of Heather McGhee."
14. Ensign and Shifflett, "College Was Supposed to Close the Wealth Gap for Black Americans."
15. Darity, "Review of Heather McGhee."
16. See Norton and Sommers, "Whites See Racism."
17. Brown et al., "If You Rise, I Fall."
18. Brown and Jacoby-Senghor, "Majority Members Misperceive."
19. Metzl, *Dying of Whiteness,* 3.
20. Ibid., 5.
21. Dovidio and Gaertner, "Aversive Racism."
22. Kendi, *Stamped from the Beginning.* See also *Stamped from the Beginning.* Netflix documentary.
23. Of course, philanthropy can also be a vehicle for genuine social impact and change. Philanthropists such as MacKenzie Scott, for example, seem very genuine in their desire to promote racial equality. Going all the way back to her college days—well before she was a billionaire—Scott showed a keen interest in social causes and challenges facing the Black community. While attending Princeton University, she studied under Toni Morrison, who later commented on how exceptional and dedicated Scott was. She assisted Morrison during her writing of the novel *Jazz.* Unlike philanthropists who "give a little and expect to be praised a lot," Scott has done the exact opposite. She has given a lot (over $1 billion) and has demanded little praise or attention.
24. Blow, *Devil You Know,* 60.
25. Ganz, *People, Power, Change,* 4.
26. Festinger, "Cognitive Dissonance."
27. This hyper-defensiveness is the subject of *White Fragility* by Robin DiAngelo.
28. Pratto et al., "Social Dominance Orientation."
29. Chow et al., "Appeasement."
30. Castelli et al., "The Explicit and Implicit Perception of In-Group Members Who Use Stereotypes."
31. To be precise, there are two types of emotional empathy—reactive and parallel (see Stephan and Finlay, "Role of Empathy"). Reactive empathy is similar to what I am calling "sympathy." Parallel empathy is experiencing the same emotions that the other person is feeling. That is what I refer to as "empathy."

32. Rogers, *A Letter to My White Friends.*
33. Kawakami et al., "Mispredicting Affective and Behavioral Responses to Racism."
34. As I stated in the introduction, being addicted to something does not preclude the possibility of change. I finally kicked the smoking habit, and there are many programs (e.g., Alcoholics Anonymous) that provide insight and guidance on how to manage alcoholism and other forms of addiction. For now, the important point is that the change process was initiated and executed by me. Nobody else had the power to force me to change. Moreover, I was finally able to quit only after many unsuccessful attempts.

Chapter Two:
St. Martin's Village: Creating "Ease of Spirit"

1. Blow, *Devil You Know,* 62.
2. Eblen, "Lexington Subdivision Opened American Dream."
3. Kaiser, "Lexington Contemplates a Life Without IBM."
4. Eblen, "Lexington Subdivision Opened American Dream."
5. Dupree et al., "Race—Status Associations."
6. St. Martin's Village is no longer a Black enclave. It and many other all-Black middle-class neighborhoods mentioned in this chapter (e.g., Oakwood) are now integrated, multicultural communities due to increasing levels of gentrification over the last twenty years.

Chapter Three:
Doing the Dance

1. Staples, "Just Walk on By."
2. Meyerson and Scully, "Tempered Radicalism."
3. Yoshino, *Covering,* ix.
4. Ibid., x.
5. Christie Smith and Kenji Yoshino, *Uncovering Talent: A New Model for Inclusion* (Deloitte, 2013).
6. Ibid., 4 (emphasis added).
7. California's CROWN (Creating a Respectful and Open World for Natural Hair) Act, a 2019 law intended to protect people against discrimination based on hairstyle or hair texture, may protect hair but not other characteristics people may feel require covering, such as an ethnic accent or manner of speech.
8. Yoshino, *Covering,* 136.
9. Ibid., 131.
10. Sidanius and Pratto, *Social Dominance.*
11. Joanne Stephane et al., *Uncovering Culture: A Call to Action for Leaders* (Deloitte, 2024).
12. Livingston and Pearce, "Teddy-Bear Effect"; Livingston and Rosette, "Stigmatization, Subordination, or Marginalization?"

13. Rhodes et al., "Facial Symmetry"; Alrajih and Ward, "Increased Facial Width-to-Height Ratio."
14. Livingston and Pearce, "Teddy-Bear Effect."
15. Koval and Rosette, "The Natural Hair Bias in Job Recruitment."
16. During our interview, Charles Blow mentioned how in liberal spaces, Black people often have what he calls "statement hair"—bold, creative hairstyles. He added that the people with statement hair are "brilliant and often attractive" and are often "being given a pass so the rule can be maintained."
17. Crenshaw et al., "Demarginalizing the Intersection"; Crenshaw, "Mapping the Margins."
18. Livingston and Rosette, "Stigmatization, Subordination, or Marginalization?"
19. Purdie-Vaughns and Eibach, "Intersectional Invisibility."
20. Glick and Fiske, "Ambivalent Alliance."
21. Thomas et al., "Women of Color at Midcareer."
22. Anderson and Kilduff, "Dominant Personalities Attain Influence."
23. Pillemer, "Strategic Authenticity."
24. Cha et al., "Being Your True Self"; Hewlin, "Wearing the Cloak"; Roberts, "Changing Faces."
25. Bailey and Levy, "Are You for Real?"
26. Yoshino, *Covering*, 189.

Chapter Four:
Twice as Good Yet Half as Far: Mastery Versus Performance

1. Rosette and Livingston, "Failure Is Not an Option."
2. Mitchell, "Identifying White Mediocrity."
3. Senko, "Mastery and Performance Goals"; Katz-Vago and Benita, "Mastery-Approach and Performance-Approach Goals."
4. Gladwell, *Outliers*.
5. Harris, *Strategize to Win*, 97.
6. Ibid., 111.
7. Ibid., 94.
8. Castilla, "Gender, Race, and Meritocracy."
9. Abouzahr et al., "Women-Owned Startups."
10. Ryan and Haslam, "Glass Cliff."
11. Lyons-Padilla et al., "Race Influences Financial Judgments."
12. Phelan and Rudman, "Reactions to Ethnic Deviance."
13. Hall and Livingston, "The Hubris Penalty."

Chapter Five:
The Necessity of Social Networks

1. Granovetter, "Strength of Weak Ties."
2. Milgram, *Individual in a Social World*.

3. Dodds et al., "Experimental Study of Search."
4. Hansen et al., "Best-Performing CEOs."
5. Putnam, *Bowling Alone.*
6. Ganz, *People, Power, Change,* 42.
7. Casciaro et al., "Contaminating Effects."
8. Ibid., 710.
9. Ibid., 712.
10. Ibarra et al., "Men Still Get More Promotions."
11. Ibid.

Chapter Six:
Playing the Game to Change the Game: Tempered Radicals

1. I informally queried people in the Black community for examples and am basing these classifications on responses that I received. However, the perception of many celebrities is based on what they do publicly. We have little knowledge of their private behaviors and do not know what is in their hearts. I do not pretend to know the reality of who Clarence Thomas, for example, is—which may be quite different from people's perception of him. Indeed, there are some who believe that Thomas is an undercover Black power operative (e.g., see Sean Illing, host, *The Gray Area,* podcast, "What Clarence Thomas Really Thinks," Apple Podcasts, August 29, 2022, https://podcasts.apple.com/nz/podcast/what-clarence-thomas-really-thinks/id1081584611?i=1000577651902).
2. The same disclaimer as in note 1, above, goes for Michael Jordan. Although he doesn't use his platform to advocate for racial justice in a public way, he may simply be quieter in his support of the Black community than other athletes, such as Muhammad Ali or LeBron James. It is known, for example, that Jordan donated $1 million to the NAACP Legal Defense Fund (he also gave $1 million to the International Association of Chiefs of Police).
3. Harris, "Rise of Respectability Politics."
4. Lorde, *Sister Outsider.*
5. Meyerson and Scully, "Tempered Radicalism."
6. Meyerson, *Rocking the Boat.*
7. Meyerson and Scully, "Tempered Radicalism," 590.
8. Dwayne Wong, "Confronting Michael Eric Dyson's Misinformation About Malcolm X," Medium, April 24, 2023. https://dwomowale.medium.com/confronting-michael-eric-dysons-misinformation-about-malcolm-x-699cc11423c.
9. Harris, "Rise of Respectability Politics."
10. Frost and Egri, "Political Process of Innovation," 242.
11. Geronimus, *Weathering.*
12. Bell, "Racism Is Here to Stay."
13. Hirschman, *Exit, Voice, and Loyalty,* 109; but see also Carmichael and Hamilton, *Black Power.*

14. Chow et al., "Appeasement."
15. Meyerson and Scully, "Tempered Radicalism."

Chapter Seven:
Confronting Social Injustice

1. Bell, "Racism Is Here to Stay."
2. Cunningham, "Argument of 'Afropessimism.' "
3. Mallett and Melchiori, "Goals Drive Responses."
4. Bergsieker et al., "To Be Liked Versus Respected."
5. Mallett and Monteith, *Confronting Prejudice and Discrimination.*
6. Kaiser and Miller, "Stop Complaining!"
7. Mitchell, "Identifying White Mediocrity."
8. Kahn et al., "Group Members Support Confrontation."
9. Wilton et al., "White's Perceptions."
10. Kaiser and Pratt-Hyatt, "Distributing Prejudice Unequally."
11. Brondolo et al., "Coping with Racism."
12. Krieger and Sidney, "Racial Discrimination and Blood Pressure."
13. Noh and Kaspar, "Perceived Discrimination and Depression."
14. Chaney et al., "Confrontation's Health Outcomes."
15. Sanchez et al., "Confronting as Autonomy Promotion."
16. Shelton et al., "Silence Is Not Golden."
17. Czopp et al., "Standing Up for a Change."
18. Mallett and Monteith, *Confronting Prejudice and Discrimination,* xxi.
19. Drury and Kaiser, "Allies Against Sexism"; Gulker et al., "Confronting Prejudice."

Chapter Eight:
The Power of We

1. Although the dialogue presented here is continuous, I have taken the liberty of inserting paragraph breaks—rather than leaving it in its long, uninterrupted transcript format—for ease of reading. It has also been lightly edited for brevity.
2. Twenge, *iGen.*
3. Lukanioff and Haidt, *Coddling of the American Mind.*
4. Van Bavel and Packer, *Power of Us,* 177.
5. Ibid., 190.
6. Ganz, *People, Power, Change,* 5.
7. Erik Pham, "Social Loafing at Work: Definition, Causes, and How to Prevent It," *Forbes,* October 24, 2023.
8. Ganz, *People, Power, Change,* 4.
9. Chenoweth and Stephan, *Why Civil Resistance Works.*
10. Ganz, *People, Power, Change,* 37.
11. Schwartz, "Overview of the Schwartz Theory."

12. Vohs et al., "Psychological Consequences of Money."
13. Bardi and Schwartz, "Values and Behavior."
14. This is also similar to the socialized versus personalized power motives described by David C. McClelland in "The Two Faces of Power."
15. As cited in Carmine Gallo, "The Power of Storytellers to Shape Our World," *Forbes,* March 17, 2024.
16. Gallo, "Power of Storytellers."
17. Ganz, *People, Power, Change,* 32.
18. Freeman, "Tyranny of Structurelessness," as cited in Ganz, *People, Power, Change,* 11.

Chapter Nine:
Eroding the Pillars of Systemic Racism

1. Desmond, "Start on the Plantation."
2. Ton, *Case for Good Jobs,* 35.
3. Daniel, " 'Turbulence Ahead.' "
4. Ton, *Case for Good Jobs,* 5.
5. Kaur et al., "Financial Concerns."
6. Bertrand and Mullainathan, "Are Emily and Greg More Employable"; Quillian et al., "Meta-Analysis of Field Experiments."
7. Yoshino and Glasgow, "DEI Is Under Attack."
8. See the OneTen website: https://oneten.org/.
9. See the Pew Research Center website: https://www.pewresearch.org/2023/12/04/wealth-gaps-across-racial-and-ethnic-groups/.
10. Johnson, "That Was No Typo."
11. Rogers, *A Letter to My White Friends.*
12. Semuels, "Freedom Through Finances."
13. Rhinehart, "Founder of $16 Billion Ariel Investments."
14. Ross, "Architects of Baby Bonds."
15. Ibid.

Chapter Ten:
Entrepreneurship: The Path to Professional Autonomy

1. Hirschman, *Exit, Voice, and Loyalty,* 30, 37.
2. Proulx, *Understanding and Helping an Addict.*
3. Rogers, *Letter to My White Friends,* 42.
4. See the "Venture Capital and Entrepreneurship" page of the Harvard Kennedy School's website: https://www.hks.harvard.edu/centers/wappp/research/past/venture-capital-entrepreneurship.
5. Janell Ross, "The Fearless Fund Is Investing in Women of Color—and Fighting in Court," *Time,* February 1, 2024.
6. Rogers, *Letter to My White Friends,* 219.

7. Luscombe, "Erin Horne McKinney."
8. Lyons-Padilla et al., "Race Influences Financial Judgments."
9. Rogers et al., "Sources of Capital."
10. Parry, "History of Anthony Johnson."
11. Zukav, *Spiritual Partnership.*
12. Gelfand et al., "Cultural Tightness-Looseness."

Chapter Eleven:
Enclaves: Incubation Is Not Segregation

1. This is also why the Marcus Garvey–Ku Klux Klan alliance was so problematic and troubled so many Black people. The surface decision was the *same,* but the sentiment was the *opposite.* White people not only didn't care about our safety, they were the source of harm.
2. Blow, *Devil You Know,* 61.
3. Rose, *Power of Black Excellence,* 135.
4. Ibid., 5.
5. Ibid., 47.
6. Arnett, "Trailblazing Leader," as cited in ibid., 48.
7. King, *Autobiography of Martin Luther King, Jr.*
8. Bretherton, "Origins of Attachment Theory."
9. Rose, *Power of Black Excellence,* 191.
10. Ibid., 148–49.
11. Ibid., 5.
12. Rogers, *Letter to My White Friends,* 90.
13. Tom Foreman Jr., "Nikole Hannah-Jones Chooses Howard over UNC-Chapel Hill," PBS News, July 6, 2021; Ssanyu Lukoma and Natalie Betts, "Ibram X. Kendi Talks New Howard Role After Facing Criticism at Boston University," *The Hilltop,* February 15, 2025.
14. Rose, *Power of Black Excellence,* 170.
15. Rogers, *Letter to My White Friends.*
16. Rose, *Power of Black Excellence,* 121.
17. Ibid., 122.
18. *Posse Alumni Report.*
19. Ross, *Divine Nine.*
20. Friedman and Holtom, "Effects of Network Groups."
21. Friedman et al., "Social Support and Career Optimism."
22. Friedman, "Employee Network Groups."
23. Ibid., 157.
24. Ibid.
25. Ani, *Yurugu,* 29.

Chapter Twelve:
Exodus: In Search of Wakanda

1. Brown and Jacoby-Senghor, "Majority Members Misperceive."
2. Cronon, *Black Moses,* 19.
3. Peery and Bodenhausen, "Black + White = Black."
4. Degler, *Neither Black nor White.*
5. Cronon, *Black Moses,* 3–4.
6. Dixon and Telles, "Skin Color and Colorism."
7. Cronon, *Black Moses,* 28.
8. Ibid.
9. Ibid., 66.
10. Ibid.
11. Foner, "First Chapter: *Forever Free,*" and Myers, "Sherman's Field Order N. 15," both cited in Rogers, *Letter to My White Friends.*
12. Rogers, *Letter to My White Friends,* 172.
13. Ibid., 173.
14. Baradaran, *Color of Money.*
15. There were two Black female senators elected in 2024, after the publication of Blow's book: Angela Alsobrooks (D) from Maryland and Lisa Blunt Rochester (D) from Delaware. Interestingly, Maryland and Delaware are two of the Southern states identified in Blow's strategy of reverse migration.
16. Blow, *Devil You Know,* 33.
17. Ibid., 27.
18. Ibid.
19. Tormala and Deaux, "Black Immigrants to the United States."
20. Waters, *Black Identities.*
21. Stepick et al., "Shifting Identities."
22. Massey et al., *Source of the River.*
23. Rimer and Arenson, "Top Colleges Take More Blacks."
24. Vickerman, Milton. 1999. *Crosscurrents : West Indian Immigrants and Race.* New York: Oxford University Press. p. 5, as cited in Tormala and Deaux, "Black Immigrants to the United States."
25. Zou and Cheryan, "Two Axes of Subordination"; Pérez et al., "Shared Status, Shared Politics?"

Epilogue:
Our Obligation to Lead a Good Life

1. See Livingston, *Conversation,* chapter 8, for a full discussion of the difference between ostriches, or individualists, who maximize self-interest, and sharks, or competitors, who maximize relative differences, sometimes at the expense of absolute self-interest. Ironically, a shark might be more willing to give another person a cigarette than an

ostrich would, because it establishes the role of "winner" and "loser"—the loser in this case being the person in the position to rely on the other's charity.

2. This phenomenon might also partially explain the much more virulent racism in Australia, compared with their neighbor New Zealand. Early White settlers of Australia were not only "losers," but criminals and convicts, back home.

3. Hirschman, *Exit, Voice, and Loyalty,* 113–14.

4. Devos and Banaji, "American = White?"

5. Anderson, "America Is Hooked."

6. Interestingly the sequence from dolphin to shark also appears to be related to the strength or prevalence of "low-road" capitalism in each country, being the strongest in the United States and the weakest in Spain. Thus, structural and cultural factors are not entirely independent of one another.

7. See for reviews: Gilbert, D. T. (2006). *Stumbling on Happiness.* Alfred A. Knopf; Seligman, M. E. P. (2011). *Flourish: A Visionary New Understanding of Happiness and Well-being.* Nicholas Brealey Publishing; Brooks, A. C. (2022). *From Strength to Strength: Finding Success, Happiness, and Deep Purpose in the Second Half of Life.* Portfolio/Penguin; Brooks, A. C., Winfrey, O. (2023). *Build the Life You Want: The Art and Science of Getting Happier.* Portfolio/Penguin.

8. Tolle, *New Earth.*

9. For example, see the discussion of "secondary trauma" and "moral injury" on page 47 of Menakem, *My Grandmother's Hands.*

10. Vohs and Goode, "Psychological Consequences of Money."

Bibliography

Abouzahr, Katie, Matt Krentz, John Harthorne, and Frances Brooks Taplett. "Why Women-Owned Startups Are a Better Bet." Boston Consulting Group. June 6, 2018. https://www
.bcg.com/publications/2018/why-women-owned-startups-are-better-bet.

Alrajih, Shuaa, and Jamie Ward. "Increased Facial Width-to-Height Ratio and Perceived Dominance in the Faces of the UK's Leading Business Leaders." *British Journal of Psychology* 105, no. 2 (2014): 153–61. https://doi.org/10.1111/bjop.12035.

Anderson, Cameron, and Gavin J. Kilduff. "Why Do Dominant Personalities Attain Influence in Face-to-Face Groups? The Competence-Signaling Effects of Trait Dominance." *Journal of Personality and Social Psychology* 96, no. 2 (2009): 491–503. https://doi.org/10.1037/a0014201.

Anderson, Carol. "America Is Hooked on the Drug of White Supremacy. We're Paying for That Today." *Guardian,* August 13, 2017. https://www.theguardian.com/commentisfree/2017/aug/13/america-white-supremacy-hooked-drug-charlottesville-virginia.

Ani, Marimba. *Yurugu: An African-Centered Critique of European Cultural Thought and Behavior.* Africa World Press, 1994.

Arnett, Autumn A. "A Trailblazing Leader." *Diverse Issues in Higher Education,* March 31, 2022.

Bailey, Erica R., and Aharon Levy. "Are You for Real? Perceptions of Authenticity Are Systematically Biased and Not Accurate." *Psychological Science* 33, no. 5 (2022): 798–815.

Baradaran, Mehrsa. *The Color of Money: Black Banks and the Racial Wealth Gap.* The Belknap Press of Harvard University Press, 2018.

Bardi, Anat, and Shalom H. Schwartz. "Values and Behavior: Strength and Structure of Relations." *Personality & Social Psychology Bulletin* 29, no. 10 (2023): 1207–20. https://doi.org/10.1177/0146167203254602.

Bell, Derrick. "Racism Is Here to Stay: Now What?" *Howard Law Journal* 35, no. 1 (1991): 79.

Bergsieker, Hilary B., J. Nicole Shelton, and Jennifer A. Richeson. "To Be Liked Versus Respected: Divergent Goals in Interracial Interactions." *Journal of Personality and Social Psychology* 99, no. 2 (2010): 248–64. https://doi.org/10.1037/a0018474.

Bertrand, Marianne, and Sendhil Mullainathan. "Are Emily and Greg More Employable than Lakisha and Jamal? A Field Experiment on Labor Market Discrimination." *American Economic Review* 94, no. 4 (2004): 991–1013. https://doi.org/10.1257/0002828042002561.

Bisson, Terry. *Fire on the Mountain.* PM Press, 2009.

Blow, Charles M. *The Devil You Know: A Black Power Manifesto.* Harper, 2021.

Bretherton, Inge. "The Origins of Attachment Theory: John Bowlby and Mary Ainsworth." *Developmental Psychology* 28, no. 5 (1992): 759–75. https://doi.org/10.1037/0012 -1649.28.5.759.

Brondolo, Elizabeth, Nisha Brady Ver Halen, Melissa Pencille, Danielle Beatty, and Richard J. Contrada. "Coping with Racism: A Selective Review of the Literature and a Theoretical and Methodological Critique." *Journal of Behavioral Medicine* 32, no. 1 (2009): 64–88. https://doi.org/10.1007/s10865-008-9193-0.

Brown, N. Derek, and Drew S. Jacoby-Senghor. "Majority Members Misperceive Even 'Win-Win' Diversity Policies as Unbeneficial to Them." *Journal of Personality and Social Psychology* 122, no. 6 (2022): 1075–97. https://doi.org/10.1037/pspi0000372.

Brown, N. Derek, Drew S. Jacoby-Senghor, and Isaac Raymundo. "If You Rise, I Fall: Equality Is Prevented by the Misperception That It Harms Advantaged Groups." *Science Advances* 8, no. 18 (2022): eabm2385. https://doi.org/10.1126/sciadv.abm2385.

Bruner, Jerome S., and Leo Postman. "On the Perception of Incongruity: A Paradigm." *Journal of Personality* 18, no. 2 (1949): 206–23.

Carmichael, Stokely, and Charles V. Hamilton. *Black Power: The Politics of Liberation in America.* Vintage Books, 1992.

Casciaro, Tiziana, Francesca Gino, and Maryam Kouchaki. "The Contaminating Effects of Building Instrumental Ties: How Networking Can Make Us Feel Dirty." *Administrative Science Quarterly* 59, no. 4 (2014): 705–35. https://doi.org/10.1177/ 0001839214554990.

Castelli, Luigi, Katia Vanzetto, Steven J. Sherman, and Luciano Arcuri. "The Explicit and Implicit Perception of In-Group Members Who Use Stereotypes: Blatant Rejection but Subtle Conformity." *Journal of Experimental Social Psychology* 37, no. 5 (2001): 419–26. https://doi.org/10.1006/jesp.2000.1471.

Castilla, Emilio J. "Gender, Race, and Meritocracy in Organizational Careers." *American Journal of Sociology* 113, no. 6 (2008): 1479–1526. https://doi.org/10.1086/588738.

Cha, Sandra E., Patricia Faison Hewlin, Laura Morgan Roberts, et al. "Being Your True Self at Work: Integrating the Fragmented Research on Authenticity in Organizations." *Academy of Management Annals* 13, no. 2 (2019): 633–71. https://doi.org/10.5465/annals .2016.0108.

Chaney, Kimberly E., Danielle M. Young, and Diana T. Sanchez. "Confrontation's Health Outcomes and Promotion of Egalitarianism (C-HOPE) Framework." *Translational Issues in Psychological Science* 1, no. 4 (2015): 363–71. https://doi.org/10.1037/tps0000042.

Chenoweth, Erica, and Maria J. Stephan. *Why Civil Resistance Works: The Strategic Logic of Nonviolent Conflict.* Columbia University Press, 2011.

Chow, Rosalind M., Brian S. Lowery, and Caitlin M. Hogan. "Appeasement: Whites' Strategic Support for Affirmative Action." *Personality & Social Psychology Bulletin* 39, no. 3 (2013): 332–45. https://doi.org/10.1177/0146167212475224.

Chronicle of Higher Education. "DEI Legislation Tracker." https://www.chronicle.com/ article/here-are-the-states-where-lawmakers-are-seeking-to-ban-colleges-dei-efforts.

Cose, Ellis. *The Rage of a Privileged Class.* Harper Perennial, 1994.

Crenshaw, Kimberlé, Katharine T. Bartlett, and Rosanne Kennedy. "Demarginalizing the Intersection of Race and Sex: A Black Feminist Critique of Antidiscrimination Doctrine, Feminist Theory, and Antiracist Politics [1989]." In *Feminist Legal Theory: Readings in Law and Gender,* edited by Katharine T. Bartlett and Rosanne Kennedy. Routledge, 1991. https://doi.org/10.4324/9780429500480-5.

Crenshaw, Kimberlé Williams. "Mapping the Margins: Intersectionality, Identity Politics, and Violence Against Women of Color." In *Critical Race Theory: The Key Writings That Formed the Movement,* edited by Kimberlé Crenshaw, Neil Gotanda, Gary Peller, and Kendall Thomas. New Press, 1995.

Crocker, Jennifer, Riia Luhtanen, Bruce Blaine, and Stephanie Broadnax. "Collective Self-Esteem and Psychological Well-Being Among White, Black, and Asian College Students." *Personality and Social Psychology Bulletin* 20, no. 5 (1994): 503–13. https://doi.org/10.1177/0146167294205007.

Crocker, Jennifer, and Connie T. Wolfe. "Contingencies of Self-Worth." *Psychological Review* 108, no. 3 (2001): 593–623. https://doi.org/10.1037/0033-295X.108.3.593.

Cronon, E. David. *Black Moses: The Story of Marcus Garvey and the Universal Negro Improvement Association.* 2nd ed. University of Wisconsin Press, 1969.

Cunningham, Vinson. "The Argument of 'Afropessimism.'" *New Yorker,* July 13, 2020.

Czopp, Alexander M., Margo J. Monteith, and Aimee Y. Mark. "Standing Up for a Change: Reducing Bias Through Interpersonal Confrontation." *Journal of Personality and Social Psychology* 90, no. 5 (2006): 784–803. https://doi.org/10.1037/0022-3514.90.5.784.

Danbold, Felix, and Miguel M. Unzueta. "Drawing the Diversity Line: Numerical Thresholds of Diversity Vary by Group Status." *Journal of Personality and Social Psychology* 118, no. 2 (2020): 283–306. https://doi.org/10.1037/pspi0000182.

Daniel, Will. "'Turbulence Ahead': Nearly 4 in 10 Americans Lack Enough Money to Cover a $400 Emergency Expense, Fed Survey Shows." *Fortune,* May 23, 2023.

Darity, William A. "Review of Heather McGhee *The Sum of Us: What Racism Costs Everyone and How We Can Prosper Together,* New York: One World 2021 415 pp." *Journal of Economics, Race, and Policy* 7, no. 3 (2024): 195–97. https://doi.org/10.1007/s41996-024-00140-8.

Darity, William A., and A. Kirsten Mullen. *From Here to Equality: Reparations for Black Americans in the Twenty-First Century.* The University of North Carolina Press, 2022.

Degler, Carl N. *Neither Black nor White: Slavery and Race Relations in Brazil and the United States.* University of Wisconsin Press, 1986.

Desmond, Matthew. "In Order to Understand the Brutality of American Capitalism, You Have to Start on the Plantation." *New York Times Magazine,* August 4, 2019.

Devos, Thierry, and Mahzarin R. Banaji. "American = White?" *Journal of Personality and Social Psychology* 88, no. 3 (2005): 447–66. https://doi.org/10.1037/0022-3514.88.3.447.

DiAngelo, Robin. *Nice Racism: How Progressive White People Perpetuate Racial Harm.* Beacon Press, 2021.

Dixon, Angela R., and Edward E. Telles. "Skin Color and Colorism: Global Research, Concepts, and Measurement." *Annual Review of Sociology* 43, no. 1 (2017): 405–24. https://doi.org/10.1146/annurev-soc-060116-053315.

Dodds, Peter Sheridan, Roby Muhamad, and Duncan J. Watts. "An Experimental Study of Search in Global Social Networks." *Science* 301, no. 5634 (2003): 827–29. https://doi.org/10.1126/science.1081058.

Dovidio, John F., and Samuel L. Gaertner. "Aversive Racism and Selection Decisions: 1989 and 1999." *Psychological Science* 11, no. 4 (2000): 315–19. https://doi.org/10.1111/1467-9280.00262.

Drury, Benjamin J., and Cheryl R. Kaiser. "Allies Against Sexism: The Role of Men in Confronting Sexism." *Journal of Social Issues* 70, no. 4 (2014): 637–52. https://doi.org/10.1111/josi.12083.

Dupree, Cydney H., Brittany Torrez, Obianuju Obioha, and Susan T. Fiske. "Race–Status Associations: Distinct Effects of Three Novel Measures Among White and Black Perceivers." *Journal of Personality and Social Psychology* 120, no. 3 (2021), 601–25. https://doi.org/10.1037/pspa0000257.

Eblen, Tom. "Lexington Subdivision Opened American Dream to Black Families in the 1950s." *Lexington Herald-Leader,* June 5, 2015.

Ensign, Rachel Louise, and Shane Shifflett. "College Was Supposed to Close the Wealth Gap for Black Americans. The Opposite Happened." *Wall Street Journal,* August 7, 2021. https://www.wsj.com/articles/college-was-supposed-to-close-the-wealth-gap-for-black-americans-the-opposite-happened-11628328602.

Fein, Steven, and Steven J. Spencer. "Prejudice as Self-Image Maintenance: Affirming the Self Through Derogating Others." *Journal of Personality and Social Psychology* 73, no. 1 (1997): 31–44. https://doi.org/10.1037/0022-3514.73.1.31.

Festinger, Leon. "Cognitive Dissonance." *Scientific American* 207, no. 4 (1962): 93–102.

Foner, Eric. "First Chapter: *Forever Free.*" *New York Times,* January 29, 2006.

Freeman, Jo. "The Tyranny of Structurelessness." In *Untying the Knot: Feminism, Anarchism & Organisation.* Dark Star/Rebel Press, 1982.

Friedman, Raymond A. "Employee Network Groups; Self-Help Strategy for Women and Minorities." *Performance Improvement Quarterly* 12, no. 1 (1999): 148–63. https://doi.org/10.1111/j.1937-8327.1999.tb00120.x.

Friedman, Raymond A., and Brooks Holtom. "The Effects of Network Groups on Minority Employee Turnover Intentions." *Human Resource Management* 41, no. 4 (2002): 405–21. https://doi.org/10.1002/hrm.10051.

Friedman, Raymond, et al. "Social Support and Career Optimism: Examining the Effectiveness of Network Groups Among Black Managers," *Human Relations* 51, no. 9 (1998): 1155–77. https://doi.org/10.1023/A:1016973611184.

Frost, Peter J., and Carolyn P. Egri. "The Political Process of Innovation." *Research in Organizational Behavior* 13 (1991): 229–95.

Ganz, Marshall. *People, Power, Change: Organizing for Democratic Renewal.* Oxford University Press, 2024.

Gelfand, Michele J., Lisa H. Nishii, and Jana L. Raver. "On the Nature and Importance of Cultural Tightness-Looseness." *Journal of Applied Psychology* 91, no. 6 (2006): 1225–44. https://doi.org/10.1037/0021-9010.91.6.1225.

Geronimus, Arline T. *Weathering: The Extraordinary Stress of Ordinary Life in an Unjust Society.* Little, Brown Spark, 2023.

Gladwell, Malcolm. *Outliers: The Story of Success.* Little, Brown, 2008.

Gladwell, Malcolm. *The Tipping Point: How Little Things Can Make a Big Difference.* Little, Brown, 2000.

Glick, Peter, and Susan T. Fiske. "An Ambivalent Alliance: Hostile and Benevolent Sexism as Complementary Justifications for Gender Inequality." *American Psychologist* 56, no. 2 (2001): 109–18. https://doi.org/10.1037/0003-066X.56.2.109.

Granovetter, Mark S. "The Strength of Weak Ties." *American Journal of Sociology* 78, no. 6 (1973): 1360–80. https://doi.org/10.1086/225469.

Greenberg, Jeff, and Tom Pyszczynski. "The Effect of an Overheard Ethnic Slur on Evaluations of the Target: How to Spread a Social Disease." *Journal of Experimental Social Psychology* 21, no. 1 (1985): 61–72. https://doi.org/10.1016/0022-1031(85)90006-X.

Gulker, Jill E., Aimee Y. Mark, and Margo J. Monteith. "Confronting Prejudice: The *Who, What,* and *Why* of Confrontation Effectiveness." *Social Influence* 8, no. 4 (2013): 280–93. https://doi.org/10.1080/15534510.2012.736879.

Hacker, Andrew. *Two Nations: Black and White, Separate, Hostile, Unequal.* Scribner, 1992.

Haidt, Jonathan. *The Anxious Generation: How the Great Rewiring of Childhood Is Causing an Epidemic of Mental Illness.* Penguin Press, 2024.

Hall, Erika V., and Robert W. Livingston. "The Hubris Penalty: Biased Responses to 'Celebration' Displays of Black Football Players." *Journal of Experimental Social Psychology* 48, no. 4 (2012): 899–904. https://doi.org/10.1016/j.jesp.2012.02.004.

Hansen, Morten T., Herminia Ibarra, and Urs Peyer. "The Best-Performing CEOs in the World." *Harvard Business Review,* January–February 2010.

Harris, Carla A. *Strategize to Win: The New Way to Start Out, Step Up, or Start Over in Your Career.* Avery, 2014.

Harris, Fredrick C. "The Rise of Respectability Politics." *Dissent* 61, no. 1 (2014): 33–37. https://doi.org/10.1353/dss.2014.0010.

Hewlett, Sylvia Ann. *Forget a Mentor, Find a Sponsor: The New Way to Fast-Track Your Career.* Harvard Business Review Press, 2013.

Hewlin, Patricia Faison. "Wearing the Cloak: Antecedents and Consequences of Creating Facades of Conformity." *Journal of Applied Psychology* 94, no. 3 (2009): 727–41.

Hirschman, Albert O. *Exit, Voice, and Loyalty: Responses to Decline in Firms, Organizations, and States.* Harvard University Press, 1970.

Hochschild, Arlie. *Strangers in Their Own Land: Anger and Mourning on the American Right.* The New Press, 2016.

Hughes, Diane, Blair Cox, and Sohini Das. "Growing Up, Learning Race: An Integration of Research on Cognitive Mechanisms and Socialization in Context." *Annual Review of Developmental Psychology* 5 (2023): 137–67. https://doi.org/10.1146/annurev-devpsych-120321-015718.

Ibarra, Herminia, Nancy M. Carter, and Christine Silva. "Why Men Still Get More Promotions Than Women." *Harvard Business Review,* September 2010.

Jackson, Regina, and Saira Rao. *White Women: Everything You Already Know About Your Own Racism and How to Do Better.* Penguin Books, 2022.

Johnson, Akilah. "That Was No Typo: The Median Net Worth of Black Bostonians Really Is $8." *Boston Globe,* December 11, 2017.

Kahn, Kimberly Barsamian, Manuela Barreto, Cheryl R. Kaiser, and Marco Silva Rego. "When Do High and Low Status Group Members Support Confrontation? The Role of Perceived Pervasiveness of Prejudice." *British Journal of Social Psychology* 55, no. 1 (2016): 27–43. https://doi.org/10.1111/bjso.12117.

Kaiser, Cheryl R., and Carol T. Miller. "Stop Complaining! The Social Costs of Making Attributions to Discrimination." *Personality & Social Psychology Bulletin* 27, no. 2 (2001): 254–63. https://doi.org/10.1177/0146167201272010.

Kaiser, Cheryl R., and Jennifer S. Pratt-Hyatt. "Distributing Prejudice Unequally: Do Whites Direct Their Prejudice Toward Strongly Identified Minorities?" *Journal of Personality and Social Psychology* 96, no. 2 (2009): 432–45. https://doi.org/10.1037/a0012877.

Kaiser, Robert L. "From the Archive: Lexington Contemplates a Life Without IBM." *Washington Post,* July 29, 1990.

Kang, Sonia K., Katherine A. DeCelles, András Tilcsik, and Sora Jun. "Whitened Résumés: Race and Self-Presentation in the Labor Market." *Administrative Science Quarterly* 61, no. 3 (2016): 469–502. https://doi.org/10.1177/0001839216639577.

Katz-Vago, Inbar, and Moti Benita. "Mastery-Approach and Performance-Approach Goals Predict Distinct Outcomes During Personal Academic Goal Pursuit." *British Journal of Educational Psychology* 94, no. 2 (2024): 309–27. https://doi.org/10.1111/bjep.12645.

Kaur, Supreet, Sendhil Mullainathan, Suanna Oh, and Frank Schilbach. "Do Financial Concerns Make Workers Less Productive?" Working Paper No. 28338. National Bureau of Economic Research, January 2021, revised December 2024.

Kawakami, Kerry, et al. "Mispredicting Affective and Behavioral Responses to Racism." *Science* 323, no. 5911 (2009): 276–78. https://doi.org/10.1126/science.1164951.

Kendi, Ibram X. *Stamped from the Beginning: The Definitive History of Racist Ideas in America.* Bold Type Books, 2017.

King, Martin Luther, Jr. *The Autobiography of Martin Luther King, Jr.* Edited by Clayborne Carson. Abacus, 2000.

Koval, Christy Zhou, and Ashleigh Shelby Rosette. "The Natural Hair Bias in Job Recruitment." *Social Psychological & Personality Science* 12, no. 5 (2021): 741–50. https://doi.org/10.1177/1948550620937937.

Krieger, Nancy, and Stephen Sidney. "Racial Discrimination and Blood Pressure: The CARDIA Study of Young Black and White Adults." *American Journal of Public Health* 86, no. 10 (1996): 1370–78. https://doi.org/10.2105/AJPH.86.10.1370.

Kunda, Ziva. "The Case for Motivated Reasoning." *Psychological Bulletin* 108, no. 3 (1990): 480–98. https://doi.org/10.1037/0033-2909.108.3.480.

Livingston, Robert W. *The Conversation: How Seeking and Speaking the Truth About Racism Can Radically Transform Individuals and Organizations.* Currency, 2021.

Livingston, Robert W., and Nicholas A. Pearce. "The Teddy-Bear Effect: Does Having a Baby Face Benefit Black Chief Executive Officers?" *Psychological Science* 20, no. 10 (2009): 1229–36. https://doi.org/10.1111/j.1467-9280.2009.02431.x.

Livingston, Robert W., and Ashleigh Shelby Rosette. "Stigmatization, Subordination, or Marginalization?: The Complexity of Social Disadvantage Across Gender and Race." In *Inclusive Leadership: Transforming Diverse Lives, Workplaces, and Societies,* edited by

Bernardo M. Ferdman, Jeanine Prime, and Ronald E. Riggio. Routledge, 2020. https://doi.org/10.4324/9780429449673-3.

Lorde, Audre. *Sister Outsider: Essays and Speeches.* Crossing Press, 2007.

Lukianoff, Greg, and Jonathan Haidt. *The Coddling of the American Mind: How Good Intentions and Bad Ideas Are Setting Up a Generation for Failure.* Penguin, 2018.

Luscombe, Belinda. "Erin Horne McKinney Is Boosting Entrepreneurship Through HBCUs." *Time,* February 1, 2024. https://time.com/collection/closers/6590701/erin-horne-mckinney/.

Lyons-Padilla, Sarah, Hazel Rose Markus, Ashby Monk, et al. "Race Influences Professional Investors' Financial Judgments." *Proceedings of the National Academy of Sciences—PNAS* 116, no. 35 (2019): 17225–30. https://doi.org/10.1073/pnas.1822052116.

Mallett, Robyn K., and Kala J. Melchiori. "Goals Drive Responses to Perceived Discrimination." In *Confronting Prejudice and Discrimination: The Science of Changing Minds and Behaviors,* edited by Robyn K. Mallett and Margo J. Monteith. Academic Press, 2019.

Mallett, Robyn K., and Margo J. Monteith. "Confronting Prejudice and Discrimination: Historical Influences and Contemporary Approaches." In *Confronting Prejudice and Discrimination: The Science of Changing Minds and Behaviors,* edited by Robyn K. Mallett and Margo J. Monteith. Academic Press, 2019.

Mallett, Robyn K., and Margo J. Monteith, eds. *Confronting Prejudice and Discrimination: The Science of Changing Minds and Behaviors.* Academic Press, 2019.

Massey, Douglas S., Camille Z. Charles, Garvey F. Lundy, and Mary J. Fischer. *The Source of the River: The Social Origins of Freshmen at America's Selective Colleges and Universities.* Princeton University Press, 2003.

McClelland, David C. "The Two Faces of Power." *Journal of International Affairs* 24, no. 1 (1970): 29–47.

McGinnies, Elliott. "Emotionality and Perceptual Defense." *Psychological Review* 56, no. 5 (1949): 244–51. https://doi.org/10.1037/h0056508.

Menakem, Resmaa. *My Grandmother's Hands: Racialized Trauma and the Pathway to Mending Our Hearts and Bodies.* Central Recovery Press, 2017.

Metzl, Jonathan A. *Dying of Whiteness: How the Politics of Racial Resentment Is Killing America's Heartland.* Basic Books, 2019.

Meyerson, Debra E. *Rocking the Boat: How Tempered Radicals Effect Change Without Making Trouble.* Harvard Business Review Press, 2008.

Meyerson, Debra E., and Maureen A. Scully. "Tempered Radicalism and the Politics of Ambivalence and Change." *Organization Science* 6, no. 5 (1995): 585–600. https://doi.org/10.1287/orsc.6.5.585.

Milgram, Stanley. *The Individual in a Social World: Essays and Experiments.* Addison-Wesley, 1977.

Mitchell, Koritha. "Identifying White Mediocrity and Know-Your-Place Aggression: A Form of Self-Care." *African American Review* 51, no. 4 (2018): 253–62. https://doi.org/10.1353/afa.2018.0045.

Mobasseri, Sanaz, William A. Kahn, and Robin J. Ely. "Racial Inequality in Organizations: A Systems Psychodynamic Perspective." *Academy of Management Review* 49, no. 4 (2024): 718–45. https://doi.org/10.5465/amr.2021.0446.

Morrison, Toni. "The Pain of Being Black." *Time,* May 22, 1989.

Myers, Barton. "Sherman's Field Order N. 15." *New Georgia Encyclopedia,* last modified September 30, 2020. https://www.georgiaencyclopedia.org/articles/history-archaeology/ shermans-field-order-no-15/.

NBC Nightly News. "John Deere Pulls Back from Diversity and Inclusion Efforts." NBC News, June 18, 2024. https://www.nbcnews.com/nightly-news/video/john-deere-pulls -back-from-diversity-and-inclusion-efforts-215196229871.

Noh, Samuel, and Violet Kaspar. "Perceived Discrimination and Depression: Moderating Effects of Coping, Acculturation, and Ethnic Support." *American Journal of Public Health* 93, no. 2 (2003): 232–38. https://doi.org/10.2105/AJPH.93.2.232.

Norton, Michael I., and Samuel R. Sommers. "Whites See Racism as a Zero-Sum Game That They Are Now Losing." *Perspectives on Psychological Science* 6, no. 3 (2011): 215–18. https://doi.org/10.1177/1745691611406922.

Oluo, Ijeoma. *Mediocre: The Dangerous Legacy of White Male America.* Seal Press, 2020.

Parry, Tyler. "The Curious History of Anthony Johnson: From Captive African to Right-Wing Talking Point." *Black Perspectives,* July 22, 2019.

Peery, Destiny, and Galen V. Bodenhausen. "Black + White = Black: Hypodescent in Reflexive Categorization of Racially Ambiguous Faces." *Psychological Science* 19, no. 10 (2008): 973–77. https://doi.org/10.1111/j.1467-9280.2008.02185.x.

Pérez, Efrén, Bianca Vicuña, and Alisson Ramos. "Shared Status, Shared Politics? Evaluating a New Pathway to Black Solidarity with Other People of Color." *Political Behavior* 46, no. 2 (2024): 1151–70. https://doi.org/10.1007/s11109-023-09863-0.

Phelan, Julie E., and Laurie A. Rudman. "Reactions to Ethnic Deviance: The Role of Backlash in Racial Stereotype Maintenance." *Journal of Personality and Social Psychology* 99, no. 2 (2010): 265–81. https://doi.org/10.1037/a0018304.

Pillemer, Julianna. "Strategic Authenticity: Signaling Authenticity Without Undermining Professional Image in Workplace Interactions." *Organization Science* 35, no. 5 (2024): 1641–59. https://doi.org/10.1287/orsc.2020.14807.

The Posse Alumni Report: The Next Generation of Leaders. The Posse Foundation, 2019.

Pratto, Felicia, Jim Sidanius, Lisa M. Stallworth, and Bertram F. Malle. "Social Dominance Orientation: A Personality Variable Predicting Social and Political Attitudes." *Journal of Personality and Social Psychology* 67, no. 4 (1994): 741–63. https://doi.org/10.1037/ 0022-3514.67.4.741.

Proulx, Andrew. *Understanding and Helping an Addict (and Keeping Your Sanity).* Recovery Folio Publishing, 2021.

Purdie-Vaughns, Valerie, and Richard P. Eibach. "Intersectional Invisibility: The Distinctive Advantages and Disadvantages of Multiple Subordinate-Group Identities." *Sex Roles* 59, no. 5–6 (2008): 377–91. https://doi.org/10.1007/s11199-008-9424-4.

Putnam, Robert D. *Bowling Alone: The Collapse and Revival of American Community.* 20th anniversary edition. Simon & Schuster Paperbacks, 2020.

Quillian, Lincoln, Devah Pager, Ole Hexel, and Arnfinn Haagensen Midtbøen. "Meta-Analysis of Field Experiments Shows No Change in Racial Discrimination in Hiring over Time." *Proceedings of the National Academy of Sciences* 114, no. 41 (2017): 10870–75. https://doi.org/10.1073/pnas.1706255114.

Rhinehart, Charlene. "Founder of $16 Billion Ariel Investments Created a School to Teach Kids Financial Literacy Through Stocks." *Black Enterprise,* April 12, 2021.

Rhodes, Gillian, Fiona Proffitt, Jonathon M. Grady, and Alex Sumich. "Facial Symmetry and the Perception of Beauty." *Psychonomic Bulletin & Review* 5, no. 4 (1998): 659–69. https://doi.org/10.3758/BF03208842.

Rimer, Sara, and Karen W. Arenson. "Top Colleges Take More Blacks, but Which Ones?" *New York Times,* January 2004. https://www.nytimes.com/2004/06/24/us/top-colleges -take-more-blacks-but-which-ones.html.

Roberts, Laura Morgan. "Changing Faces: Professional Image Construction in Diverse Organizational Settings." *Academy of Management Review* 30, no. 4 (2005): 685–711. https://journals.aom.org/doi/10.5465/amr.2005.18378873.

Rogers, Steven S. *A Letter to My White Friends and Colleagues: What You Can Do Right Now to Help the Black Community.* Wiley, 2021.

Rogers, Steven S., Stanley Onuoha, and Kayin Barclay. "Sources of Capital for Black Entrepreneurs." Harvard Business School Case #319-117. May 2019.

Rose, Deondra. *The Power of Black Excellence: HBCUs and the Fight for American Democracy.* Oxford University Press, 2024.

Rosette, Ashleigh Shelby, and Robert W. Livingston. "Failure Is Not an Option for Black Women: Effects of Organizational Performance on Leaders with Single Versus Dual-Subordinate Identities." *Journal of Experimental Social Psychology* 48, no. 5 (2012): 1162–67. https://doi.org/10.1016/j.jesp.2012.05.002.

Ross, Janell. "The Architects of Baby Bonds Are Finally Seeing Some Momentum." *Time,* February 12, 2024.

Ross, Lawrence C., Jr. *The Divine Nine: The History of African American Fraternities and Sororities.* Kensington Books, 2000.

Ryan, Michelle K., and S. Alexander Haslam. "The Glass Cliff: Evidence That Women Are Over-Represented in Precarious Leadership Positions." *British Journal of Management* 16, no. 2 (2005): 81–90. https://doi.org/10.1111/j.1467-8551.2005.00433.x.

Sanchez, Diana T., Mary S. Himmelstein, Danielle M. Young, Analia F. Albuja, and Julie A. Garcia. "Confronting as Autonomy Promotion: Speaking Up Against Discrimination and Psychological Well-Being in Racial Minorities." *Journal of Health Psychology* 21, no. 9 (2016): 1999–2007. https://doi.org/10.1177/1359105315569619.

Schwartz, Shalom H. "An Overview of the Schwartz Theory of Basic Values." *Online Readings in Psychology and Culture* 2, no. 1 (2012): 1–20. https://doi.org/10.9707/2307-0919.1116.

Semuels, Alana. "Freedom Through Finances." *Time,* February 12, 2024.

Senko, Corwin. "When Do Mastery and Performance Goals Facilitate Academic Achievement?" *Contemporary Educational Psychology* 59 (2019): 101795. https://doi .org/10.1016/j.cedpsych.2019.101795.

Shelton, J. Nicole, Jennifer A. Richeson, Jessica Salvatore, and Diana M. Hill. "Silence Is Not Golden: The Intrapersonal Consequences of Not Confronting Prejudice." In *Stigma and Group Inequality: Social Psychological Perspectives,* edited by Shana Levin and Colette van Laar. Taylor & Francis, 2006.

Sidanius, Jim, and Felicia Pratto. *Social Dominance: An Intergroup Theory of Social Hierarchy and Oppression.* Cambridge University Press, 1999.

Sinclair, Lisa, and Ziva Kunda. "Reactions to a Black Professional: Motivated Inhibition and Activation of Conflicting Stereotypes." *Journal of Personality and Social Psychology* 77, no. 5 (1999): 885–904. https://doi.org/10.1037/0022-3514.77.5.885.

Staples, Brent. "Just Walk on By: Black Men and Public Space." In *50 Essays: A Portable Anthology,* 5th ed., edited by Samuel Cohen. Bedford/Saint Martin's, 2017.

Stephan, Walter G., and Krystina Finlay. "The Role of Empathy in Improving Intergroup Relations." *Journal of Social Issues* 55, no. 4 (1999): 729–43. https://doi.org/10.1111/0022-4537.00144.

Stepick, Alex, Carol Dutton Stepick, Emmanuel Eugene, Deborah Teed, and Yves Labissiere. "Shifting Identities and Intergenerational Conflict Growing Up Haitian in Miami." In *Ethnicities: Children of Immigrants in America,* edited by Rubén G. Rumbaut and Alejandro Portes. University of California Press, 2001.

Tatum, Beverly Daniel. *Why Are All the Black Kids Sitting Together in the Cafeteria?* Basic Books, 1999.

Telford, Taylor. "As DEI Gets More Divisive, Companies Are Ditching Their Teams." *Washington Post,* February 18, 2024.

Thomas, Kecia M., Juanita Johnson-Bailey, Rosemary E. Phelps, Ny Mia Tran, and Lindsay N. Johnson. "Women of Color at Midcareer: Going from Pet to Threat." In *Psychological Health of Women of Color: Intersections, Challenges, and Opportunities,* edited by Lillian Comas-Díaz and Beverly Greene. Praeger, 2013. https://10.5040/9798216002536.ch-014.

Tolle, Eckhart. *A New Earth: Awakening to Your Life's Purpose.* Dutton/Penguin Group, 2005.

Ton, Zeynep. *The Case for Good Jobs: How Great Companies Bring Dignity, Pay, and Meaning to Everyone's Work.* Harvard Business Review Press, 2023.

Tormala, Teceta Thomas, and Kay Deaux. "Black Immigrants to the United States: Confronting and Constructing Ethnicity and Race." In *Cultural Psychology of Immigrants,* edited by Ramaswami Mahalingam. Psychology Press, 2006. https://doi.org/10.4324/9781315820934.

Twenge, Jean M. *iGen: Why Today's Super-Connected Kids Are Growing Up Less Rebellious, More Tolerant, Less Happy—and Completely Unprepared for Adulthood (and What This Means for the Rest of Us).* Atria Books, 2017.

Twenge, Jean M., and Jennifer Crocker. "Race and Self-Esteem: Meta-Analyses Comparing Whites, Blacks, Hispanics, Asians, and American Indians and Comment on Gray-Little and Hafdahl (2000)." *Psychological Bulletin* 128, no. 3 (2002): 371–408. https://doi.org/10.1037/0033-2909.128.3.371.

Van Bavel, Jay J., and Dominic J. Packer. *The Power of Us: Harnessing Our Shared Identities to Improve Performance, Increase Cooperation, and Promote Social Harmony.* Little, Brown Spark, 2021.

Varley, Pamela, and Robert Wilkerson. "Embracing the Uphill Struggle: Marc Morial's Quest for Corporate Diversity." Harvard Kennedy School Case #2242.0. October 25, 2021.

Villarosa, Linda. *Under the Skin: The Hidden Toll of Racism on American Lives and on the Health of Our Nation.* Penguin Random House, 2022.

Vohs, Kathleen D., Nicole L. Mead, and Miranda R. Goode. "The Psychological Consequences of Money." *Science* 314, no. 5802 (2006): 1154–56. https://doi.org/10.1126/science.1132491.

Waters, Mary C. *Black Identities: West Indian Immigrant Dreams and American Realities.* Russell Sage Foundation Books at Harvard University Press, 1999.

Wilderson, Frank B., III. *Afropessimism.* Liveright, 2020.

Wilkerson, Isabel. *Caste: The Origins of Our Discontents.* Random House, 2020.

Wilton, Leigh S., Aneeta Rattan, and Diana T. Sanchez. "White's Perceptions of Biracial Individuals' Race Shift When Biracials Speak Out Against Bias." *Social Psychological & Personality Science* 9, no. 8 (2018): 953–61. https://doi.org/10.1177/1948550617731497.

Yoshino, Kenji. *Covering: The Hidden Assault on Our Civil Rights.* Random House, 2006.

Yoshino, Kenji, and David Glasgow. "DEI Is Under Attack: Here's How Companies Can Mitigate the Legal Risk." *Harvard Business Review,* January 5, 2024.

Zou, Linda X., and Sapna Cheryan. "Two Axes of Subordination: A New Model of Racial Position." *Journal of Personality and Social Psychology* 112, no. 5 (2017): 696–717. https://doi.org/10.1037/pspa0000080.

Zukav, Gary. *Spiritual Partnership: The Journey to Authentic Power.* HarperOne, 2010.

Index

About the Author

Robert Livingston is a race scholar who serves on the faculty of the John F. Kennedy School of Government at Harvard University. He is the author of *The Conversation*, selected as a *Financial Times* Best Book of 2021 and nominated for a 2022 NAACP Image Award for Outstanding Literary Work. His research has appeared in *The New York Times, The Wall Street Journal, Time, Newsweek,* and *Harvard Business Review.* For more than two decades, he has served as a diversity consultant to over a hundred Fortune 500 companies, public-sector agencies, and nonprofit organizations. He has lived in six countries and speaks four languages.

robertwlivingston.com

McGraw-Hill Education's

Nursing Spanish Visual Phrasebook

Neil Bobenhouse, MHA, EMT-P
with Dean Meenach, RN, BSN, CEN, CCRN

New York Chicago San Francisco Athens London Madrid
Mexico City Milan New Delhi Singapore Sydney Toronto

1 2 3 4 5 6 7 8 9 10 CTP/CTP 1 0 9 8 7 6 5 4 3

ISBN   978-1-260-02673-3
MHID   1-260-02673-6

e-ISBN   978-0-07-180891-0
e-MHID   0-07-180891-4

Library of Congress Control Number 2013930338

NOTICE

This book is not intended to provide medical advice or to substitute for the advice of a licensed medical professional, and readers should consult an appropriate medical practitioner for all matters relating to their health. Medicine is an ever-changing science. As new research and clinical experience broaden our knowledge, changes in treatment and drug therapy are required. The authors and the publisher of this work have checked with sources believed to be reliable in their efforts to provide information that is complete and generally in accord with the standards accepted at the time of publication. However, in view of the possibility of human error or changes in medical sciences, neither the authors nor the publisher nor any other party who has been involved in the preparation or publication of this work warrants that the information contained herein is in every respect accurate or complete, and they disclaim all responsibility for any errors or omissions or for the results obtained from use of the information contained in this work. Readers are encouraged to confirm the information contained herein with other sources. For example and in particular, readers are advised to check the product information sheet included in the package of each drug they plan to administer to be certain that any information contained in this work is accurate and that changes have not been made in the recommended dose or in the contraindications for administration.

Credits appear on page 152

McGraw-Hill Education products are available at special quantity discounts to use as premiums and sales promotions or for use in corporate training programs. To contact a representative, please visit the Contact Us pages at www.mhprofessional.com.

This book is printed on acid-free paper.